T0313953

BUBBLES AND CRASHES

BUBBLES AND CRASHES

The Boom and Bust
of Technological Innovation

Brent Goldfarb and David A. Kirsch

STANFORD UNIVERSITY PRESS

Stanford, California

Stanford University Press

Stanford, California

© 2019 by the Board of Trustees of the Leland Stanford Junior University.
All rights reserved.

No part of this book may be reproduced or transmitted in any form or by any
means, electronic or mechanical, including photocopying and recording, or in any
information storage or retrieval system without the prior written permission of
Stanford University Press.

Printed in the United States of America on acid-free, archival-quality paper

Library of Congress Cataloging-in-Publication Data

Names: Goldfarb, Brent, author. | Kirsch, David A., author.
Title: Bubbles and crashes : the boom and bust of technological innovation /
    Brent Goldfarb and David A. Kirsch.
Description: Stanford, California : Stanford University Press, 2019. |
    Includes bibliographical references and index.
Identifiers: LCCN 2018037966 (print) | LCCN 2018040063 (e-book) |
    ISBN 9781503607934 (e-book) | ISBN 9780804793834 (cloth : alk. paper)
Subjects: LCSH: Technological innovations—Economic aspects. | Business cycles.
Classification: LCC HC79.T4 (e-book) | LCC HC79.T4 G645 2019 (print) |
    DDC 338/.064—dc23
LC record available at https://lccn.loc.gov/2018037966

Typeset by Newgen in 11.25/16 Baskerville

Cover design: Rob Ehle
Cover image: iStock | dkidpix

Mom and Dad, thanks for always cheering me on throughout the many years. Elena and Nathaniel, your brightness keeps me going. Beth, nothing would be possible without your endless love, patience, and support. 17. —BDG

Jacob and Isabel, thank you for your company on this and so many journeys. Andrea, I look forward to keeping you company when they have left the nest. Dad, I miss you. —DAK

CONTENTS

ACKNOWLEDGMENTS

It pains us to write that this book took many years to complete. It was always a big endeavor, one that grew bigger the deeper and longer we dug. During this time, there has been a long parade of excellent and dedicated students who have assisted us with our research. It would not have been possible to complete this project without early assistance of Pablo Slutzky, Heidi Nalley and Haley Nalley, Fardad Golshany, Jen Fortini, Ami Trivedi, Dana Haimovitz, Aayushi Shah, Dillon Fletcher, Pierre Souchet, Candice Ho, Mahum Hussain, Mary Nguyen, Solen Kebede, Nafeez Amin, Stanley Portillo, Liana Alvarez, Brian Zimmerman, Sanil Shah, and Devika Raj. We also called upon several of our outstanding doctoral students. Robert Vesco helped organize the digitization of the stock prices from the curb market; Liyue Yan and Sandeep Pillai were instrumental at critical moments, oftentimes putting aside their own work to finish this task or the other. Without complaint! The care these students put into this project helped make it a reality. Our local administrative team kept us organized: thank you, Barbara Chipman, Tina Marie Rollason, Kristine Maenpaa, and Mary Crowe.

We received constructive comments from seminar participants at multiple universities, including the University of Wisconsin, the Wharton School at the University of Pennsylvania, Tsinghua University, Hong Kong Polytechnic, UCLA, UC Berkeley, Rutgers, the University of Toronto, London Business School, Ivey Business School, New York University, Universidad de los Andes in Buenos Aires, Boston University, and the University of Chicago. Avi Goldfarb (no relation), Dan Gordon, Jerry Hoberg, Sarah Kaplan, David Kressler,

Chris Rider, John Riley, Melissa Schilling, Amanda Sharkey, David Sicilia, Ezra Zuckerman, and four anonymous Stanford University Press reviewers provided invaluable specific feedback. Ajay Agarwal, Ashish Arora, Iain Coburn, Gary Dushnitsky, Daniel Friel, Javier Garcia Sanchez, Naomi Lamoreaux, Dan Raff, Violina Rindova, Zur Shapira, Wes Sine, Scott Stern, Alex Triantis, Roberto Veloso, Marc Ventresca, Dan Wadhwani, and Mark Zbaracki provided encouragement and helped us avoid many pitfalls that were obvious to them, less so to us.

Particular thanks are due to Richard Rumelt (David) and Nathan Rosenberg (Brent) for their guidance and inspiration. Thank you, Rajshree Agarwal, Christine Beckman, Serguey Braguinsky, Wilbur Chung, Christian Deszo, Waverly Ding, Anil Gupta, Rachelle Sampson, Evan Starr, and David Waguespack for creating and sustaining the generative scholarly community we cherish.

Victor Reinoso came up with the title, aided by the crowd. The Reinoso-Nicolet clan has been supportive throughout.

We have been working on this book long enough that we have inevitably failed to mention someone who provided a useful suggestion, comment, or criticism. Our apologies for this oversight.

We also thank the editorial and production staff at Stanford University Press. When we began this project, we did not know how to write a book such as this. Margo Fleming made it possible. She believed in the book, scolded us when necessary, and without question, upped our game.

We are grateful for financial support from the Smith School (across multiple administrations), the National Science Foundation, the Dingman Center for Entrepreneurship, and the Richard M. Schulze Family Foundation.

No work is perfect. With regard to all remaining problems in the book, empirical, theoretical, or interpretive, the buck stops with us.

College Park, Maryland
June 2018

BUBBLES AND CRASHES

INTRODUCTION

"WE'RE LOSING MONEY FAST ON PURPOSE, to build our brand," Toby Lenk, chief executive officer of eToys.com, proudly proclaimed. Lenk claimed that revenues were increasing an astounding 40% monthly. While most consumer purchases were still made in buildings called "stores," in Toby Lenk's world, the new economy had arrived. It was February 2000 and eToys was trading at $86 a share, implying an enterprise valuation of $7.7B, 35% more than bricks-and-mortar industry leader Toys "R" Us. Lenk believed he understood: the internet was changing the business world; traditional retailers would soon be a thing of the past; we would soon be buying groceries, or at least toys, in our underwear. The new economy was inevitable.

This was an astounding proposition given that in 1999 eToys' revenues were $30 million. In 1999, Toys "R" Us took in $30 million in a single day. Not to mention, Toys "R" Us was profitable, earning $376 million that year, with a respectable, if not particularly remarkable, margin of 6.2%.[1]

The key to e-commerce was to buy high and sell low, in order to generate volume. With volume, costs would decline and profits would ensue. The revenue growth of eToys' was extraordinary. These revenues came from "eyeballs," or website traffic. Investors fit this fact into a narrative that justified losses to attract this traffic: get big fast. Build it, and they will come, costs will drop, and profits will follow![2] Get big fast was a narrative shared by the entire dot-com sector.

Meanwhile, *Fortune* magazine reporter (and later TechCrunch editor) Erick Schonfeld, was struggling with a different question: How much is a customer worth? In the heady days before costs had dropped to support profits, it was all guesswork. For example, in February 2000, a few weeks before the dot-com crash, a Yahoo! customer was valued at three times the value of an Amazon customer. To make sense of this, investors came up with stories to justify stock market valuations. The margins of Yahoo! would be higher than Amazon's because online advertising is not as competitive as retail. And while pricing power had proved considerably stronger in advertising than in retail, Yahoo! was a long way from winning the online advertising space (if you don't believe us, just Yahoo! it).

Was eToys overvalued? If it was, then we might have a bubble. More precisely, if eToys was worth more than the sum total of all the profits that it would make in the future, it would be a *bubble*. Toby Lenk didn't think so. And who was to say he was wrong? To support his cause, Lenk proclaimed himself the expert: despite his lack of experience in retail, he was "a grizzled veteran."[3] He had a story too! According to Lenk, the e-commerce market was a land grab, and eToys was grabbing land and worrying about the rest later.[4]

For eToys, getting big fast required overcoming multiple challenges. The organizational challenges of building a multibillion-dollar business, which are difficult in any low-margin business, would be insurmountable for most new ventures. Timing the build-out of infrastructure to match the unpredictable growth in demand while buying high and selling low further complicated the challenge. The audacity of the bet, trying to sell all toys to all people, instead of focusing on a high-margin niche to start, complicated the mission. By November 2000, the game was almost over. eToys' stock had fallen from $86 to $6.25 a share, and the "get big fast" narrative was showing cracks.[5] Without investors who were willing to continue to make sense of the world through Lenk's narrative, there would be no way for the company to assemble the funds it needed to survive, let alone grow. With its stock further falling to trade at $.09 a share, eToys shut down in March 2001.[6]

The eToys story was built on the "get big fast" narrative. And while the magnitude of eToys' rise and fall is exceptional, the fact that it was built on a story is not. Generally, entrepreneurial capitalism is built on narratives that strive to make sense of imagined futures. These narratives, or stories, do much more than interpret the present; they shape the future. Not all narratives are equal. The logic of capitalism constrains which narratives will be convincing and to whom. For example, all investments require supporting narratives that are plausible to someone, but only a subset of these narratives produce eToys-style bubbles. Hence, understanding why and how narratives, and in particular speculative narratives, form is critical to understanding when there are—and when there are not—bubbles.

eToys was just a subplot in a much larger narrative that included other parallel subplots such as Webvan (groceries), Value America (general retail), CDNow (compact discs) and, of course, Amazon. com.[7] These stories had a magnificent effect on the financial markets. The plot accelerated on August 9, 1995, when the browser company Netscape had its initial public offering. That day, the NASDAQ Composite Index closed at 1,005. On March 10, 2000, driven by a host of eToys-like subplots in the larger "get big fast" narrative, the index peaked at 5,132, more than 500% higher. Two and a half years after that, on September 23, 2002, the same index closed at 1,185, marking a loss of nearly 77% from its peak. This decline wiped out $4.4 trillion in market value. Accounting for inflation, it was not until January 2018 that the NASDAQ recovered its value.[8]

This collapse was much more severe in the tech-heavy NASDAQ than in the broader Dow Jones Industrial Average, which collapsed from 14,164 to 6,547.05 (a mere 54% decline), or the Standard & Poor's 500 which fell from 1,516 to 800 (only 48%). If we look exclusively at a dot-com index the contrast is even starker. An index of four hundred dot-com stocks increased tenfold from the end of 1997 to March 2000, only to lose 80% of its value in the following nine months.[9] The dot-com bubble was concentrated almost exclusively in, well, dot-com and closely related sectors.[10]

The events of the dot-com era fit into a long line of boom and bust episodes in the prices at which these types of assets change hands. Historical boom and bust episodes, popularly known as "bubbles," often define their economic eras. For example, relative to the size of the British economy in the mid-nineteenth century, the "Railway Mania" bubble was several times the size of the dot-com bubble. The Roaring Twenties and, subsequently, the Great Depression scarred an entire nation; it was almost two generations before the next major speculative episode hit Wall Street in the form of the "'tronics" boom in the 1960s.[11] Bubbles are important, undeniable facts of life for citizens living under entrepreneurial capitalism. However, bubbles are both inefficient (from a strictly economic perspective) and potentially damaging to the individual interests of those who are caught up in them. Our inability to avoid bubbles suggests that our understanding of them is incomplete.

A closer look at the investors in dot-com firms on the NASDAQ reveals additional curiosities. First, inexperienced investors threw around large sums of money. Many retail investors, usually viewed as less experienced than professional investors, were trading in dot-com firms.[12] These investors were particularly bullish on dot-com firms and took bigger risks. For example, investors trading on E*Trade—the online, no-frills brokerage catering to retail investors—were over seven times more likely to trade on margin than investors who kept their assets with the full-service brokerage Merrill Lynch.[13] One suspects that these margin investors not only were trading online but also were more invested in internet stocks. Second, many Wall Street investors were also inexperienced. While only 12% of professional money managers were younger than the age of 35 in 1997, these younger, less experienced mutual fund managers were more likely to invest in technology stocks than were their more seasoned colleagues.[14] Third, many of those providing the initial funding to the dot-com firms that later went public were also inexperienced. From 1990 to 1994, the share of investments made by venture capitalists in the business for less than five years was 10%.[15] By the year 2000, recent entrants to the VC space made 40% of all VC investments. Fourth, the entrepreneurs themselves were inexperienced. In earlier work, together with our student Michael Pfarrer, we estimated that between 1998 and 2002, fifty thousand would-be entrepreneur-millionaires founded dot-coms.[16] We do not have good statistics on whether dot-com founders themselves were first-time entrepreneurs, but we do know that none of these founders had ever built an internet business—no one had.

What was the lure of dot-coms for investors? Why did they think their investments in dot-com ventures would pay off? For one, it seemed clear that the internet was going to be big. It was flashy, in the news, and most of all already *familiar*—investors used the new technology. Unlike products and services that targeted industrial buyers, the World Wide Web engaged Main Street, which made its potential value quite tangible to many of those who chose to invest. For example, investors in eToys could purchase toys on eToys.com. As we have documented extensively elsewhere, with economist David Miller, investors *thought* they knew that the "get big fast" narrative was a good bet.

In retrospect, it proved quite difficult to imagine and implement business models that turned the internet, the next big thing, into profitable businesses. As a young business school professor, David would ask his students questions like "How are entrepreneurs expecting to 'appropriate' or capture part of the value that was being created by the internet?" Students often responded that generating a positive bottom line was no longer a relevant business metric. Investors and entrepreneurs were fighting for "eyeballs," not dollars. These entrepreneurs, analysts, and investors (and, apparently, students) believed that they understood the new economy. It was an urgent land grab, and the land was inherently, inevitably valuable. This confidence is puzzling, given that in the late 1990s few dot-com businesses had generated profits. There was still profound uncertainty about how to value them. It was not merely unknown if and how such metrics would translate into bottom-line profits—it was *unknowable*.[17]

The eToys story epitomizes the interaction of unknowability and consequent narratives that are used to divine the unforeseeable future.

Understanding this interaction provides clues as to how to identify when a bubble is occurring and, perhaps, how to avoid the most destructive excesses of rampant speculation. For a given opportunity, is it known which business models will be profitable? Can we identify why entrepreneurs, investors, and analysts believe what they believe? Are such beliefs based on real, relevant past experience, or are they simply guesses? Do the players proclaim the future with certainty? Are investors and entrepreneurs making similar bets based on the same emergent, urgent narratives built on flimsy foundations? Do they all look to one another for social proof they are doing the right thing?

If this first set of questions explores attributes of a given opportunity, a second set asks who is investing. For any asset or class of assets, if many novice investors are investing when asset values are fundamentally unknowable, this is reason for concern. Such investors are unlikely to have access to information that would allow them to provide sound reasons to be bullish and are more likely to make decisions based on what others have told them. That is, novice investors are unlikely to understand what is unknowable. Thus, understanding who else is investing and why is critical to making an informed evaluation of whether an asset or class of assets is being traded at unjustifiably inflated prices.

While we hope you find this interpretation of the dot-com bubble intriguing, generalizing from a single convincing story is unwise. There are many problems with making the leap from statements like "entrepreneurs didn't know how they were going to convert eyeballs into profits" and "there were novices investing in dot-coms" to a causal statement such as "there were novices investing in dot-coms who thought they understood how dot-com entrepreneurs would convert eyeballs into profits, and this was a significant factor in causing the bubble." This leap requires not only a plausible cause-and-effect argument that links investor type and beliefs as well as the nature of uncertainty to investment decisions and asset prices, but also some "counterfactual" evidence to convince us that the dot-com bubble might have been avoided altogether in the absence of novice investors and the narrative that emerged.

More generally, one strategy to help convince a skeptical reader would be to demonstrate that novice investors were systematically not investing in the companies commercializing early-stage technologies that were *not* associated with bubbles, and conversely, that novices were active investors in new industries that experienced bubbles. We would then need to demonstrate that when novices were present but there were no compelling narratives, bubbles were less likely to form. To find examples of each of these situations, we would need to sample across a wide range of assets with varying financial histories. This exercise is the intellectual journey of this book.

Our principal methodological challenge is fundamental to the scientific method: identifying causal links requires that we observe instances when the outcome of interest does not happen. For example, imagine that we wanted to breed faster thoroughbreds and so examined the dietary histories of all horses that had won the Triple Crown. Further, imagine we discovered that most Triple Crown winners were found to have received more oats and grains than vegetables. Is this sufficient to change the recommended diet of all racehorses? Hopefully not. It could be that the horses that finished last in every Triple Crown race also received more oats and grains than vegetables. To conclude that diet was an important causal determinant of the outcome of the races, we would need to compare the diets of winning and losing horses, and show that horses that won had different diets from those that lost.[18] Similarly, identifying causal factors requires an analysis of assets that were associated with speculative episodes and those that were not associated with speculation at all. Although there are many prior studies that relate the theory of market speculation to the existence of a bubble, we have been unable to identify studies that systematically compare such speculative episodes to historical instances when broad-based market speculation might have occurred but did not.[19]

To do so, we need a class of assets that appears to be at similar risk of sparking speculative episodes. The category "major technological innovations" meets our requirements. Major technological innovations, as defined in the literature on long waves in economic activity, are interesting and important precisely because they are hypothesized to be economically and socially significant.[20] We examine a subset of major technological innovations identified in the long-wave literature so as to observe when bubbles do and do not occur. Then, we relate those observations to, among other things, whether novices were present and whether technological narratives were available that might have aligned investors' and entrepreneurs' beliefs in support of speculative activity. In this way we identify robust conditions for the appearance of a bubble.

We analyze fifty-eight major innovations appearing between 1850 and 1970 that may or may not have led to speculative activity. For each, we delve into the history of the innovation and its commercialization—with a particular focus on the uncertainty surrounding how entrepreneurs and businesspeople would make money in the emergent industries. Such uncertainty accompanied many, though not all, new technologies. We then examine the contemporaneous press coverage and historical accounts to understand how entrepreneurs, investors, and the public perceived the market opportunities associated with the innovation. Which types of technology and investment narratives could a given innovation support? We provide the list of technologies in Table A.1 in the Appendix. The table has many fields, which we describe in the forthcoming chapters.

Our interpretation of investment activities would be incomplete without a close examination of the market institutions of the day. Many technology stocks were floated in the early part of the twentieth century when financial market regulation was nonexistent, and trades were literally conducted "on the curb" outside the New York Stock Exchange building in Lower Manhattan. The historical contexts help us understand the level of market access enjoyed by different classes of investors, and understanding the nature of the technology and its related narratives provides windows onto investor composition and entrepreneurial beliefs.

Early on in our study, we discovered important practical barriers to the identification of bubbles associated with the introduction of new technologies. First, there was no comprehensive database of stock market movements that covered the periods of introduction of such profoundly important technological innovations as the telephone or the steel industry. Sometimes, though, we were able to supplement our use of existing databases with indices derived from primary sources. Second, our focus on beliefs and the narratives that string them together required a similar window into public perceptions of the various technologies under study, one that allowed for cross-technology comparisons to find the presence or absence of bubbles, as well as the identification of events that may have coordinated beliefs about the promise (Charles Lindbergh's successful transatlantic flight) or limitations (the *Hindenburg* disaster) of a new technology. Understanding these narratives required a careful reading of contemporaneous press accounts. It is doubtful that this exercise would have been possible without the digitization of historical newspapers. Our next step is to clarify precisely our definition of a bubble, then outline when we think bubbles are more likely to occur.

Bubbles, Booms, and Busts

A bubble refers to the rise and fall in asset prices such that prices deviate from "fundamental" or "intrinsic" value. Defining "fundamental" value is hard, so financial economists have tried to tie it to something real, the asset's future discounted returns. This is easy when considering a bond with a fixed interest rate but much harder to think about when we consider a new, highly uncertain start-up.

But we are getting ahead of ourselves. Simply predicting rises and falls in asset prices—which we call boom and bust episodes—would be sufficient for any practical use. However, such cycles are much more interesting when the price movements fail to reflect underlying intrinsic value; that is, when they are irrational, inspired by "animal spirits" or the "madness of crowds." Financial economists call such episodes "bubbles," and so will we.[21]

Distinguishing between bubbles and mere boom and bust cycles requires a statement about the rationality of traders. This in turn requires some idea of what might have been reasonable to believe at the time trades were made. One has to have a theory of what is reasonable to believe about a future profit stream. The problem is, though, that one can come up with a justification to explain any price as rational. For example, if one has good reason to believe that the $7.7 billion eToys valuation in February 2000 was a reasonable assessment of eToys' future profits from selling toys on the web, then the eToys episode is properly classified as a boom and bust cycle, not a bubble. In general, many stories are plausible in highly uncertain settings. To quote the famed baseball philosopher Yogi Berra, "It's tough to make predictions, especially about the future."[22] This prediction challenge has led to claims that even the most excessive price fluctuations, such as those of the dot-com bubble, were not examples of irrational exuberance but measured decisions of thoughtful traders.[23] Such arguments rely on an options-based logic that suggests that prices should increase with uncertainty; in this view, high prices reflect the possibility that a given venture might be the next General Electric or Apple while also taking into account the fact that losses are limited—stock prices can't fall below $0. However, rational theories do not explain why the presence of novice investors increases the likelihood of the phenomenon, nor do such accounts square well with contemporaneous descriptions of bubbles and other market anomalies. They do not incorporate the role of narratives and stories in human decision making. While we will be more precise about these arguments and our definitions in later chapters, we use the term "boom and bust episode" to refer to a substantial increase and subsequent decrease in prices. We label such an episode a "bubble" if we find that the boom and bust occurred at a time with a substantial influx of novice investors and was also accompanied by identifiable narratives.

Causal Factors

What causes technology bubbles? Inevitably, this is the bottom-line question that drives our study, haunts investors in their sleep, and has brought you this far. As noted already, we can offer only probabilistic statements. We identify four principal factors that, taken together, increase the likelihood of a speculative bubble forming around a given technological innovation: the nature and degree of uncertainty surrounding the innovation, the existence of "pure-play" firms whose fortunes are tightly coupled with the commercialization of the innovation, the availability of narratives that coordinate and align beliefs about the likely development of the innovation, and the presence of novice investors to fund those firms. We take up each of these factors in depth in the body of the book but give a brief overview here.

Uncertainty

The arrival of a major technological innovation is often associated with uncertainty about how firms will capture value from the innovation and which firms will profit. The financial economics literature has suggested that bubbles are more likely to occur under greater uncertainty and that speculation will end as this uncertainty is resolved.[24] If positive beliefs are both pervasive and, in hindsight, misplaced, then a boom and a bust will follow. In retrospect, this will appear to be speculative.[25] Unfortunately, existing research says little about how uncertainty will manifest in the context of new technologies, and if and to what extent institutional and market features will mitigate or exacerbate the effect of uncertainty on the likelihood of a speculative bubble forming.

For example, there might be considerable uncertainty regarding which business model will prove to be an advantageous means to exploit a new technology.[26] A business model describes the way businesses will make money selling or using the new technology. It depends on the entire economic system used to deliver value to the end user. Do the best opportunities come from selling cars to consumers or tires to car manufacturers? Although it might appear counterintuitive, when investors have trouble understanding how a new technology will fit into this system, or alternatively, when it is surmised that a new technology might displace extensive portions of a value chain, then this will encourage investment. If there is uncertainty about which part of the value chain will be able to appropriate returns, then we can rest assured that there will be a variety of opinions, and those opinions will be woven into stories justifying investment. Moreover, if firms are replacing greater proportions of a value chain, they may have a better chance of appropriating more value. Different types of investors will get caught in the different webs of stories generated to make sense of each idea about capturing value. This dynamic will push up the entire sector.[27] For example, in the case of radio, it was unclear how anyone would make money in broadcasting. In the early 1920s department stores produced broadcasts as a loss leader to attract customers to their store, and the Radio Corporation of America (RCA) began broadcasting as a means to increase demand for its primary product, radio sets. But this also encouraged entry of dozens of independent radio broadcast and receiver producers, and the airwaves were quickly filled with many stand-alone, privately financed radio stations. Contemporaneous observers did not know whether great profits would emerge in broadcasting, radio production, or the production of radio broadcast equipment, although there were opportunities to invest in any of those segments. This variation may have appealed to different investor segments, thereby increasing overall demand for stock in the sector.[28]

Similarly, electric lighting was demonstrably useful and a sight to behold when all one had experienced was lower quality gas lighting.[29] It was first introduced before a metering technology existed and before it was well understood whether electricity should be transmitted using direct or alternating current, or for that matter, whether value would be appropriated by light-bulb producers or electricity suppliers.[30] It was also unknown whether electricity would most profitably be sold on a per-light, per-watt, or subscription basis. Different firms and their subsidiaries each pursued different potential solutions (e.g., Brush, Edison, Westinghouse).[31]

Counterintuitively, knowing who might profit from an innovation might reduce the likelihood of a bubble. Because all bets are tied up in one firm, the bet is more closely aligned with the success of the technology, as opposed to different segment or monetization strategies associated with the new technology.[32] There is less room for competing narratives to appeal to different populations and thereby drive up the entire sector. For example, once the US Supreme Court upheld Alexander Graham Bell's broad patent claims on the invention of the telephone, uncertainty surrounding the fate of other inventors' claims was reduced. Bell had successfully prevented their entry into the market. Thereafter, the expected value of their ideas and ventures decreased, even if the exact business model that American Telephone and Telegraph (AT&T) would follow had yet to become clear.[33] In general, strong intellectual property protection may reduce uncertainty regarding who will profit, even before the precise mode of profit is known.

Uncertainty is necessary for the existence of a boom and bust episode. Without it there are no surprises, and hence neither booms nor busts.[34] As we discuss in further detail in Chapter 2, technological innovation is not the only source of uncertainty, but uncertainty is the sine qua non for the formation of a bubble. Uncertainty does not last forever. We expect the likelihood of asset bubbles to wane as appropriate business models are discovered, and it becomes clear who will profit. These periods map closely onto stages in industry evolution that are identified in the strategic management literature.[35]

Pure Plays

For a bubble to form, pure-play firms—firms tightly coupled to the commercial fate of the technology or innovation—must exist, and investors must be able to buy and sell shares in them. This factor highlights several important features of the landscape that predict the presence or absence of a bubble. First, the existence of pure plays is tied to the degree of uncertainty. Uncertainty is higher when it is not understood whether the skills and capabilities of existing firms will be necessary or useful in the commercialization of a new technology. The presence of pure-play firms indicates that uncertainty may be exploitable by new entrants. Second, pure plays make good stories. Given an interest in, say, electric vehicles, it is more exciting to invest in Tesla than in General Motors, despite the fact that both companies are deeply involved in the electrification of transportation. Conversely, the public and the media are less likely to attend to technology stories that lack a pure-play protagonist. Finally, for a bubble to form, there must be a way for investors to literally buy into the story. This point emerges from our sampling methodology of technologies. Many important technologies were not commercialized by publicly traded companies, or if they were, the companies' fortunes were broadly diversified. If there are no tradable financial assets that closely track the fortunes of the technology, then there can be no market speculation. Without a pure-play investment opportunity in a given technology, it is simply not possible for a speculative bubble to form for that technology. Simply put: a market must already exist for there to be a market bubble.

Coordination or Alignment of Beliefs Through Narratives

As pointed out in theories of herding and in studies of fads and fashions, beliefs must be sufficiently focused to drive up the value of a class of assets; investors with heterogeneous beliefs must become aware of the opportunity to participate in an emerging market for a new technology. On the one hand, attention must be focused on a particular market. On the other hand, uncertainty is necessary. Bubbles are rarer when attention is focused on a single means of generating returns and more likely when there is uncertainty about how to exploit the new opportunity.

Beliefs are coordinated through stories that circulate in the media and among investors. These stories or narratives piece together different facts, ideas, and guesses about a new technology and its potential profitability. Toby Lenk of eToys told a compelling story that was believable because of the uncertainty surrounding the viability of e-commerce and whether niche players could survive in online retailing. Some ideas and technologies are better subjects of narratives. It was easier to tell a story about human flight than the world's first synthetic plastic, Bakelite. The degree to which technologies lend themselves to storytelling is an important factor in driving bubbles.

The arc of a narrative is often propelled or stalled by particular actors and events. There are many historical examples of events that appear to have propelled narratives by aligning investor beliefs about the potential profitability of an opportunity. For instance, President James K. Polk, prior to the California gold rush, publicly confirmed the veracity of the rumors of gold in California in his State of the Union address.[36] Similarly, Charles Lindbergh's transatlantic flight was followed by a wave of 127 IPOs of airline and aircraft-related stocks, just like in 1995 the successful Netscape IPO brought increased attention to internet opportunities.[37] The *Hindenburg* disaster halted interest in airships. For other technologies, such as polyester or the laser, neither of which generated a boom and bust cycle, we find no associated coordinating event and no set of plausible entrepreneurial narratives.

Novice Investors

The fourth and final causal factor that contributes to the likelihood of speculation is the presence of novice or unsophisticated investors. Overoptimism or overconfidence may lead to poor buying decisions, thereby increasing demand for risky assets. Certain populations may be especially vulnerable to such biases. This thinking dates back at least to 1841, with Charles MacKay's *Extraordinary Popular Delusions and the Madness of Crowds*.[38] Contemporary scholars have explored this idea and observed that investors possess different levels of sophistication. Less sophisticated investors, sometimes called "noise traders," may be overly bullish, and individual traders appear less sophisticated than professional investors.[39] We expect that noise traders are especially likely to invest when the technology or its application is something they can understand, even if it is unclear how one might profit from the new technology. For example, in the late 1990s it was evident to the casual observer or investor that the internet was useful, although it was unclear who might profit from its adoption and how.

With this in mind, we argue that potential investors are more likely to buy an asset when they believe that they understand how value will be appropriated. If investors are more likely to invest in something they think they understand than in something they do not, then we suspect that at a minimum, the commercial potential of an innovation, or at least its usefulness, needs to be comprehensible and accessible to the investor. For example, relatively obscure developments in science such as the Nipkow disk in 1885 did little to stimulate the public imagination, despite the fact that the innovation was critical to the eventual development of television. In contrast, the public broadcast of the Metropolitan Opera on the radio in 1922 was accessible to the general investor and may have helped stimulate and align investor beliefs about the commercial prospects of radio.[40] Thus, retail-facing innovations may be more likely to grab the attention of a broad set of investors, even when that retail-facing quality is not perfectly correlated with profitability.[41] This observation is in line with evidence that individuals tend to invest in assets with which they are familiar.[42] We expect (and find) that speculative activity is more likely in innovations or ideas that are familiar and understandable based on common experience. The role of familiarity is exacerbated when the arrival of a retail-facing innovation coincides with an influx of novice or unsophisticated investors.[43]

The ebb and flow of new investors depends on many factors. Of course, each generation brings new investors to the market. Other factors, such as new investment technology (e.g., the stock ticker, E*Trade) or changes in regulation (e.g., bans on insider trading or the Jumpstart Our Business Startups Act and its influence on crowdfunding in the United States), may increase the influx of novices. To assess the importance of novices, we proceed with direct and indirect measurement. We piece together estimates of the number of households investing across our time period. We then supplement this direct measurement by developing a timeline of innovations and structural changes that increase (or decrease) market access for equity investments. These supply-side innovations lower barriers to entry for investors and reduce transaction costs. To help quantify this across our time periods, we put together a long-term series of the months of labor it takes the average worker to buy the average share traded on the New York Stock Exchange. We put these factors together to identify periods in which the number of possible participants in a financial market increase, thereby allowing us to identify influxes of novice or unsophisticated investors into markets. We term this process "market democratization."

Moreover, the performance of the market itself will attract or discourage investors. A bull market will attract more novices, and a level of optimism will persist among participants who have yet to experience a bear market. In contrast, a bear market will not only drive investors from the market but also discourage new entrants. The most dramatic of these events is the bull market of the 1920s and the investment desert that prevailed during the Great Depression. We summarize major events in the democratization of investment in Chapter 3.

While the first factor, uncertainty, may lead to rational boom and bust episodes, the fourth factor, the presence of novices, is associated with bubbles: rational models from financial economics do not explain why the presence of novices might be associated with price fluctuations. As we discuss in Chapter 3, these two factors, uncertainty and novice investors, may interact in ways that exacerbate the likelihood of a bubble, because uncertainty exacerbates the liabilities of inexperience in investing.

An Illuminating Example

A single example should never convince us of the importance of these institutional features—there are simply too many other factors that can plausibly explain one event. Nevertheless, such an exposition can illustrate our approach. We develop the four-factor model for two similar cases: the commercialization of Brush electric arc lighting in Cleveland and in London.

Electric lighting, a novel and, to contemporary observers, amazing technology, was demonstrated in Cleveland, Ohio, on April 29, 1879, when Charles F. Brush, backed by Cleveland financier George Stockly, lit up Public Square—then known as Monumental Park—with twelve arc lamps. As reported at the time, Brush's streetlights turned night into day and were visible for miles. The demonstrations were widely covered in the media and served to coordinate beliefs around the potential of this marvelous new technology.[44] A narrative emerged about the inevitability of electrical lighting. The eventually successful Brush Electric Company was capitalized at $3 million.

Nevertheless, investors were still unsure how to profitably exploit the innovation. Given the general uncertainty surrounding the technology, and the difficulty investors may have had in assessing the ability of entrepreneurs to exploit it, investors looked for endorsements of prominent businesspeople. Indeed, the Brush Electric Company was funded by what would be known today as business angels. These wealthy investors, mostly Cleveland's business elite, were connected to Brush through social networks.[45] More generally, Brush Electric and its numerous competitors were financed through informal, private equity networks.

The success of the Brush company sparked entry. However, the market for new equity investment in quality firms was limited to these individuals. For example, Brush spin-off Linde was subscribed by "prominent Cleveland businessmen."[46] Not only were investors in these assets relatively sophisticated, at least by the test of using endorsements as signals of underlying quality; they also had strong incentives to make sure that the underlying assets were of long-term value. There was a very illiquid market for shares in early high-technology enterprises in Cleveland, as described by economic historians Naomi Lamoreaux, Margaret Levenstein, and Kenneth Sokoloff:

> The wealthy Clevelanders who bought shares in these new high-tech enterprises seem to have been motivated by the returns they expected to earn from owning and holding them rather than the profits they could reap by selling them after an initial run-up in price. Although a few investors cashed out their investments relatively early, the practice seems uncommon. Before the formation of the CSE [Cleveland Stock Exchange] in 1900, the only firms associated with the Brush network for which share prices were quoted in Cleveland papers were Brush Electric itself and the Walker Manufacturing Company. Even after the formation of the exchange, we do not see much trading in equities of concerns associated with the hub. The one major exception, National Carbon, was listed on the exchange from the very beginning, but by that time it was a consolidation of a large number of previously competing firms.[47]

While it is clear that the most promising opportunities were funded through Cleveland's angel investor network, it is possible that smaller, individual investors funneled money into ventures of inexperienced entrepreneurs (or worse). The same authors report that there were perhaps forty attempts by fly-by-night artists to raise money in pursuit of dubious electric lighting companies in Cleveland. However, there is little evidence that they raised much money.[48] Although public beliefs were aligned in the presence of uncertainty, the structure of the Cleveland investment market limited the influx of new investors and stifled speculative activity.

A remarkably different history can be told about the Anglo-American Brush Company (AABC), founded in London in 1882. This company, established to commercialize Brush's arc lighting system in Britain, generated a number of "little Brushes," each receiving territorial exclusivity to establish central stations and supply lighting. Through a political process, monopoly rights were granted to central stations for a period of seven years, which, at the time, was predicted to provide sufficient time to generate a return for investors, although later, in August 1882, this was amended to twenty-one years under pressure from business interests. AABC became part of a larger speculative bubble in electric company assets in the spring of 1882. In the first five months of 1882, British electrical companies registered with authorized capital of £9 million, reflecting investments of £7 million. In mid-May shares of the Anglo-American Brush Electric Light Corporation dropped £600,000 in three days of trading (though they remained above par value).

Why was there a bubble in Britain but not in the United States? While it was clear that lighting was valuable, it was not clear in the 1880s which business model would sustain a lighting company. Would money be made on light bulbs or by selling electricity? (Electricity meters were not yet invented.) To what degree were inexperienced investors interested in this innovation? The historical record is clear that lighting generated interest, if not awe, among contemporary observers. Early entrepreneurs lit up prominent areas of both Cleveland and London (and other cities as well). However, there is reason to suspect that inexperienced investors had much greater market access in London than in Cleveland. The London Stock Exchange (LSE) was a very democratic institution that accommodated smaller, less sophisticated traders. First, commissions on the LSE were lower than on the New York Stock Exchange (NYSE). Second, perhaps more important, trades were settled in London every fortnight. Thus, London traders enjoyed a two-week "float"; they could "buy" for the account what they could not afford and sell short as well. This increased liquidity and allowed for greater speculation. While there was no market in Cleveland, stocks may have been floated in New York on the NYSE. However, in New York trades settled the following day. What's more, the NYSE had a policy of monopoly that held down the number of securities that were traded.[49] By contrast, the London exchange would list any security for which there was a market, and hence traded smaller companies' shares. Even as late as 1914 the average capitalization of the NYSE was $24.7 million, whereas the average LSE listing was capitalized at one-fifth that amount ($£$1.03 million, or contemporaneously approximately $5 million). Importantly, the inability to list on the NYSE also made smaller-capitalization stocks less available as collateral for other margin purchases.

Through this example we see that even when the specific asset in question is the same—that is, investors in Cleveland and London were investing in the same underlying technological system—the potential for speculation can be determined by the institutional and organizational context through which investors access the relevant financial market. In this case, the specific features of the LSE supported, perhaps encouraged, speculation. In Cleveland, because shares of Brush and related companies were not readily traded, speculation was certainly harder to engage in, if not impossible.

The London bubble had deleterious effects on the British electric lighting industry and on the British economy more generally.[50] In the aftermath of the bubble, and with the help of entrenched interests (gas lighting companies), the British Parliament passed the Electric Light Act of 1885. Not only did this law retard the adoption of the new lighting systems, but perversely, the more "developed" London capital markets set up the darkness exploited by Jack the Ripper. London remained dark well into the 1890s while other worldly cities such as Paris and New York were lit. This episode also deprived British entrepreneurs of valuable opportunities to move down the learning curve with the new technology. This latter cost is quite difficult to quantify.

The fact that public investors in London were able to invest easily in the electric lighting companies itself became part of the story of electric lighting. While journalists in America focused on the magic of the electric light, their British counterparts overlay on this a narrative of investment opportunities. This reporting, in turn, fed the narrative of speculation.

Road Map

In the chapters that follow, we summarize our studies of the history of the commercialization of fifty-eight major technological innovations. This sample—which we describe in greater detail in Chapter 1—contains variation in the features in which we are interested and allows us to generate the causal model we have described here. In the spirit of our previous work with David Miller, our analysis is stochastic.[51] Even if all the potential causes are present, a bubble still may not form— and a bubble may form even if few potential causes are present. A successful theory of bubbles will identify factors that, when present, imply that a bubble is more likely to occur. We identify such factors. In no place do we claim or mean to imply that these conditions are sufficient or necessary to generate asset bubbles.

To evaluate whether our ideas have any external validity—that is, to see if the theory applies beyond our initial fifty-eight technology "training sample"—we then test the theory on a different set of thirty more recent technologies that includes the internet, laparoscopic surgery, and liquid crystal displays. Because at this point our framework was fixed, this exercise allowed us to assess how well the framework works outside the historical settings of the initial sample. We then consider whether the theory helps us understand recent events such as the housing crisis and the Great Recession (Chapter 5).

Our work puts the role of narrative at center stage. We cannot understand real economic outcomes without also understanding when the stories that influence decisions emerge and under which conditions they are most likely to be created. Much to the dismay of economists such as the Nobel laureate Robert Shiller, the history of much of economics has been an attempt to assume away the role of stories; they have no space for a rational decision maker.[52] However, our analysis suggests that ignoring stories and narratives makes it much harder to understand important economic phenomena such as bubbles.

Independent of our theoretical interpretation, our basic finding—that certain major technological innovations are associated with speculative bubbles and others are not—affirms our methodological approach. This establishes a point of departure for subsequent debates about the possible causes of speculative behavior, regardless of whether one agrees with the specific conditions we describe. To understand the antecedents of bubbles, we must examine when there are and when there are not bubbles. Although we believe that our analysis and interpretation advance theoretical and practical understanding of the causes of bubbles, one might plausibly disagree with these implications, yet still accept the basic empirical framework we set forth. Other explanations of why some but not all major technological innovations lead to speculation are possible.

Chapter 1

BUBBLES AND NON-BUBBLES ACROSS TIME

What Is a Bubble?

In January 1926 a share of the Radio Corporation of America (RCA), the leading radio manufacturer, patent holder, and broadcaster of the day, could be had for $43 on the New York Stock Exchange. The same share peaked at $568 in September 1929 but cost only $15 in 1932. RCA's dividend-adjusted price did not recover to 1929 levels until the 1960s. By that time, the company was making most of its money from television rather than radio. By any measure imaginable, investors were better off avoiding RCA stock in 1929.

The RCA story is not unique. In early 1637, prices for some tulip bulbs in Amsterdam were briefly on the order of seventeen years' wages, before collapsing by 99.99%. For a time in 1998, plush toys known as Beanie Babies sold for $5,000 each, and trading in such toys accounted for 10% of eBay transactions.[1] Today, most of these toys can be had for $10, a 99.998% collapse. Were these bubbles? If not, it is hard to imagine what would qualify as one.

This question of whether an event is a bubble is confusing without some discussion of what we mean by *bubble*—and we will have difficulty answering the central question of our book, "When are there not bubbles?" without careful attention to this. Therefore, we take a moment here to define what we mean by a bubble. This becomes even more interesting when we consider that *bubble* is a loaded term in some academic circles. Some financial economists contend that bubbles do not exist at all!

Academics who study financial markets traditionally define a bubble as a deviation from fundamental value. A subset of these scholars, the true believers in efficient markets, deny that prices can deviate from fundamental value. They do not deny that prices rise and fall; rather, they contend that prices always reflect nothing but investors' reasoned beliefs about the asset's fundamental value. But the prices must summarize the beliefs that investors have about future profits or value. Most economists call price expansions and collapses bubbles only if investors are paying more than future profits or expected share-price increases would justify—or, more specifically, more than a reasoned or "rational" investor would expect the market to price the asset in the future. If investors purchase an investment asset that they know will be worth less when they expect to sell it, this is clearly foolish.[2] For example, paying full price for a Christmas tree on December 26 with the purpose of reselling it is foolish, or in academic speak, "irrational." Following common practice, we define bubbles as extreme price fluctuations associated with fools and foolish behavior.

To stay true to this terminology, we refer to a rise in prices followed by a sharp decline as a boom and bust episode.[3] Bubbles are those boom and bust episodes in which investors drive up prices and get fooled. Perhaps the investors are newcomers or naïfs, but however we identify them, their essential behavior consists in getting fooled. If reasonable beliefs justified the high prices, then boom and bust episodes are better thought of as examples of investors making reasonable bets that turn out poorly.

The distinction between a foolish investor and one making a bad bet may seem arbitrary. Were the ill-fated investors who bought RCA stock in 1929 buying because they were irrational (and therefore foolish), or did they simply overestimate the expected value of future cash flows accruing to the company? Both look the same in hindsight—a high price followed by a collapse, with many people losing money.

However, for financial economists and the policy makers they advise, assumptions about investor beliefs are critical: if the cause was foolishness, perhaps we should consider a policy response to prevent such events in the future. In contrast, if the rearview mirror is showing us just a reasoned bet gone bad, then there is no room for any policy response. In this view, the result is not a bug but a feature of capitalism. We need to experiment to find the correct solution, and capitalist incentives are funneling money to such experiments. To summarize, a boom and bust episode is a bubble if it is associated with an increase in investors who are unlikely to have the tools or experience to understand whether any given price is reasonable, or if we have compelling evidence that investors were justifying their investments on the basis of particularly foolish arguments.

Although bubbles can arise in many different asset classes, this book is about technologies. It is simply much more interesting for us, and intellectually compelling for you, to learn about the history of airplanes as we study bubbles than, say, the history of Beanie Babies. Airplanes shape our experience today to a much greater extent than cute stuffed animals.[4] In Chapters 5 and 6, we argue that because the causes of bubbles are based in fundamental characteristics of markets, human psychology, and the interaction of those two things, our conclusions generalize to many different asset classes, including Beanie Babies, real estate and mortgage-backed securities, and other objects of speculation.

To compare episodes across time periods and industries, we also need to take into account the fact that some stocks will be naturally more volatile than others. When ventures are inherently hard to assess because they are trying to do something that is actually new, investors will find it difficult to find similar ventures to which to anchor their assessments of value—but unless investors' analogies are close, the resulting assessments of value will rarely be accurate. Because of this, every bit of new information causes investors to reassess. If the information is ambiguous or the analogy imprecise, investors will arrive at different opinions about the value, which will lead to volatile trading patterns: there will be numerous price movements as investors trade on their various guesses. That is, we will see volatility. Contrast this to, say, a stable, boring utility business that is well understood. New information is unlikely to be weighted as heavily given a reliable and predictive track record. Different opinions about value will be rare, and volatility lower. With more uncertain stocks, it will take more severe swings to raise our scholarly suspicions that something is amiss. Alternately, better-understood assets will trigger our interest with more modest deviations in value, simply because such patterns are likely to be more exceptional with respect to historical price trends.

Over the course of the next few pages, we introduce several cases, each an instance of a significant technological innovation that either was or was not associated with the formation of a boom and bust episode. Not only do we find the cases interesting in their own right; these examples also provide context for us to introduce the sample of technologies that we will analyze throughout the book. For each one, we spend some time contextualizing how the technology and investment opportunity was viewed in the day and documenting the price fluctuations. We then consider how we might compare episodes across time and technology.

"Talking at a piece of sheet iron": The Telephone, 1878–1889

"The very idea of talking at a piece of sheet iron was so new and extraordinary that the normal mind repulsed it. Alike to the laborer and the scientist, it was incomprehensible. It was too freakish, too bizarre to be used outside the laboratory and the museum. No one, literally, could understand how it worked; and the only man who offered a clear solution to the mystery was a Boston mechanic, who maintained that there was 'a hole through the middle of the wire.'"
HERBERT N. CASSON, *THE HISTORY OF THE TELEPHONE*, 1910

Historically, the conditions necessary to create a bubble have been rare simply because the markets for assets have been limited. The investment history of the telephone illustrates this clearly. When Alexander Graham Bell demonstrated the telephone on August 4, 1876, the ability to transfer voice in real time across distance was incredible, if rudimentary. The telephone business model was neither obvious nor uncontested, and success of the platform was not ensured. Even Bell's inner circle was unsure of how to build a profitable business around the invention. In mid-1879—three years after Bell first demonstrated the device—when National Bell sought additional working capital to support geographic expansion, investor demand was weak. Par-value shares priced at $100 fetched only $50 in the contemporary equivalent of a failed IPO.[5] We do not know whether investors were uncertain about the basic functioning of the technology or doubted demand for the initial value proposition or worried about potential competition. All three concerns would have been valid. The feasibility of the telephone as a network connecting any subscriber to any other subscriber was still very much a work in progress. The exchange-based architecture that supported any-to-any communication had only been introduced in New Haven, Connecticut, in 1878. Telephone numbers were introduced in 1879. Challenges to the enforceability of Bell's patent were looming, as was competition from the leading telegraph operator of the time, Western Union. Investors likely debated all these issues, resulting in the first tranche of Bell shares being overpriced relative to market demand.

Soon thereafter, however, Western Union and National Bell Telephone Company settled outstanding legal claims and agreed not to compete in each other's respective lines of business. Investor interest strengthened, and as Stehman describes it, "a mad rush for the stock" followed. Within a matter of months, the final tranche of the same $100-par-value shares that had been hard to place at $50 sold for $600 each. The fact that the agreement with Western Union calmed investors' fears suggests that investors had doubted Bell's ability to successfully compete with a well-capitalized incumbent. As noted, Western Union and Bell would soon come to occupy distinct lines of business, but at this early stage, basic features of the telephone industry were not yet fixed, and investors saw the resolution of the potential competitive threat from Western Union as an important positive signal for Bell.[6]

Was there a bubble in Bell stock? On the one hand, the reported stock price surged 1,200% in less than a year, and it is unlikely that the investors who purchased shares in the final tranche at $600 profited from their investment for some time.[7] But who were the buyers, and were they investors participating in a bubble or simply rewarding the firm for having successfully resolved underlying uncertainties and thereby paving a path for successful growth? Unfortunately our sources do not enable us to definitively answer these questions.

What we do know, however, is that it was difficult to invest in telephone stocks until at least 1881. Shares of the early Bell companies like New England Bell Telephone Company (1877), National Bell Telephone Company (1879), and American Bell Telephone Company (1881) were placed privately, with scant secondary trading on the Boston Stock Exchange. There were 338 investors who owned the 8,500 shares of National Bell Telephone and 12 who owned 4,795 shares (56.4%), but even the remaining "small" investors had average holdings larger than 11 shares each (more than $1,100 in 1879 at par value).[8] We note that at this point in time, $1,100 was three times the amount an average American worker earned in an entire year.[9] Thus, direct, public access to the Bell stock book was limited.

Access to the market was easier after the American Bell Telephone Company's private placement was complete. An index of telephone stocks from the 1880s was not available, so we dug into old Boston newspapers to reconstruct one on our own. We pick up the price trend on October 22, 1881, when the price was $145 per share. The price rose to $296 by March 1883. In late 1883, Bell's general manager Theodore Vail announced to shareholders, "The telephone business has passed its experimental stage."[10] Nevertheless, the price dropped by 50% to $150 by the summer of 1884, perhaps because patent litigation continued to cast a shadow on the company's prospects. It wasn't until 1887 that the Supreme Court granted Bell expansive rights over all transmission of voice using wires and electricity.[11] Thereafter, the price rebounded, hovering around $200–$230 through late 1889. The stock was volatile. Should we call this a bubble?

Resurrection: Insulin, 1920–1923

In 1919, diabetes was a devastating disease, especially for children. Individuals with juvenile diabetes faced a "ghastly choice between death from diabetes or a few more months of famished life before dying of starvation."[12] It was in this setting that Elizabeth Hughes, the eleven-year-old daughter of US Secretary of State Charles Hughes, was diagnosed with diabetes. Following the state-of-the-art treatment of the day, diabetes specialist Frederick M. Allen put Hughes on a four-hundred-calories-per-day diet to limit her blood-sugar levels. By 1922, young Elizabeth had outlived the life expectancy of childhood diabetes by two years, although her weight had dropped from seventy-five to forty-five pounds. The Hughes family prepared to bury their daughter.

Situations such as young Elizabeth's were nothing new and had stimulated the search for a cure for diabetes for many decades. At the time diabetes affected, by some estimates, 1 million people in the United States. However, the childhood version of the disease was particularly insidious in that it was both more severe than the adult version and the victims were, well, children. The search for a cure was in full swing. Fifteen years earlier it had been recognized that the pancreas produced something that helps metabolize carbohydrates and control blood-sugar levels. By the early 1920s several teams were trying to isolate that factor. In Toronto, the amateur scientist Frederick Banting conceived of an experimental method to extract and isolate the pancreatic factor known to be associated with metabolizing carbohydrates. He approached his former teacher J. J. R. Macleod, a professor at the University of Toronto, who arranged for lab assistant Charles Best to help on the project. Banting's insights proved amateurish, and later that year, senior scientist J. B. Collip was added to the team. Collip developed a technique to isolate the pancreatic secretion that came to be known as insulin. Initial treatment focused on children who were in a diabetic coma. The results were nothing short of miraculous. Early observers reported that insulin treatment appeared to "resurrect" the stricken. This dramatic impact was soon picked up in the press.

Elizabeth's mother, Antoinette, petitioned the Toronto team to treat her daughter. She was rebuffed. The Toronto process was experimental, and the team was unable to produce insulin in quantity. A desperate Antoinette then asked her husband to use his position to intervene. The secretary of state thought it unethical to use state power to intervene on his own child's behalf, but he did so at his wife's behest. In mid-August 1922, Elizabeth arrived in Toronto emaciated. The fourteen-year-old began receiving two insulin shots a day. Her recovery was nothing short of miraculous. She gained two pounds during her first week of treatment and quickly recovered strength. She then did what any child would like to do: she went to the movies.

Insulin's transition from remedy for the few to salvation for the many required a series of technological and business processes. First, despite concerns that patenting medical technology would violate the Hippocratic oath, the University of Toronto patented the process. A partnership with Eli Lilly and Company was soon formed to produce the drug. Scaling production was difficult, but by 1923, insulin was becoming widely available. The ability to transform a severe, debilitating, often fatal illness into a manageable condition was a major achievement of modern medicine. In October that same year, Banting and MacLeod shared the Nobel Prize in Physiology or Medicine.[13] Elizabeth Hughes was one of the first individuals with juvenile diabetes to live a full life. She graduated from Barnard College, was active in civic affairs throughout her life, married, had children, and lived to the age of seventy-three. Over the course of her life she injected an estimated forty-five thousand doses of insulin.

Despite these accolades, the estimated million people in the United States who were living with the disease at the time, and the undeniable advance to human health that insulin represented, we found no evidence of market speculation in companies that were producing insulin.[14] The patent protection eliminated any uncertainty regarding who would control the technology. Eli Lilly was not traded publicly at the time, so there was no way for the public to invest in the company behind this dramatic new business opportunity. Therefore, despite the miracle of resurrection, there was no bubble in insulin.

The new remedy did attract fraudsters, a phenomenon we observed across many exciting new technologies. Although a few firms tried to market alternatives to insulin (using deliberately confusing names like "Insulans" that were superficially similar to Lilly's branded insulin), the clarity of the biological mechanism quickly revealed these frauds for what they were. Only insulin—the "magic hormone"— would keep diabetics alive. It was easy to verify whether a substance would keep a patient alive, and no one would invest in a company whose product did not keep people alive.[15] We highlight this historical footnote because if there had been opportunities to invest in the new space, fraudsters would have likely exacerbated any bubble potential as they did in other settings.

"When virtually nothing was fixed": Radio, 1898–1933

If insulin is on the non-bubble end of the spectrum, radio is on the frothier end. Radio was the first, live, mass-media technology. The ability to transport voice into living rooms and parlors satisfied a primal human need of social connection. It allowed people to feel part of broader society while in the intimacy of their homes. However, the original turn-of-the-century radio inventors did not imagine broadcast, and early radio technology could transmit only Morse code, not voice. Even once the idea of radio broadcast took hold, it was still unclear how to build and support the necessary infrastructure—nor was it obvious how radio firms would make money. The historian Susan Douglas eloquently captures the uncertainty in the 1920s radio industry:

> These were the frothy "boom" years of radio, when virtually nothing was fixed—not the frequencies of the stations (although at first

everyone was supposed to broadcast at the same wavelength), not the method of financial support, not the government regulations, and not the design or the domestic location of the radio itself. There were no networks—known in the 1920s as the chains—and there was very little advertising on the air. With a few exceptions, like the Sunday broadcasts of church services, there was not a predictable program schedule. Instead, stories geared for children might be followed by a lecture on "hygiene of the mouth"; or "how to make a house a home," which would in turn be followed by a phonograph music of "Madame Burumowska, formerly of the Moscow Opera" singing Rimsky-Korsakov's "Hymn to the Sun." Department stores, newspapers, the manufacturers of radio equipment, colleges and universities, labor unions, socialists, and ham operators all joined the rush to start stations.[16]

And the rush was intense. In January 1922, 8 new stations were licensed. In February, 24 new stations added, March, 77 and then 76, 97, and 72 in April, May, and June, respectively. By July there were 76 more, and by the end of 1922, there were 690 radio stations broadcasting across America.[17]

In this environment, one could weave many stories about the potential profitability of a venture designed to build out any part, or a combination of parts, of this emerging ecosystem: radio broadcast stations, broadcast equipment, programming, and radio sets. The industry was filled with experimentation. For example, the closest technological precedent was the telephone, and the early radio pioneer David Sarnoff sought to replicate Bell's model with RCA through aggressive patent protection and by charging radio listeners a fee to tune in.[18] This proved difficult, because unlike the case of the telephone, there was no way to know who was tuning in. Alternatively, RCA sought to derive profits from the sales of magazines with programming information. Eventually, RCA derived the bulk of the company's revenues through programming and the licensing of radio patents.[19]

Without question, radio had one of the most dramatic boom and bust episodes that we examine. In 1925, radio stocks traded on the New York Curb Market (yes, there really was a stock market located on the street curb; it moved inside in 1922 and was eventually renamed the American Stock Exchange, or AMEX, in 1953). We have calculated a price index of radio stocks traded on the Curb. This index rose from a base of 5 in January of 1924 up to 30 in January 1925 and back to 7 in January 1926. But the real drama came later in the decade, an episode epitomized by the rise and fall of RCA stock with which we opened this chapter: RCA stock rose thirteen-fold and then lost 97% of its value within seven years. There is nothing in our depiction that helps us understand whether this was a bad bet, and hence a simple boom and bust episode, or a bubble. We'll need some patience to answer that question, which requires considering who was investing in the stock market generally and in radio stocks in particular in 1929—a task we take up in Chapter 3.

Visual Radio, 1926–1951

The story of television is quite different from that of radio, even though ultimately the business models of the two broadcast technologies are similar. The first television demonstration occurred in a London department store on January 27, 1926—a time when radio was entering the mainstream in the United States. This was a simplistic demonstration, with no more than rough shapes transmitted in motion. Nevertheless, although early televisions were low-resolution, mechanical devices, many thought that television would cannibalize theater and other live productions. Commercialization and widespread adoption awaited the development of the electronic television and broadcasting systems, along with the standardization of the broadcasting format by RCA in 1941. At the end of World War II, the television craze hit. While there was great excitement around television, and there is no doubt that the advent of television was a major historical event, indices of TV stocks and radio broadcast stocks exhibit only modest evidence of speculation. An index of TV and radio broadcasters reached a peak in January 1946 and lost half its value by the summer of 1947. A similar pattern is seen in the parallel index of radio and TV and electronics manufacturers. Because many firms were active in both the radio and the television industries, it is hard to know whether investors were trying to invest in the TV industry, the radio industry, or both. In 1947 few individuals owned televisions and radios were pervasive. This is not simply a flaw in our ability to measure; rather, it reflects the difficulty an investor had in trying to make a pure-play investment in the television industry. Many, if not most, of the industries in our study never overcame this difficulty. We improvise a partial solution by assembling an index of firms that manufactured exclusively TVs, even though this captures only part of the industry's activity.[20] But it was possible to invest in this set of stocks only after 1948, and between 1948 and 1960 the greatest sustained decline in these stocks was 30% in the mid-1950s. All these indices recovered their lost value in the late 1950s and far exceeded this value going forward. TV stocks were volatile, but the investor experience was very different from the earlier radio episode.

Comparing Boom and Bust Episodes Across Technologies

Comparing the investment histories of radio and TV poses an additional challenge. The peak radio stock prices occurred during the run-up in prices of 1929 and can be understood only in the context of the historic stock market crash and depression that followed. Thus, the 97% collapse in the value of radio stocks must be understood in the context of the 81% general average decline in stock value during the same period. In contrast, the 30% drop in television stocks in the mid-1950s occurred at a time when the market was much flatter. On the one hand, in a relative-to-market sense, the fluctuations in TV stocks in the late 1940s are more striking than those of radio stocks in the late 1920s. On the other hand, it might be more relevant to investors and practitioners to keep our focus on the percentage decline: if forced to choose, most of us would prefer to lose only 30% of our money rather than 97% of it.

How different were these episodes? Which should we consider a boom and bust episode? Which was a bubble? To make progress in understanding the causes of these fluctuations, we need a concrete, objective way to compare the introduction, commercialization, and societal and market responses to technologies as disparate as the telephone, insulin, radio, and television. How do we know if one is "frothier" than the next while also taking into account market conditions? Maybe the radio crash was just part of a larger macroeconomic process, and the observed fluctuations were due to factors that were unrelated to our variables of interest. At a minimum, any solution must take into account the movements of technology-linked stocks relative to the broader market.

To compare stock market fluctuations across time and technology we measure their *frothiness*. Formally, *frothiness* is the number of standard deviations from the predicted stock or index trend. We classify an episode as a boom and bust when frothiness is greater than 2, that is, 2 standard deviations above the trend, where the "trend" is the predicted stock price looking forward and backward seven years.

It is helpful to think of frothiness as a stock's temperament.[21] For example, some people are quick to anger and others are relatively calm. When someone who is quick to anger gets angry, we might brush it off, saying, "Oh, that person is a hothead; he reacts at the slightest provocation," whereas when someone with a calm demeanor loses their temper, we really notice, because it is exceptional and likely indicative of something wrong. Consider the index of rubber and tire companies in the early part of the last century, shown in Figure 1.1. There are three lines—solid, dashed, and dotted. The solid line is the realized price index. The dashed line is the projection based on a window that looks forward and back seven years. One can think of it as the long-term average value of an index.[22] The dotted line is the bubble line—or the line that at every point in time is exactly 2 standard deviations above the trend.

We see in Figure 1.1 that in the case of tires and rubber, the index was at a record high in 1920. Through the lens of history it becomes clear that the entire run-up in stock prices was erased by the mid-1920s. Prices rebounded in 1929, but that was erased too. The prices went well above the trend line. In July 1919, the tire and rubber index peaked at 301, whereas the predicted trend was only 129. This implied a frothiness of 3.19 (or 3.19 standard deviations above the trend). This

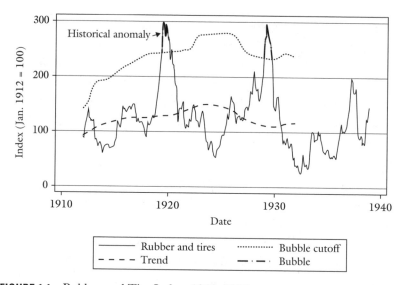

FIGURE 1.1   Rubber and Tire Index, 1912–1938

Sources: Authors' calculations based on A. Cowles, *Common-Stock Indexes* (Bloomington, IN: Principia Press, 1939), Automobile Tires & Rubber Goods, Series C, p. 202. *Notes:* Index is normalized to 100 in January 1912. Index takes into account stock dividends.

is well above the bubble line, which marks two units of frothiness from the underlying trend. To emphasize this, we've darkened the stock trend line when frothiness is above 2. Tires and rubber had two boom and bust periods, one in 1920 and the second in 1929.[23]

These trends may be different even with two related technologies. Looking at Figure 1.1, we see that rubber and tires peaked at about 300 in both 1919 and 1929. This peak was three times the value in 1912. In Figure 1.2, we graphed the same data that is in Figure 1.1 on the left panel. You can see the two boom and bust periods, but they appear very small. This is because we have scaled the graph to depict the history of automobile stocks. Automobile stocks moved together with tires and rubber, but in 1919 the index almost hit 1,900, more than six times the level of the corresponding tire and rubber index. Both products exhibit a bust period in 1921. Evidently, despite Ford's great success, it was not entirely clear how profits would be distributed through the industry, and it was not yet possible to invest in Ford stock anyway. General Motors was in the index, but it was still very much a challenger to Ford's dominance. By the mid- to late 1920s, it was clear that tires were a commodity; consequently, tire companies would not enjoy great pricing power. In 1929 automobiles and trucks hit 11,000, or 110 times the 1912 value. Profits (and shareholder returns) would clearly concentrate in successful automobile manufacturers rather than in their suppliers. With this forward knowledge, the automobile movements do not measure as frothy. In our analysis, the frothiness of the automobile index peaked in 1920 at 2.5 standard deviations above the index's trend at a time when the market was also at 2.5. But the events of 1929 and the Great Depression dwarf these patterns. Automobiles experienced a boom and bust period in 1929, as did tires. But how do we compare these episodes? In 1929, tires peaked at 3.34, whereas automobiles only 2.66. Tires were frothier than automobiles, and both were frothier than the general market frothiness of 2.15.

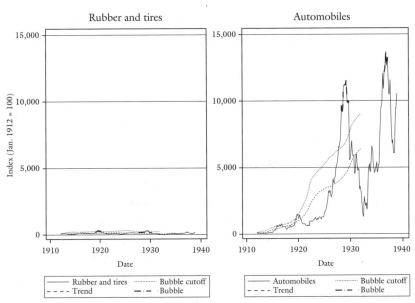

FIGURE 1.2   Rubber and Tire and Automobile manufacturer indices, 1912–1938
Sources: Authors' calculations based on A. Cowles, "Common-Stock Indexes," 1939, Automobiles & Trucks, Series C, p. 240; Automobile Tires & Rubber Goods, Series C, p. 202.
Note: Both indices take into account stock dividends and are normalized to 100 in January 1912. For frothiness data, see the Appendix.

When Are There Not Bubbles?

We can now almost answer the question of when there are not bubbles, at least for these technologies. Taking the four cases explored in the previous sections as a minisample, we can measure and compare frothiness, and thereby assess whether there was a boom-and-bust period for each one, but we cannot yet determine whether each boom and bust episode was a bubble. So we can say when there are not bubbles, but we cannot yet say when there are. That is the "almost" sense. According to our calculations, Bell stock was frothy, peaking at 1.92, just shy of our bubble cutoff. But it did not stay there for long, very few shares were traded at this price, and it fell just 52%. This contrasts with the case of insulin. Here, it was not possible to trade in insulin companies, as Lilly was a private company at this time. So we cannot even construct a frothiness measure, and there was no possibility of public speculation. The radio index was extraordinarily frothy. Indeed, it was one of the frothiest industry indices we found in all our studies. Radio stocks peaked in 1929 at 3.35 and subsequently lost 97% of their value. Moreover, the frothiness of radio remained above 2 for eleven consecutive months. By contrast, television wasn't nearly as frothy. At its peak, the index peeped just above 2 for a single month in 1946. Subject to the limitations of our data, we can now rank these episodes from most frothy (definite boom and bust period) to least frothy (no boom no bust): radio, television, telephone, insulin.

With our measure of frothiness in hand, we can compare historical episodes to each other. But which to compare? Imagine that we chose a set of speculative bubbles, such as radio, dot-com, and other historical bubbles, such as the seventeenth-century Dutch Tulipmania and the eighteenth-century British South Sea Bubble, and then analyzed and compared the episodes to identify the underlying causes of bubbles. As intuitive as this may sound, it would be an error—indeed, an affront—to the scientific method.[24] We need what social scientists call a "sampling strategy," a way of choosing assets, events, what-have-you, that were at comparable risk of leading to a boom and bust episode. We could then compare times when bubbles happened to times when they did not in order to understand what is different about each case.

To understand why a sound sampling strategy is needed, it is helpful to consider what might happen if we did not carefully define our sample. Assume for the moment that we embarked on a study of technology bubbles and found out that there was a large population of novice investors investing in high numbers in each bubble. Assume further that we then concluded that novice investors were a cause of bubbles. This would be a gross error of inference. It may be that there was a large population of novice investors investing in most new technologies, but many of these technologies did not experience a bubble at all. Because in our hypothetical example we examined only cases of bubbles, we would never know that novices are generally investing in all new technologies and therefore cannot explain why some new technologies are associated with bubbles and some not. This leads to the obvious conclusion that one cannot understand underlying causes of bubbles without making comparisons of assets that were associated with bubbles to assets that were not.

Given that market speculation appears more likely when something important happens, though, we needed a group of assets (in our case, technologies) that were actually important. If not, we might sample a large set of technologies (say, every new patent) and find so few associated with bubbles that we would not be able to say much at all about underlying causes. Thus, we must find a set of important assets that might have generated sufficient interest to spark speculation but were not chosen *because* they generated speculation.

Economics is generally not considered a particularly dangerous profession, but here we are aided by the legacy of one economist who lost his life because of his ideas. In 1938, following ten years' imprisonment, the leading Russian economist Nikolai Kondratiev was sentenced to death and executed by firing squad. Kondratiev was one of hundreds of thousands of individuals who lost their lives as part of Stalin's catastrophic Great Purge. Stalin was threatened by Kondratiev's ideas, which recognized that technological change was a key ingredient of economic growth. Kondratiev tried to explain economic growth through "long waves"—or, as he called it, long cycle theory. The theory postulates that new innovations spawn technological revolutions that in turn give rise to new industries. Industries first grow, then stagnate, and eventually decline, leading to aggregate patterns of the business cycle. While Stalin was able to eliminate Kondratiev, his ideas sparked many decades of research in which scholars assembled inventories of new and important technologies and attempted to link them empirically to growth rates and the business cycle. This voluminous research has not been particularly successful in supporting Kondratiev's hypotheses because it has proven exceptionally difficult to relate aggregate growth to specific technologies.[25]

However, buried in this tragic history is great news for our project. We need a list of technologies that we can compare to one another to try to relate characteristics of new technologies to the appearance of boom and bust episodes and bubbles. The list items cannot have been chosen because the history of the associated technologies generated bubbles. The long-range theorists' legacy of lists of "major technological innovations"—whose criteria for selection was that the included technologies were economically important without consideration of whether they were associated with market speculation—is ideal for our task.[26]

We identified three timelines of technology and technological innovations that were produced as chapters for a volume on long waves and technological change.[27] Each of the three individual chapters includes a list of important technological innovations from 1840 to 1967.[28] Because the long-wave scholars sought to identify innovations associated with consequential, durable shifts in the world economy, we infer that they would have made a good-faith effort to prepare exhaustive inventories of important technological innovations. Also, the scholars were recognized experts in this area. Therefore, if the authors erred, it was likely that they counted too many major innovations rather than too few. We joined the three lists and identified those innovations that appear on at least two, resulting in a list of fifty-eight innovations. We took this list as our baseline set of major technological innovations that were at risk of creating financial boom and bust episodes. We then went to work figuring out what happened to each innovation.

The results—which appear in Table A.1 in the Appendix—warrant closer inspection. We list the name of the technology, the window during which a bubble might have formed, an aggregation of factors based on our research as to whether it was likely a bubble would form, and whether there was a company or companies in which to invest. If there were publicly accessible investment options, we report peak frothiness, percentage decline from peak to trough, and the decline relative to the S&P 500 Index (post-1926) or the Cowles industrial index (pre-1926).

Investors need investment targets for there to be speculation. For many of these technologies, there was no way, or no direct way, for investors to speculate. Sometimes, bubbles happen mostly outside the public markets, as private investors invest in new start-ups that are not traded publicly. We will note when we find some evidence that this has happened, but we cannot easily track asset prices in private markets, especially historically. Some technologies are explored by large diversified firms, which limits the ability of the independent investor to narrowly target investment in the new thing.[29]

We then list the year in which much of the uncertainty about the technology and the associated business model disappeared because a dominant business model emerged. We get into how this resolution of uncertainty plays out and what we mean by it in Chapter 2. We call this period between initial investments and the resolution of business model uncertainty the *window of bubble opportunity*. Of course, there is quite a bit of judgment required in putting a date on something like this. Our reasoning for these dates is in our online Appendix available at the Stanford University Press website (http://www.sup.org/bubbles andcrashes). Nevertheless, we need to put time limits on our measurement because—as we will explore—bubbles feed on uncertainty. New windows can open when, say, economic relationships change in a related market, as in the case of rubber and the market for automobiles. Our sample includes television, which was introduced after World War II but was soon eclipsed by a second item on our list, the color television, in the 1960s. The introduction of color television closed the window for television as subsequent stock movements of television manufacturers would be associated with color television as opposed to the earlier technology. Similarly, the first commercial class of antibiotics, sulfa drugs, was eclipsed by penicillin after only a few years on the market. We stop our analysis of a technology when the initial window of bubble opportunity closes; future fluctuations may be caused by confounding factors that we do not track.

Finally, even if we find signs of speculation in the index, it does not necessarily imply that these movements are caused by the factors in our theory—or even that the movements are associated with the given technology. This is because for some of the technologies, it is difficult to construct an index that properly maps the opportunity and the technology in question. To remedy this, we do two things. First, we cross-reference stock movements with the emerging narrative in the press. If widespread excitement about a new technology is moving stock prices, then this would have been reported in the press.[30] Therefore, for each speculative episode that we identify, we examine what was being discussed about the technology in the press, as well as how the stock movements were being described. We report how the movements were perceived in our online Appendix.

Examining the discourse trends over time also allows us to identify periods during which there might have been speculation that we fail to pick up in stock indices. For example, drilling for oil caused a clear speculative episode in Titusville, Pennsylvania, in the mid-1800s. This episode was widely reported in the contemporary press. However, there was no way to publicly invest, as securities markets were primitive relative to today.

Spanning nearly 130 years, the list of major innovations includes many that obviously had a large impact on society, such as the incandescent lamp, the telephone, the airplane, television, and penicillin. Although at least three of these are themselves evolving with the continuing information technology revolution, it is difficult to argue that these were not transformative technologies. However, the list also counts some innovations that might not, at first blush, seem as important: rayon, the electric record player, the pesticide DDT, and the automatic watch. Some are simply underappreciated. For example, we were amazed to learn that DDT was instrumental in eradicating malaria in large parts of the world. Without exaggeration, and notwithstanding the fact that DDT was ultimately abused and overused as an agricultural pesticide, DDT saved the lives of millions of people across the globe.

To remove all subjective judgment in the selection of technologies to study, the sampling strategy of "appear on two of three lists" is a hard-and-fast rule that we must follow. We cannot pick and choose those that seem most interesting to us now, as that might lead to sampling only those that were associated with bubbles. Furthermore, this variation in perceived importance is what we need to test for the presence or absence of speculation, and it is exactly what has been missing from prior studies of bubbles.

Although this sampling strategy is theoretically sound, implementation is a messy, imprecise endeavor. The biases of past economic historians, the complexity of history, and the ambiguity in what we actually mean when we categorize technologies as well as the interdependencies among technologies create a host of research challenges. One of these difficulties stems from the same reasons long-wave theory failed. Technologies are interdependent, and sometimes speculation in one is associated with a rise in perceived opportunity afforded by another. So it may be that an observed pattern in one industry may be due to developments in a related one, even long after the original innovation occurred. For example, both the internal combustion engine and vulcanized rubber appear on our list. The process to create vulcanized rubber was discovered by Charles Goodyear in the 1840s. Goodyear was half-mad and totally obsessive, and he engaged in behavior that would torpedo many a good marriage, conducting many of his chemical experiments in the kitchen. However, at first rubber was a solution in search of a problem. A modest industry emerged making things like raincoats and galoshes, and demand was easily met by tapping rubber trees that grew naturally in the Amazon rain forest. The "killer app" of vulcanized rubber—automobile tires—did not materialize for another sixty years. Against the backdrop of international industrial espionage in which a British subject earned his knighthood by stealing rubber tree saplings from Brazil in the 1870s, the first decade of the twentieth century witnessed speculation in Malaysian rubber plantations on the Shanghai and London exchanges. The speculation in Shanghai was so rampant and the potential crash so severe that at one point trading was halted on the exchange for several months! But it is impossible to understand this event without considering the transformative effect of the automobile.

Somewhat surprisingly, the automobile does not appear on our list. But the internal combustion engine and the assembly line do. We suspect that the internal combustion engine is there because it enabled the automobile—as well as tractors, trucks, airplanes, and many other applications. Early applications of the assembly line emerged in the second half of the nineteenth century in the manufacture of sewing machines and bicycles and in the meatpacking industry. We are left with the question of whether we should consider the rubber boom and bust episode in 1907 a delayed reaction to Goodyear's invention or a manifestation of the automobile craze associated with the internal combustion engine and the assembly line. Reading contemporaneous newspaper reports as well as secondary history indicates that speculation in rubber was an attempt by investors to hop on the automobile bandwagon, and this is how we view it. Most of the uncertainties associated with the technology of rubber, as well as its industry, were resolved decades earlier; the window of bubble opportunity had already closed. We therefore associate the later boom and bust episode in rubber-related assets with internal combustion and the explosive growth of the automobile. By contrast, in the 1840s, asset markets were not sufficiently developed to leave us records with which to detect anything except the most notable episodes of speculation. Hence, we are unable to measure frothiness for vulcanized rubber during the window of bubble opportunity. This is reflected in Appendix Table A.1.

Internal combustion illustrates an additional aspect of technological interdependence: because of the linkage between engine makers and final assemblers, investors had limited options for investing in pure-play internal combustion engine manufacturers. In fact, we have few records of stand-alone producers of internal combustion engines. Instead, the technology was embedded in automobiles and other applications. In such cases, we take a broader view of the technology and investigate whether there was speculation in the internal combustion engine by examining the auto industry. In so doing, we also view this as an investigation of the moving assembly line, which was first applied to automobile production in the production of the Ford Model T between 1908 and 1913. We do so recognizing that Buick implemented a static assembly line, and that the assembly line had a longer history dating back to the production of rifles as well as the disassembly of cow carcasses in the meatpacking industry.[31] However, the basic idea was brought to an entirely new level in the production of the Model T. We view any attempts to speculate in this technology as embedded in purchases of those automobile manufacturers adopting the technology, such as Ford, EMF, and General Motors.[32] We describe the specific companies in our indices in the Appendix of this book, but fuller explanations can be found in our online Appendix, where we describe the historical basis of our coding.

Even so, the history of the automobile industry illustrates one final empirical challenge. Like Eli Lilly at the time it brought insulin to market, Ford was a private company at the time it rose to prominence. Until 1912, public investors were shut out of the automobile market and hence had little opportunity to speculate. Although investors might have been able to buy shares in a few automobile companies on the Detroit Stock Exchange, we have been unable to re-create price indices for this early period in Detroit. For the assembly line, investors could have invested in related companies that were likely to implement this innovation, such as US Motors and General Motors. Whether we are able to detect any speculation in automobile companies, and whether that speculation reflects speculation in the underlying technologies of internal combustion and the assembly line, is a matter of judgment. We present the facts regarding any such episodes as they are and provide our interpretation, but we also make clear the assumptions and judgments on which these interpretations rely.

On the bright side, for many of the technologies in our sample, we have relatively good records of asset prices during the window of bubble opportunity. Take, for example, the case of radio, a technology with an especially long window that extended across the entire period from earliest invention to the development of the capacity to transmit spoken language to the development of broadcasting. The first radio company, the Marconi Company, was founded in 1897. Guglielmo Marconi's vision was to use the technology for wireless telegraphy. In 1902, Reginald Fessenden developed voice communication, a process improved by Lee de Forest in 1908 with the invention of the triode. Experimentation in radio broadcasting began in 1908, and the advertising business model was first tried in 1916, but public broadcasting began expanding only in 1920. The number of radio receivers increased quickly throughout the decade, expanding from 100,000 in 1922 to 4.4 million in 1929, when equipment sales reached $843 million. In 1919, RCA was established with the goal of pooling and licensing critical radio patents to producers General Electric and Westinghouse. However, between 1923 and 1926, strong demand and negligible barriers to entry encouraged several hundred firms to enter the radio market while ignoring or inventing around RCA's patents. Although we are unable to trace the financing of most of these firms, the business historian Mary O'Sullivan documents that eighteen companies, including RCA, raised money on the Curb market by 1925.[33] These, we observe. Additional producers may have had successful offerings on the regional exchanges that proliferated through the country as well. These we do not observe. By the 1930s, both the technology and business models associated with radio were sufficiently understood, and the window of bubble opportunity closed.[34]

Despite these limitations, and others that we share in the course of the ensuing chapters, these results represent an important advance in our collective ability to think about the demography of bubbles. Appendix Table A.1 is the point of departure for the deeper explorations of the causes of bubbles that follow, and the summary results support a raft of positive and comparative statements in the next chapters. Of the fifty-eight technologies in our sample, investors in nine experienced bubbles, three got close, three did not, and investors could not invest in forty-three.

As previously noted, all fifty-eight technological innovations were associated with more or less uncertainty. We turn to this critical determinant of speculative interest in Chapter 2.

Chapter 2

UNCERTAINTY AND NARRATIVES

"Before a company exists, it is a story
about an imagined future."
ELLEN O'CONNER, *STORYTELLING TO BE REAL:*
NARRATIVE, LEGITIMACY BUILDING AND VENTURING, 2004

TODAY, THE CITY OF AUSTIN, TEXAS, is home to seventeen moonlight towers, relics of a path not taken on the way to the widespread use of electric light. The arc lights, mounted in 1895 on 145-foot towers, burned carbon filaments that showered smoldering ash on unsuspecting, awe-filled bystanders. The light was so bright that observers were known to use parasols to shield themselves from its harsh effects. Nevertheless, for most people living in a world that had previously contented itself with oil lamps and gaslight, this was the initial, profound experience of electric light.[1] In retrospect, it is clear that electric lighting was still a primitive technology in 1895, full of false starts. For electric lighting to become what it is today, the capitalist process needed to figure out how this marvel of electricity would be turned into a sustainable business proposition.

Most major technological innovations come into the world like electric arc lighting—wondrous, challenging, sometimes dangerous, always raw and imperfect. Inventors, entrepreneurs, investors, regulators, and customers struggle to figure out what the technology can do, how to organize its production and distribution, and what people are willing to pay for it. As marvelous as the electric light was, the American economy would spend the following five decades figuring out how to fully exploit electricity. Along the way were many dead ends, seemingly promising opportunities that ultimately came to naught. In this chapter, we explore the various dimensions of uncertainty that characterize the commercialization of major new technologies.

A key element of new industries and new technologies is that it is difficult to predict how the product and the market through which it is bought and sold will develop. Over time uncertainties are resolved. But in the meantime, the risk increases of a boom and bust episode and, potentially, a bubble. Two factors account for this risk: first, uncertainty implies that there is a chance for very high returns to materialize. This is in part why, for example, the value of options increases with the uncertainty (volatility) of an underlying asset. The second reason is that when there are few facts upon which to ground beliefs, investors can spin optimistic tales of favored outcomes to justify their decisions. These narratives can have real effects on the emergence of speculative episodes. The resolution of uncertainty does not occur at a set pace. In some cases, technical or market developments happen quickly and the role of uncertainty is limited, while in other settings, uncertainty can persist for years.

Recognizing that uncertainty is a fundamental feature of the entrepreneurial dynamic, we explore how different types of uncertainty accompany the emergence of new industries. Each type of uncertainty—technological, competitive, business model and value chain, and demand—is introduced through a series of technology case studies. We mostly build on earlier discussions of technologies discussed in the introduction and Chapter 1: aviation, rubber, the telephone, internal combustion, and radio. Along the way, we look at how entrepreneurs and investors experience different types of uncertainty and how that experience differs from technology to technology, as each technology fits into existing and emergent industries in different ways. The details of how different types of uncertainty interact influences the likelihood that investors will see high-return outcomes as more or less likely and attend to the possibility that their outlook may be wrong. That is, to understand the likelihood of a bubble, we must first understand the setting in which investors construct the stories they tell themselves about uncertainty.

Imagined Futures

All things being equal, uncertainty can lead to higher asset valuations because of the option effect. The logic is straightforward: all limited liability investments (including investments in corporations) have some of the central features of options; the upside is unlimited, but one can lose only the amount invested.[2] When an asset is highly uncertain, there is a chance that some of the more optimistic scenarios might materialize, and this possibility increases its value. This feature of modern capitalism is interesting because most new businesses fail, especially those in new industries. For example, there is a chance that a new three-dimensional printing business may be a big hit, but there is a much greater probability that it will tank. An investor can lose only her investment. However, losing a bet does not necessarily equate to making a bad decision. The bet may have been the best guess, given the information at a specific point in time.

But we should not assume that is the case. Psychologists, sociologists, and behavioral economists have given us many reasons to believe that individuals may systematically make bad bets, and these bets are justified through stories, or narratives.[3] The Nobel laureate Robert Shiller coined the term *narrative economics* and used his presidential address to the American Economics Association in early 2017 to call for greater study and understanding of the "spread and dynamics of popular narratives, the stories, particularly those of human interest and emotion, and how these change through time, to understand economic fluctuations."[4] Shiller's emphasis on the role of narratives is admittedly reluctant and the result of a long, intellectual journey through rich literatures in other social sciences. These views depart from mainstream economics in a fundamental way, and perhaps this is what makes Shiller uncomfortable. Instead of viewing uncertainty as a menu of possible futures to be discovered, these approaches view the narrative as a potential tool to shape the future.

As noted in the epigraph to this chapter, Ellen O'Connor, in her 2004 ethnography of the earliest days of a Silicon Valley tech start-up, begins her account as follows: "Before a company exists, it is a story about an imagined future."[5] The more this "imagined future" resonates with potential stakeholders (e.g., investors, customers, regulators, prospective employees), the more funding, employees, and customers the stakeholders will be able to gather, and the more likely the company will arrive at the future its founders imagined. In the case of our sample of major technological innovations, we are interested in technological narratives and the role these narratives play in market speculation. Narratives are defined here as "temporally sequenced accounts of interrelated events or actions undertaken by characters."[6] For our technologies, a narrative is a story about how each imagined event in a technology's future leads to the next. A technological narrative is compelling when it is a story or account of a future state of the world in which the technology in question or the venture that is its vector is legitimate and successfully embedded. For instance, when Elon Musk talks about the prospects of Tesla Inc., he relies on a technological narrative; the story of Tesla describes a future in which a significant fraction of total vehicle miles traveled (VMT) is provided by battery-electric vehicles. Consequently, in that future, Tesla is a successful, established, and—most important—profitable automobile manufacturer. No market participant—inventor, entrepreneur, consumer, or especially investor—will contribute to an emergent and uncertain technological system in the absence of a narrative in which the innovation is understood to be capable of producing meaning or value. For investors in an uncertain tech start-up like Tesla, the value of the firm is inextricably linked to its technological narrative.

What makes a technological narrative successful? Recent work in the sociology of expectations offers some help: an effective technological narrative generates expectations—"statements about the future" that are "performative"; statements about the future can alter behavior of market participants; "they do something."[7] One important performative effect is that expectations can be self-fulfilling.[8] If investors believe Elon Musk's technological narrative, they will be more inclined to buy and hold Tesla stock. The more people accept Musk's narrative, the more people buy and hold Tesla stock, and the more resources Musk has at his disposal to make his vision a reality. Many successful technological narratives share this feature: the more broadly they are believed, the more likely they are to produce the envisioned result. The most compelling narratives foster an illusion of inevitability, and the more people who jump on a particular narrative's bandwagon, the more real this illusion seems and even becomes.[9]

Surely Elon Musk tells a good technological narrative, and ceteris paribus, inventors or investors would probably rather have Musk describing the future of their firm than almost anyone else. But as we look across the technologies in our sample, some better lend themselves to successful narratives than others. What determines the attractiveness of a given technology's narrative to potential speculators?

First, we can ask, how many different narratives are consistent with the success of the technology? For instance, there was only one basic technological narrative about insulin. As we saw in Chapter 1, this narrative was incredible: "the resurrection cure" woke dying children from diabetic coma to live normal lives. But that was about it. There was not much else to be done with insulin other than save the lives of people with diabetes. However, other technologies lent themselves to multiple narrative interpretations. Multiple narratives accompanied the super-frothy 97% evisceration of radio stocks in 1929 that is described in Chapter 1. As Susan Douglas describes the early days of radio, many possible technological narratives were available to potential entrepreneurs and their investors. Would radio be loss-leading marketing for department stores? A public service for broadcasting Sunday sermons? An ad-supported medium for entertainment? All were possible. All were the subjects of technological narratives. From an expectations perspective, these different possible narratives are "bids," forward-looking bets about how the future will unfold.[10] Assuming that the investing public possesses heterogeneous tastes for different narratives, the more technological bids we can construct about each technology, the more people are likely to be interested in potentially investing in a venture intended to create each particular "imagined future." More potential narratives means more bids, and different bids will appeal to varied investor tastes. By sweeping up a larger, more varied set of investors, a technology that can support more narratives is likely to generate speculation.

Second, the time it takes for competing technological narratives to be resolved varies by technology. Questions related to single (or limited) narratives can be resolved relatively quickly, whereas technologies that support multiple narratives take longer to shake out. Here, compare the case of insulin to that of the electric light. With access to a single technological narrative, would-be insulin entrepreneurs needed to demonstrate their product's performance in the insulin narrative. Electric lighting—which required the development and construction of electrical networks, regulations, and hardware—was different. Would profits accrue to producers of light bulbs, suppliers of electrical equipment, or sellers of electricity? Would networks be alternating or direct current? For each narrative, entrepreneurs raised funds from different sets of investors at specific moments in time. The resulting bids were then enacted over time, with resolution coming slowly as each venture's economic hypothesis was more or less effectively tested in the marketplace. The longer it takes for these competing narratives to be resolved, the more time is available for speculation to develop. In the context of our model, the longer the uncertainty persists, the longer is the window of bubble opportunity (introduced in Chapter 1). Some technologies have longer windows than others. Technologies with short windows will generate narratives that are quickly resolved and, therefore, are less likely to produce a bubble.

Third, technological narratives may vary in their accessibility or availability to potential stakeholders.[11] As the Princeton psychologist and Nobel laureate Daniel Kahneman states, "The core of the illusion is that we believe we understand the past, which implies the future also should be knowable."[12] Kahneman points out that our understanding of the past is infused with false narratives—but familiarity helps determine the degree to which a narrative will take root. For instance, narratives about the transformative effect of catalytic cracking or modern steelmaking are relatively inaccessible. Not only do such narratives describe processes rather than products, the processes themselves are abstract, occur in large industrial settings, and are remote from the final products that consumers know and buy. By contrast, for new products that consumers can understand (and buy), technological narratives will be more accessible and more likely to prompt action. There is a relevant past experience with which to make sense of the future.[13] The sociologist Donald Mackenzie describes a "trough of uncertainty": those who are closest to the technology know the fragility and contingent nature of the promised benefits. Meanwhile, those who are farthest from the innovation are least likely to even have been exposed to the narrative to know about the technology and are, therefore, more likely to reject it. In both extremes, the technological narrative is less likely to generate support. But as the sociologist Harro van Lente observes, those in the middle—"direct stakeholders . . . such as clients or prospective users . . . accept the promise but lack insight into the details that may hinder the realisation."[14] For these actors, the illusion is most dangerous: perceived uncertainty may be relatively low, and these individuals may be more inclined to accept proffered narrative bids. They think they understand.

Fourth, and finally, sociologists have identified a relationship between expectations and the coordination of beliefs, especially in the presence of fundamental uncertainty.[15] The self-fulfilling prophecy, noted earlier, is one manifestation, whereby behavior based on expectation of a particular narrative coming to fruition coordinates actors around that narrative and increases the likelihood of it happening. However, in the case of our sample, we also observe the converse: coordinating events can align expectations around given technological narratives. We see this in Chapter 3, where the Lindbergh transatlantic flight generated a self-reinforcing series of public events that aligned beliefs around a technological narrative that supported the growth of the aviation industry. In other cases, events intended to coordinate beliefs around a narrative of technological success failed: in 1968, the National Geographic Society sponsored a journey by hovercraft from Manaus, Brazil, to Port of Spain, Trinidad, billed as the "Last Great Journey on Earth." The team successfully navigated the treacherous rapids of the Orinoco River, encountering all manner of interesting trials along the way, but the expedition failed to capture public imagination and coordinate beliefs in support of a pro-hovercraft technological narrative. Few cared, and although a small number of hovercraft were placed in service shuttling travelers across the English Channel, the more optimistic technological narrative never came to pass.

Speculation requires the clear and direct embodiment of narrative bids in investment targets. For our purposes, this implies the existence of publicly traded stocks that are "pure plays" in the new opportunities. Pure plays match entrepreneurs and investors with similar beliefs. Most important, pure plays open up the story line to an additional set of stakeholders: investors. Now the technological and industry story is of prime interest to consumers of investment news, whereas before it may have been of interest to technological enthusiasts but of lesser interest to a general investor. This dynamic can turbocharge the narrative, as the narrative will now command more media attention. This process, in turn, will attract more resources to the ventures commercializing the new technology. Thus, the existence of pure plays has a double-whammy effect on the emergence of speculation: without a pure play, it is difficult for investors to find a vehicle for speculation, but without a proper market, speculation will not occur. With pure plays, not only are there vehicles for speculation; their existence has the potential to turbocharge the narratives, and hence the extent, of speculation.

These factors—number of narratives available, time to resolution, comprehensibility or proximity of narrative to actor, and extent of coordination—can predict whether and to what extent a given set of technological narratives will be "sticky" or "contagious." To be sure, narratives are not technologically determined. For a given technological innovation, more creative entrepreneurs will craft more compelling narratives, but there are many factors outside the control of entrepreneurs that make it more or less easy to craft these narratives.

The degree of uncertainty allows for the construction of multiple and more varied speculative narratives, and in turn, the uncertainty varies across technological domains. For example, it is easier to create a narrative that explains exponential growth in a new three-dimensional printing venture than it is for a single Subway sandwich franchise. The fate of a particular three-dimensional printing play, and for that matter three-dimensional printing in general, is at the time of this writing unknowable. A Subway franchise is limited by capacity and a known distribution of outcomes for other franchises that are different only in location and management. We could look for the best-performing Subway franchise and think of this as an upper bound on the potential performance of a new one. This upper bound constrains the narrative. Not so for the 3-D printing business. A skilled storyteller would envision a future and then a place for the new company in that vision. Imagine printing your steaks at home instead of going to the butcher!

In other words, we cannot construct equally believable narratives about all possible futures. It is easier to form narratives around something that plausibly creates and delivers value—even if the business case for whether and how that value will be appropriated is poorly understood and unknowable. In fact, it is precisely cases in which value can be imagined but how that value might be delivered is unclear that we see an onslaught of entrants and investors. This happens not only because narratives can be readily constructed about the potential of an opportunity but also because those narratives are more likely to be believed. We want to believe we are going to be part of the project that will change the world. To borrow the language of longtime Stanford professor and student of organizations James March: "Clarity of vision protects deviant imaginations from the disconfirmations of experience and knowledge. Attachment to fantasy converts the ambiguities of history into confirmations of belief and a willingness to persist in a course of action."[16] Stratifying the nature of uncertainty—seeing it as a family of types—helps us understand when narratives are more likely to take off; we can more clearly see the various dimensions around which narratives might be constructed. That is, unpacking uncertainty allows us to estimate both the likelihood of the option effect mentioned earlier, as well as the likelihood of fantastic narratives. Both can lead to boom and bust episodes, but only the latter can lead to a bubble.

Technological Uncertainty

Will it work? After experimenting with gliders and wind tunnels for the better part of four years, on December 17, 1903, the Wright brothers' plane the *Flyer* managed three test flights of 120 feet, 175 feet, and 200 feet—about the range of distance of a typical fly ball in baseball. The *Flyer* flew six miles per hour and was unflyable by any except the Wright brothers.[17] It was a rudimentary device. Between the recognition that these devices were in their infancy and the high fatality rate of early aviators, investment in aviation came slowly. The industry received an infusion of government capital during World War I. Approximately $400 million ($8 billion in 2015) worth of airplanes were purchased as part of America's war effort. Unfortunately, the technological improvements associated with this influx of cash were underwhelming.[18] The severe drop in demand at the end of the war led to intense competitive pressures. So much so that, to stimulate development, Congress decided to subsidize the industry through airmail. This subvention encouraged investment, which, together with the establishment of the private Orteig Prize for the first successful, nonstop crossing from New York to Paris, led to the technology that enabled Charles Lindbergh's famous first transatlantic flight.

Insiders who knew the technology well issued honest and public opinions about the prospects of the industry. In June 1928, a year after Lindbergh's flight, and just three months into an aviation IPO wave that would last into 1930, Daniel Guggenheim—a lead benefactor of aeronautics demonstrations and research—reallocated all of his foundation's funds to basic aviation research. He explained his decision bluntly: "The populace understood the great potential of airplane flight, they overestimated the speed in which this potential might be obtained."[19] That is, as we noted earlier, narratives were most likely to take hold in the populace with a superficial as opposed to deep understanding of the emergent field. Six months later, investment pages warned the average buyer: "Reading constantly about this or that development in the industry, hearing about some achievement, discussing the general subject with his friends, he reaches the conclusion that 'someone is going to make a lot of money out of aviation.' He wants to get in on the ground floor and his lack of knowledge of the subject makes him an especially fallow field for the cultivation of the high-pressure salesman."[20] There were several such warnings in this vein in the mainstream press,[21] but they were lost in the stream of more superficial, optimistic news. For example, not three weeks earlier, the following short note was offered to investors in the *Wall Street Journal*: "In 1925 it is estimated that airplane manufacturers turned out 600 planes. This past year producers reached a schedule that called for 600 planes a month. The total number of planes that will be pro-duced and sold during 1929 is estimated at 12,000. Several large com-panies had announced their schedules for next year. Many of them have already sold all that they can produce: It is now impossible to buy a plane under three weeks to a month."[22] Technological uncertainty, when discussed at all, was often framed as opportunity, not risk. For example, in late May 1929, one headline screamed "Engine Makers Take the Lead." The article described how speculation would turn to companies' experimenting with the "manufacture of engines," since "much sooner than expected, the manufacture of airplanes has . . . definitely passed from the experimental era."[23] The article then briefly described the leading companies developing airplane engines.

The emergent picture is that the future of aviation was inevitable and happening in that moment. Early problems in the manufacture of airplanes were already in the rearview mirror, and the focus was on optimizing performance of components. The fact that the backlog in airplane delivery was due to orders from pilot schools who sought to train pilots for the new industry was lost at the time, as was the fact that the profitability of aviation companies—if it existed at all—was entirely dependent on government subsidies.[24] For a brief moment, the narrative was driving real demand in the industry.

Investment continued unabated as prices peaked in May 1929, held steady until October, and then dropped 96% by May 1932. The dive might have been worse had the federal government not made airmail subsidies more generous in early 1930 in an effort to stave off a complete collapse of the aviation business. It was still too expensive to fly passengers profitably. In 1935, after almost thirty years of government underwriting, subsidies were cut completely. By that time, sufficient development in passenger air transportation had taken place, and the industry was able to climb to profitability.[25] Indeed, prices recovered somewhat and stood at close to 35% of the 1929 peak in 1941, when the United States entered World War II. But like the rest of the market, investors who put money into airplane and airline stocks at the 1929 peak would need to wait until June 1954 to avoid even nominal losses. Arguably, by then stock prices reflected the hope of the jet engine, suggesting that internal-combustion planes never fulfilled their promise. Even if investors sold when Guggenheim issued his warnings (well before the peak), they might have purchased an air transport index at less than the June 1928 price for the following fourteen years.

In other words, whereas expert investors appreciated correctly the importance of airplanes and air travel, the narrative of inevitability largely drowned out their caution. Technological uncertainty was framed as opportunity, not risk. The market overestimated how quickly the industry would achieve technological viability and profitability.

Competitive Uncertainty

In Chapter 1, we discussed how the emergent automobile industry drove a derivative boom and bust in rubber in the early 1900s. The history of this episode is illustrative of the way narratives often underemphasize the role competition will have on profits. For decades, Brazil monopolized the rubber supply by harvesting latex from naturally occurring rubber trees. However, a shady royal subject, the subsequently knighted Sir Henry Wickham, sowed the seeds of competition by spiriting dozens of rubber-tree saplings from South America to London in the 1880s.[26]

Nevertheless, increased demand driven by automobile tires made the Brazilian monopoly much more lucrative as increased demand for automobiles led to a steady increase in raw rubber prices throughout the first decade of the 1900s. Rubber transformed cities. By 1910,

Akron, Ohio, the new center of the tire industry, had become a booming metropolis that imported 70% of the world's natural rubber supply.[27] While increased demand stimulated a search for alternative supplies of latex, workers forayed deeper into the Brazilian Amazon in search of undiscovered trees.[28] But they couldn't keep up: by 1910, supply had doubled, but prices had quadrupled. To seize this financial opportunity, British capitalists—exploiting Wickham's biopiracy—planted more than 70,000 acres annually between 1905 and 1911, driving up productive acreage to 542,877 in the Malay states. These plantations financed their operations by floating joint-stock companies on the London and Shanghai Stock Exchanges.[29]

The uncertainty came from the nature of rubber trees. In 1910 half a million acres of rubber trees had been planted, but few were productive. It takes six years from planting to the first latex harvest. That meant that investor returns depended on prices six years in the future. Narratives about the inevitability of profits were based on available information—current rubber prices. All but the experts ignored the larger picture. In essence, investors in the new Malay rubber plantations were betting that rubber prices—several years in the future—would be sufficiently high to cover their investment. For this to happen, demand for rubber would have to increase quickly enough to absorb the massive capacity that was coming on line. To complicate this picture, suppliers not only reacted by increasing raw production; they also made production more efficient. The combination of new rubber trees coming on line and better use of raw materials led rubber prices to plummet 75% between 1910 and 1913, even in the face of increased demand for automobiles. This caused a bust. To this day, the inflation-adjusted price of natural rubber in 1910 remains the historical apex. Free entry into the production of rubber ensured that supranormal profits would never return to the rubber market.

Why didn't entrepreneurs and investors who were pouring their money into Malay rubber plantations anticipate the likely effects of competitive uncertainty? It is hard to argue that entrants were completely unaware of the extent of competition, but it is also clear that information was far from precise. For example, the president of the

Firestone Tire and Rubber Company, H. S. Firestone, suggested that rubber prices would remain high in 1909.[30] Firestone, whose job it was to understand rubber prices, enticingly noted that the price of rubber was approaching a third that of silver, that there were supply problems in the Brazilian Amazon, and that demand was driven by the automobile. He failed to mention the forthcoming arrival of Malaysian rubber on the global market. The narrative of the inevitability of high rubber prices is surprising in a subsequent short piece, also in the *New York Times*, that describes in the same paragraph both the Brazilian government cornering the market for rubber and speculation in London. The article does not consider that the plantations represented by the London stocks would likely break the Brazilian stranglehold and lead to a reduction in prices.[31] Speculation in the rubber market itself likely also contributed to the boom and bust.[32] The fact that the Southeast Asian plantations would come on line was known; but even when reported, it was buried in the tenth paragraph.[33]

These plantation pure plays, traded publicly on the London and Shanghai exchanges, were reported in both the trade and the popular presses as subjects of wild speculation. In contrast, the same press reports suggest that, in 1910, there was no clear consensus about how much planting was under way. Even when this information was reported, it was downplayed. The heart of the narrative was about prices.

The example of the rubber boom is attractive because it is pure—in the sense that there was no narrative about whose rubber was best. Malay and Brazilian rubber came from the same tree species, and hence was of similar quality. Speculation arose from the difficulty in understanding and anticipating the effect of free entry on long-term prices.

In contrast, the lack of free entry often restricts speculation because it limits the potential variety of narratives—that is, the potential bids. If different stories with the same overall conclusion appeal to different potential investors, multiple technology narratives—or bids—may lead to greater speculation. The case of the telephone—our example of an almost bubble from Chapter 1—helps illustrate this point. Here, certain types of uncertainty remained unresolved over time (business model, technological) while other types of uncertainty (competitive, value chain) were resolved more quickly through legal maneuvering.

In 1879, investors initially framed Alexander Graham Bell as competing against the well-established Western Union; the original telephone patent was even titled "Improvements in Telegraphy." Indeed, Bell modeled the telephone after the telegraph, envisioning it as a premium telegraph service for business that would be offered from centralized locations. No one yet imagined the telephone as the building block of an entirely new industry, and investor interest in a slightly improved telegraph was limited. The specter of competition with Western Union spooked investors, especially given the pending-patent dispute with the telegraph monolith. It was only after the resolution of outstanding patent disputes between Western Union and National Bell Telephone Company that investor sentiment improved.[34] This narrative was simple: Bell was David and Western Union Goliath. Once Goliath was subdued, Bell looked more attractive. This is true despite the fact that it was unclear precisely how Bell's business model would work.

What happened then is an important lesson in the role of free entry and market structure in producing broad-based market speculation. Under normal conditions, after seeing Bell's initial success, investors and entrepreneurs would have started competing firms in a race to exploit and populate the newly proven market space. Each company would represent a different experiment in creating value, a unique bid. Most would eventually fail, but not before many would have generated convincing narratives describing their future success, leading to successful funding and—if the resulting stocks were publicly tradable—potential speculation. But instead, the Bell companies fiercely defended the primacy of Bell's pioneering patent, bringing up to six hundred infringement lawsuits against would-be competitors.[35] We can interpret the fact that it took Bell's legal department six hundred lawsuits to keep new entrants out of the telephone industry as an indication of the speculative opportunity that entrepreneurs saw in the new technology. Nevertheless, the rate of adoption for the telephone was slowed by the presence of a strongly defended patent supporting a monopolist, and it is likely that many more than six hundred competitors would have been started had the Bell interests not fought so hard to quash them. The short-term successes of a small handful of well-capitalized potential competitors—Molecular Telephone Company (1883), Pan-Electric Telephone Company (1884), and People's Telephone Company (1880), to name some of the most prominent—also underscore the public appetite for telephone securities. Each of these entrants was able to craft a plausible narrative that placed its prospects beyond the reach of the Bell patents. Until the US Supreme Court finally upheld the Bell position in March 1888, these ventures had more or less successfully tapped into widespread public fascination with the telephone, raising significant capital. Thereafter, however, the plausibility of these alternative narratives collapsed, and future entrants would need to wait for the expiration of the founding Bell patents to craft a convincing entry story. Thus, the regulatory environment and government action—in this case, the judicial branch— had a large effect on competitive outcomes.

By the time Bell's patent expired in 1892, the bulk of the technological and business model uncertainty had been resolved, and the window of highest uncertainty had passed. Without the entry barrier of the patent, a degree of market structure uncertainty was reintroduced to the telephone sector. Although thousands of independent telephone companies were formed in the 1890s, the prospect of a speculative bubble was limited. Bell's dominance was no longer in doubt.

In the case of rubber, even though plantation entrepreneurs and investors observed their peers' behavior, it is possible to believe that few knew the full extent of entry and, therefore, the fact that they themselves were fueling oversupply. This tendency may have been exacerbated by a well-known bias from which many investors and entrepreneurs suffer: overconfidence in their abilities and overrating their chances of success.[36] If there are more competitors, this bias is more likely to manifest. So, we should expect this phenomenon in a free-entry context like rubber but not with the telephone. Even if investors accurately predict the extent of entry, they may fail to consider how increased competition might affect prices. To understand the effect on prices, a well-developed model of supply and demand is needed—or at least a good heuristic. In the emerging, global market setting of rubber, neither was available. Such forces may lead to mass entry and a subsequent decline in prices as investors and entrepreneurs overlook the dynamics of market entry and its potential effect on prices. In the case of telephony, the forces of patent law and effective intellectual property strategy eliminated such a dynamic. Hence, we should expect bubbles to be more likely when free entry is possible—when all producers need, for instance, is the ability to plant trees as opposed to inventing around a telephone patent.

The examples of rubber and the telephone demonstrate the importance of competitive uncertainty for the development of a financial bubble. High competitive uncertainty—either in the form of unregulated entry as we saw with rubber or uncertain regulation of entry, as was the case with the telephone—will encourage speculative activity.

Business Model and Value Chain Uncertainty (and Regulatory Uncertainty, Too)

In Britain, a "wireless" is a radio set. When radio inventor Guglielmo Marconi founded the Marconi Company in 1897, his goal was to commercialize wireless telegraphy. Advances by Reginald Fessenden and Lee de Forest allowed voice transmission and opened the door to the possibility of broadcast. However, imaginations are limited: at the time no one could conceive of broadcasting anything but religious services. Indeed, the idea of broadcast did not take hold until after World War I.[37] Early broadcasts re-created performance and lecture situations in which many listened to a few. For instance, in the 1910s and 1920s, many universities established radio stations to broadcast educational content, and a few contemporary observers predicted the end of the modern university. However, it was quickly discovered that universities did more than simply provide venues for lectures—and the university survived, as did many university radio stations. How would radio manufacturers make money? Would they sell radio subscriptions? Perhaps value would be created through production of radio content? Amid the early radio euphoria, newspapers, churches, universities, and even a laundry started broadcasting.[38] Some department stores experimented in broadcasting radio as a loss leader to bring in customers.

Throughout the 1920s, David Sarnoff—at the helm of the Radio Corporation of America, or RCA—attempted to replicate Bell's telephone strategy, whereby RCA, through its use of patents, would control every radio set sold. However, unlike a one-to-one telephone connection, one-to-many radio broadcasters had no way of knowing if a given radio set was receiving content. And while Sarnoff was able to generate a formidable patent portfolio, it proved difficult to enforce. Radio sets were not difficult to assemble, and there was no way of controlling who tuned in on the radio. There were dozens of radio producers in the 1920s. Although early radio sets were major household expenses, innovative telemarketing and sales techniques moved product.[39]

In addition, the role of government was unclear. The proliferation of broadcasts led to crowded airwaves. How and when would the crowding of these airwaves be resolved? There was regulatory uncertainty. Regulation of the radio spectrum by the commerce secretary, Herbert H. Hoover, made it easier to control and monitor who was using broadcast equipment and also improved the likelihood that listeners would hear something intelligible—Hoover's policies favored larger players such as RCA. This increased the value of RCA's patent portfolio. But RCA could not profit by charging listeners when they tuned in. They had no idea who was actually doing so!

If a radio subscription model was infeasible, and broadcasters themselves were barely covering the cost of expensive broadcast equipment and operations, would anyone in the industry make money? At the time, the idea of commercial radio—supported by advertisers willing to pay to reach listeners—was simply unknown. It took several years and many false starts for broadcasters to develop the innovation of commercial radio. Not only did they have to work out which types of programming would attract listeners; early broadcasters also needed to convince potential advertisers that people would listen and respond to ads.[40] Developing capabilities to sell ads took years.[41] Over time, it did become clear that money could be made in broadcasting. Companies learned how to advertise, and the Radio Corporation of America became profitable. However, early uncertainty created a frenzy of speculative activity. Investors in radio at the peak in mid-1929 would recover only $0.30 on the dollar in the late 1950s.

The uncertainty about how money would be made in the new radio industry allowed several narratives of inevitability of radio profits to emerge. Consequently, radio companies across the value chain were able to sell stock on the exchanges. In our language, each pure play was a different bid that might have appealed to a different set of investors who liked that particular story. For example, Hazeltine was a pure-play manufacturer of radios, while RCA was also experimenting in broadcast. Sonatron advertised its "radio," or vacuum, tubes in the *Saturday Evening Post*. Using them would apparently "bombard [you] with energy."[42] Perhaps if Sonatron had enacted an early version of "Intel Inside," they might have become a household name. Not knowing how money would be made and where in the value chain it would concentrate made spinning multiple narratives easier, and investors could choose from RCA, Hazeltine, and Sonatron stocks, among others. That is, just because a product or service goes on to become wildly popular, not all businesses related to that product or service will make money on it. A successful business must position itself in an advantageous part of the market ecosystem, even as that ecosystem is forming. Since the eventual form of this ecosystem is often unknowable, the business and its investors must be both good and lucky. Note the contrast among the different industries: radio, telephone, and rubber. Telephone was a single-firm play: Bell's patent strategy allowed it to control the entire ecosystem. If you wished to speculate in the telephone business, Bell and its subsidiaries quickly emerged as the only way to do so. If you wished to speculate in rubber, you might have purchased shares in similar plantations all producing a commodity—or you might have purchased the commodity directly. Finally, any single speculative play in radio required a choice of a specific part of the value chain and business model: broadcast and patents, the sale of radio sets, or the sale of set components. It was uncertain!

Demand Uncertainty

The internal combustion engine (ICE) might have been a minor technology without its killer app: the automobile. Interestingly, though, from the first commercial production of the automobile in 1896 to the realized superiority of the ICE in about 1904, it was unclear whether automobiles should be propelled by an internal combustion, electric, or steam engine.

In 1897, Ransom E. Olds founded the Olds Motor Vehicle Company in Lansing, Michigan, and placed his bet on internal combustion. Olds was betting on the failure of some powerful business interests. In early 1899, the New York–based businessman William H. Whitney and his fellow investors capitalized their own nascent electric vehicle empire at $200 million ($5 billion in 2015). The Electric Vehicle Company (EVC) offered a fee-for-service model, where the central company would own the vehicles and lease them for hire to wealthy consumers. EVC projected that it would have 4,200 vehicles in service by 1900. The projection was audacious, as only a hundred or so cars had been manufactured for sale at that point. Thus, Olds was not only betting on internal combustion; he and his backers were betting on the particular business model prevalent today, in which users own their cars. The EVC and its subsidiaries around the country put only 850 vehicles into service. Fragile cars and dubious business practices revealed the business model to be, at best, marginally viable.[43] The decline in electric vehicle stocks started in late 1899 and heralded the end of the early electric vehicle experiment. By 1901, every sixth automobile sold was an Olds. Although only 425 Oldsmobile Curved Dash models were sold that year, the growth of the internal combustion automobile market was exponential. By 1910, 250,000 cars were produced; by 1916, 1 million. Electric vehicle production never scaled beyond a few thousand units per year. But the market was still evolving; the high price of early autos left the product out of reach for most consumers.[44] The extent of the market and whether cars could be produced at a price that would appeal to a larger, mass market were open questions. Betting on growth implied a bet as well that demand would be high if a product could be offered that provided sufficient quality at the right price. As we now know, this was a good bet. In contrast, it was a much poorer bet for airplanes in the late 1920s. They were too dangerous and expensive for mass appeal until the jet age, and other technologies on our list, such as airships, failed altogether.

Demand uncertainty is complicated by value chain and business model uncertainty. For example, even if investors or entrepreneurs could have predicted automobile demand, where in the supply chain should they have invested? Raw rubber producers? Tire manufacturers? Automobile producers? Where was competition destined to be least intense? We are experiencing a very similar situation today when we consider autonomous vehicles. It is unclear which companies will make money, where the bottleneck will be, and which company, if any, will control the bottleneck. Should we place bets with ride-sharing companies such as Uber or Lyft, legacy automobile manufacturers such as Ford and GM, diversified tech firms like Google and Apple, upstarts such as Tesla, or technology specialists such as Intel, which purchased the leading sensor provider Mobileye?

Similar questions plagued investors in the earlier days of the automobile industry. In 1917, there were forty-five automobile securities actively traded in New York and Detroit. But the financial news editors did not, or perhaps could not, meaningfully separate the companies along the value chain. For example, on a representative day in October, listings of "automobile" security prices in the trade periodical *Automotive Industries* included twenty-four automobile companies but also ten tire producers and eleven other suppliers producing auto bodies, wheels, engines, and lights.[45] This mixing was, in retrospect, misleading for investors. Whereas a single dollar invested in an automobile index in 1917 would be worth $19 in 1938, a similar investment in auto accessories would return "only" $7.50, and an investment in tire companies would return a meager $1.20.[46] It was, apparently, difficult to foresee the low returns of companies like Goodyear, Firestone, Goodrich, and US Rubber after the 1922 advent of corded tires.[47] As a result of poor patent protection, these tire manufacturers all soon offered similar products, and automobile manufacturers exploited the similarity of the big-four tire manufacturers' products to keep supplier margins low. Even though together the four suppliers controlled 80% of the market by 1929, margins on tires have never recovered.

Given the excitement around automobiles, it is not surprising that investors extrapolated from the unprecedented profits and returns on assets being earned in the automobile industry to other parts of the value chain. It fit into the narrative of inevitability that surrounded the automobile.

To summarize, we have seen that uncertainty is more than a binary description of the state of the world. Rather, uncertainty can be decomposed into components—technological, competitive, business model and value chain, regulatory, and demand uncertainty. This decomposition leads to specific questions that we can ask when applying our framework, which is set forth in Table 2.1. Uncertainty is understood only when applied to specific contexts. It is only then that we might consider *what* is uncertain. What might entrepreneurs and investors disagree about in the first place?

Our minds like stories, and we make sense of new and uncertain technological innovations through narratives, some of which can lead to speculation. The imagined future is inevitable! When there are more types of uncertainty, it becomes easier to weave these stories, and the stories themselves may be more plausible.

But sometimes the narratives themselves shape the course of technological development. Narratives are bids to create a particular version of reality. If the bid is compelling and plausible, investors offer

TABLE 2.1   Types of uncertainty

Uncertainty	Questions
Technological uncertainty	
The nature of technological development	How will the technology evolve to solve a useful problem? Where will the bottlenecks be in a technology's subcomponents?
The speed of technological development	How quickly will a common design be established and margins eroded?
Competitive uncertainty	
Potential entrants	How many firms will enter the market and what will their capabilities be? When should we expect pricing pressure?
Business model and value chain uncertainty	
Monetization	How will the solution be monetized? Are there many different bets in the market?
The boundaries of the firm	If the product is complex and built from many components, how will the market be vertically structured?
Future market structure and power	Can current players effectively restrict entry through intellectual property rights or other means? Will product differentiation matter and firms have pricing power, or not?
Which parts of the value chain will profit	Will competition be more intense in upstream or downstream markets?
Regulatory uncertainty	
Government actions	Will government regulation slow down the market and determine winners and losers? Will safety or other fairness considerations force the government to intervene?
Demand uncertainty	
Market demand	How quickly will demand develop? Will technological convergence accelerate or retard demand?

their resources to help support a given imagined future. If there is only one narrative, uncertainty will be limited, and the spread between the known and the imagined will be minimal. In other cases, however, multiple technology-specific narrative bids may be supported, indicating greater and more diverse sources of uncertainty.

For these reasons, we consider the levels of uncertainty when the various technologies in our sample came to market, as well as when these uncertainties were resolved. This approach allows us to understand both the speculative potential of each technology and the time period, the window of bubble opportunity, in which we should look for speculation associated with these factors.

Chapter 3

NOVICES, NAÏFS, AND BIASES

"Question: I am a daily reader of your valued column
in The Tribune, and your knowledge on investments
has commended itself to me. The great impulse given
to wireless telegraphy by the wireless concerts given
daily at Newark and elsewhere suggest to me the
advisability of making a modest investment in some
wireless equipment stock that has potentialities. Could
you name a few such stocks that I might invest in with
reasonable assurance of large returns later on? What
do you think of Radio common?" —Mrs. W. C. B.
"SPECULATING IN WIRELESS AGE," *NEW YORK TRIBUNE,*
MARCH 27, 1922, 15

Novices

In the previous chapter we discussed how narratives affect investors' choices. In theory, financially literate investors choose their stocks on the basis of a deep understanding of the market and knowledge of the investment opportunity. That is, investors build well-informed, reasoned narratives to justify their choices. While figuring out whether a company will generate profits is almost impossible except in the short term, some investors might have a better sense of which companies or industries are good bets. In practice, our very humanity makes this worse. This humanity manifests in what psychologists like to call decision-making biases. The psychologists' list of biases is long, so we focus on a few that have outsized influence on investment decisions. First, we are more likely to buy into narratives that draw analogies to things with which we are familiar. That is because in we tend to falsely believe that the past always predicts the future. But often, new opportunities are difficult to understand, and sloppy analogies lead to bad decisions. These biases are exacerbated by the nature of stock picking. There are an overwhelming number of potential stocks to buy, and we are drawn to those that attract our oft-fleeting attention, for whatever reason. Experience is about learning to restrain and override these very biases; it is about not constructing specious narratives.

When investors are inexperienced and less financially literate, they may be beguiled by opportunities that are new and seem exciting—as is often the case with new technologies. The (new) internet (new) economy will change EVERYTHING! Blockchain will eliminate firms! Bitcoin will end government currencies! But just because something is new, exciting, and the subject of buzz does not make it a good investment. In fact, as we discussed in the preceding chapter, newness is often associated with uncertainty, uncertainty leaves room to generate narratives, and it's easier to generate these narratives when we know less about the opportunity. Sometimes, we investors—even experienced ones—collectively fixate on such new shiny objects. Call it herding, a fad, or fashion, but either way, this behavior can lead to bubbles. Perhaps a parable will better illustrate what we mean.

In the spring of 1993 a cocky twenty-four-year-old Israeli undergraduate student in economics and computer science discovered the Tel Aviv stock market. In Israel before the internet, trades were done through a phone call to your bank, and the trade came directly out of your checking account. So if you had a bank account and signed a few papers, you could dabble in the stock market. Hearing a tip that a locally traded oil exploration company, Isramco (currently trading as ISRL on NASDAQ), was searching for oil in the Mediterranean, he and his friend bought some shares in the stock—about $1,000 worth each. Everyone with a passing interest in the market appeared to be focused on it, so it seemed like a good bet. The neighboring Egyptians had found oil. And of course, everyone knew that the Persian Gulf countries were the epicenter of the global oil industry. By analogy, there should be some oil in Israel, too. After all, Israel *is* in the Middle East. The students had constructed a neat, clean narrative with a nice analogy.

Simile and metaphor are critical to the construction of narratives. The use of analogies is typical in trying to understand an uncertain world. While working together at New York University, scholars Daniel Beunza and Raghu Garud studied how famed investment advisers Henry Blodget and Jonathan Cohen developed different analogies to help them make sense of Amazon in 1998. Cohen thought of Amazon as analogous to Barnes & Noble and felt it should be valued like a bookstore. Because bookstores had relatively low margins, he valued Amazon at $50 a share. Blodget suggested that Amazon was more like Dell Computers, which was earning a healthy 8% margin at the time. With this in mind, Blodget arrived at a $400 valuation.[1] Given the information available in 1998, both analogies yielded plausible narratives. There are ways in which both Cohen and Blodget got the analogy right, but the point is that their assumptions led to wildly differing conclusions. Unfortunately for our student stock pickers in Israel, the use of analogies is where their similarity to this Amazon comparison ends.

Whether the "Israel is like the Persian Gulf countries" analogy made sense or not was far beyond the students; they knew nothing about the geology of oil deposits, or, for that matter, geology. But they were making sense of a really attractive comparison. Why should their country be the only one impoverished by lack of oil?

This idea was what Stanford professor Chip Heath and his brother, Dan Heath, of Duke University, would call "sticky."[2] Even in the face of countervailing evidence, sticky ideas have some or all of the following six attributes: simple, unexpected, concrete, credible, emotional, and (finally) part of a story. *Simple* means that the idea has a brisk message, even if the underlying reality is complex. The idea of offshore oil appears simple, even if the geology and economics of offshore oil extraction are not. *Unexpected* is something that makes an idea shiny, interesting. That Israel might have oil was unexpected in the sense that part of the mythos of Zionism is self-reliance and hard work. Oil would have been manna from heaven, which contradicted this mythos. The idea of oil is *concrete*. Oil is a commodity, and everyone buys it—even if the actual logistics and market structure of the industry are opaque.[3] The story may not have been particularly *credible*, but the naïve students were credulous enough to accept that the company had committed to bring an oil rig to Israeli waters. The *emotional* content came from the combination of expected profits (who doesn't want to win the lottery?) with a vague nationalistic idea that oil would be beneficial to the country as a whole. Indeed, the company founders had chosen a name, Isramco, to exploit this very idea. The name combined the name of the nation, *Israel*, with *Aramco*, the name of the Saudi national oil company. That is, the company had purposefully chosen a name to leverage the Middle East oil narrative. Finally, it was easy to put the entire episode into a narrative, a story. This story had more than one level. First, the analogy to the oil-rich Persian Gulf countries is a story in and of itself, just as the analogies of Amazon to Barnes & Noble or Dell Computers result in two competing stories. But the Israeli oil story was extra slick. The idea of offshore oil bringing a valuable natural resource to a country without many natural resources—a resource that might signal independence from world oil markets dominated by Israel's enemies—is a very good and sticky story. This was the sort of story novices might accept.

Sticky ideas are social phenomena. One of the Heath brothers, Chip, together with the financial economists Brad Barber and Terrance Odean have made the case that sticky ideas are more likely to catch on in groups, as opposed to individuals, who decide alone.[4] Barber and Odean later summarized a host of studies suggesting that stocks are more likely to be purchased when they are either in the news or experiencing sharp movement in a short period of time. That is, when they are part of a popular narrative. In their own analysis, Barber and Odean find that the least sophisticated retail investors bought almost twice as many shares of the most heavily traded stocks than they sold, whereas sophisticated investors bought only 10% more.[5] In other words, the least sophisticated, least experienced investors appear the most likely to react to salient facts that bring a stock to their attention.[6] Novices are most likely to buy into these types of narratives.

Indeed, the students might as well have been subjects in Barber and Odean's study. They considered Isramco following a tip. This was reinforced by news stories and the general sense that the stock was "hot." The choice of what to buy is daunting; there are hundreds or thousands of securities traded on the market. In contrast, the choice of what to sell is restricted to what one actually owns. Thus, once a story about a stock spreads, some investors will short-circuit an expansive, reasoned search and focus on salient stocks as investment targets. Isramco was psychologically "available," easily digestible, and buzz laden. The students interpreted the general interest as (social) proof that Isramco was a winner; sticky ideas flow through social channels.[7]

The students contributed to a self-reinforcing process—indeed, they became part of the narrative. Retail investors buy popular stocks and in the process make them more popular. Financial economists have astutely noted that self-reinforcement is enhanced when investors realize that this process is happening, and then try to cash in on the cycle—further driving up the price with the hope and expectation of selling near the peak. As the stock starts to move, it becomes more interesting and further propels the story. The two processes, whereby investors invest in newsworthy stocks, and thereby en masse make them more newsworthy, work together. Novices learn of their friends' and acquaintances' market exploits and enter the market, while more sophisticated investors try to take advantage. The part of the process whereby investors believe that they can sell to later investors at inflated prices is often labeled the "greater fool theory," and this theory has been, deservedly, the subject of many treatments of bubbles. Unfortunately, the greater fool theory has an important shortcoming. It doesn't consider whether there are times when fools might more likely be attracted to the market. Because of this, we can identify that there were greater fools only in hindsight—and we lack the tools to predict when they will appear.[8]

Nevertheless, with hindsight, we can identify specific events that make people hyper-aware of certain opportunities. These events catalyze and magnify the process. For example, President James K. Polk's fourth annual message to Congress in 1848 included this extraordinarily sticky and contagious passage: "It was known that mines of the precious metals existed to a considerable extent in California at the time of its acquisition [1848]. Recent discoveries render it probable that these mines are more extensive and valuable than was anticipated. The accounts of the abundance of gold in that territory are of such an extraordinary character as would scarcely command belief were they not corroborated by the authentic reports of officers in the public service who have visited the mineral district and derived the facts which they detail from personal observation."[9] Polk's statement was the clearest signal in a long series of reports emanating from the first gold strike at Sutter's mill in January of that year. Would-be prospectors who might have heard rumors about gold in California felt confirmed in the truth of the claim by none other than the president of the United States. Polk took a naturally sticky idea and put it on steroids—perhaps single-handedly catalyzing the California gold rush. In 1849, some three hundred thousand "49ers" left for California. Most 49ers found little gold but perhaps would have been consoled by the fact that they did inspire the name of a National Football League team. We call events like President Polk's address *coordinating events*. They are rare, but they are important in that they are events or series of events that can draw attention to a particular opportunity and transform a loose set of ideas into a shared narrative that can then affect markets and economic behavior on a grand scale. Coordinating events direct traffic in the most expansive sense; they focus attention on particular narratives and in so doing propel the narratives forward—or even create the narratives. They can also catalyze bubbles.

Our Israeli students knew little about the geology of oil deposits; the 49ers (neither prospectors nor the football team) knew even less about the practicalities of extracting gold from remote foothills. Nevertheless, similar forces were at work to entice their participation in the respective markets. Just outside the main Tel Aviv University gate was a bank. Israeli banks, which made money off commissions, encouraged interest in trading by generating printouts of prices throughout the day. It was the 1990s version of the ticker tape. The students ate it up. Every day, they would go to the bank to see what had happened to their investments. To stay informed, they followed the news, including a story that Isramco might, in fact, have secured that oil rig that could perhaps, *maybe*, be brought to the area to start exploration.

Soon, the student and his friend noticed that there was too much money in their account, given that the price of the shares had not risen very much. Confused and certain that the bank had made an error in their favor, they met with a bank manager, who happened to be another friend's father. The bank manager generously explained to them that Isramco had split their stock after it had appreciated—there was no error. That is, the company had created two new shares for each old share and had halved the price. On paper, each student had more than doubled his investment as speculators had driven up the value of the stock. By chance, one student was planning a trip to Turkey. Needing funds for his trip, the student sold his shares and enjoyed a month-long backpacking trip in Asia Minor. That student was one of your authors, Brent.[10]

Brent was very lucky (at least on this trade). He was financially illiterate; he did not understand the basic mechanics of stocks to the extent that he could not read a simple account statement. He did not know that something like a stock split existed. His luck notwithstanding, he had as much business investing in the market as he did panning for gold or playing professional football.

Brent's decision-making process was typical of inexperienced, unsophisticated investors. We quote Mrs. W. C. B. at the start of the chapter as an example of this type of decision making. Like Brent's Isramco gambit, Mrs. W. C. B. was attracted to radio stocks because the idea of radio was salient and sticky. It was simple: the radio could be manufactured and sold. It was unexpected: the idea of transmitting voice invisibly through the air was exceptional and miraculous. There had been public demonstrations and broadcasts of the radio; these made it concrete. Moreover, she could hear the radio and see the miraculous device. It was exciting; that is, she had an emotional reaction to the new product. And there was a good story: radio was amazing; it would become popular, so set producers would make money. But she short-circuited her search process to focus on one small subset of the industry. She did not realize that the business model for radio was not well understood at the time. (As discussed in Chapter 2, even the ultimate insider, RCA's president David Sarnoff, didn't yet know how to make money on it!) It was unclear whether profits would accrue to any or all of the radio producers, radio stations, content producers, networks, or patent holders who were active in the market. Mrs. W. C. B. did not entertain the idea that any type of company other than the manufacturers of radio receivers could be an interesting investment target. She had focused her attention very narrowly—in this case to her detriment.

But let us not judge Mrs. W. C. B. too harshly, for we are all susceptible. The celebrated early twentieth-century economist Irving Fisher publicly proclaimed that the stock market had hit a permanently high plateau and was bullish on the market. Unfortunately, Fisher said this just six days before the market crash that sparked the Great Depression. Arguably, Fisher was prognosticating outside his area of expertise—which was monetary policy and neoclassical economics, not the vagaries of the stock market. So although he may have believed he was an expert and his narrow worldview told him one thing, in terms of the stock market, he turned out to be more of a novice.

In general, novices are more likely to follow the crowd. For example, during the 1990s internet boom, novice investors were more likely to invest in well-publicized internet stocks than were those with investing experience.[11] Novice investors were more swayed by the publicity and excitement about the "new way of doing business"—while more sober-eyed, experienced investors, especially those who had lived through the bear market of the late 1980s—were skeptical about the promises of the internet. Similarly, Mrs. W. C. B.'s financial illiteracy was also evident when she was considering radio stocks. She believed that "reasonable assurance of large returns" was possible. With this conception of investing, Mrs. W. C. B, like Brent, should not have been investing at all.

What swayed her? Mrs. W. C. B. could tell herself a story in which it made sense to invest in radio. She was aware of "the wireless concerts given daily at Newark and elsewhere." She had become familiar with the new medium, and familiarity implies comfort and encourages investment.[12] Some technologies translate into sticky ideas and stories more readily than others. For an idea to be sticky, at minimum, the commercial potential must be understandable to the investor. The public broadcasts of the Metropolitan Opera on the radio were sticky, and the public concerts made the technology accessible and understandable not only to Mrs. W. C. B. but also to general investors. Indeed, such public demonstrations may have been coordinating events that aligned investor beliefs about the commercial prospects of radio.[13] Retail-facing inventions that people actually use or might use are more likely to attract attention of investors and breed familiarity, especially for novices. Thus, we offer the general prediction that retail-facing innovations are more likely to be associated with bubbles.[14]

Just as sticky ideas about new, emerging technologies can envelop novice investors, so, too, can incomplete information. Nobel laureate Daniel Kahneman points out that stories are easier to concoct when the facts are sparser.[15] The less we know, the more we supply from our own imagination, which is influenced by our biases. To paraphrase former US secretary of defense Donald Rumsfeld, the young Brent was not just ignorant of known unknowns; he was also unaware that there was such a thing as unknown unknowns. A known unknown is, for example, the fact that Brent did not know what a stock split was. An unknown unknown? Brent did not even comprehend the scope of his financial illiteracy when he gambled $1,000 before a costly trip abroad. Perhaps Brent should take comfort in the fact that Mrs. W. C. B. made a similar error. We saw in Chapter 2 that there was significant business model and value chain uncertainty in radio. At the time, however, Mrs. W. C. B. did not know what she did not know, that profits might be generated from different parts of the radio broadcast value chain such as content producers, the emerging broadcasting stations, and advertisers—not just radio set producers. Mrs. W. C. B. assumed away this uncertainty altogether with her assumption that money would be made selling radio sets.

Evidently, Rumsfeld was channeling Bertrand Russell: "The fundamental cause of trouble in the modern world today is that the stupid are cocksure while the intelligent are full of doubt."[16] In an attempt to account for the modern world's toxic brew of ignorance and overconfidence, MIT Sloan School's Dražen Prelec created a "Bayesian truth serum"—an algorithm that overweights the opinions of those who recognize the limits of their own knowledge.[17] Together with the Princeton neuroscientist Sebastian Seung and MIT student John McCoy, they have formalized a method to detect who has more awareness, or "metaknowledge," as they call it, and then weight those meta-knowing, non-cocksure doubters' opinions more heavily. Doing so turns out to lead to more accurate predictions, at least in experimental settings. By implication, we expect that novices are more likely to not know what they don't know, and therefore make less accurate investment decisions.

Although it might be intuitive that novices are more likely to make judgment errors when they buy securities, it is not clear whether novices will have sufficient influence on the market to affect prices. At the end of the day, it is doubtful that Mrs. W. C. B. was investing enough capital to affect the price of radio securities, and certainly Brent's small investment did not affect the aggregate market for Isramco shares. We should expect novices to affect the market only when a relatively large number of them go for gold—as in the case of the gold rush.

Financial economists like to call these novices "noise traders." According to Russell, Rumsfeld, and, more recently, Prelec and his colleagues, those who are full of doubt, the sophisticates, will outperform the noise traders. Indeed, if markets are working with no frictions at all, these sophisticates can borrow shares from those who own them and sell them on the market. This practice is referred to as short selling or shorting. Shorting is often very difficult to do, and risky as well, because if the price goes up, the lenders might get nervous about getting their shares back and so recall them. This scenario would force the short sellers to repurchase these appreciated shares at a loss. It is especially likely when novices and naïfs flood the market. This added risk makes the sophisticates less likely to short the market, contributing to the observed price rise.[18]

New technologies make this problem worse, as nobody can be a "grizzled veteran" in new things. The arrival of new technology both attracts new (novice) investors and devalues existing expertise, thereby rendering even experts like David Sarnoff or Irving Fisher more like novices. The shock of the new makes novices more plentiful. Technological innovation creates noise traders.

This leads to the natural question of when an investor loses their naïve status? When do they become sophisticated? The experimental economist and Nobel laureate Vernon Smith and his many collaborators have investigated the role of experience in the lab. The emergence of bubbles is surprisingly robust to a variety of real-world conditions in the lab; many types of investors, such as small business owners, securities brokers, and corporate executives create bubbles in markets. Simple number of years trading does not appear to be a good proxy for becoming sophisticated. Doctoral students in economics, who study fundamental value and are trained to make such calculations, were able to stave off bubbles in their experimental markets.[19] That is, if the fundamental value is explicit and investors are trained to think about this concept and calculate it, we can avoid bubbles. These subjects were probably as close to "rational" as a neoclassical economist could hope. However, it is never possible in the real world to calculate the fundamental value of an asset, particularly in an emergent technology industry. And such rational calculations become even more difficult when the assets are embedded in creative narratives. What *is* robust and replicable is that once participants experience a bubble and a crash, they are chastened and tend not to overbid for assets anymore.[20] Theoretically, bubbles should become more likely as the share of inexperienced investors and assets they control increases because naïfs overwhelm the sophisticated investors' abilities to arbitrage the market. Consistent with this idea, bubbles become more likely as the time since the last bear market increases.[21]

Intriguingly, some of the very technologies that have the greatest speculative appeal—think telegraph, telephone, computer—also had the effect of making it easier for investors to invest and thereby magnified this appeal. Of course, it wasn't all technology. The share of novices in the market has increased over time, with macroeconomic growth and the changing organization of investing having made

trading cheaper, more accessible, and more transparent. This progress, though halting and nonlinear, has slowly opened up investment
to an increasing share of the populace in a process that is commonly
called *market democratization*.[22] When market democratization speeds
up, we will be more likely to see a greater influence of novices on the
market and, therefore, more likely to see bubbles. This means that
to understand when bubbles are most likely, we need to understand
the process of market democratization in all its fits and starts. If we
assume that investment opportunities arrive randomly, and if an investment opportunity happens to coincide with an influx of novices,
we expect the likelihood of a bubble to increase. Conversely, if an
opportunity arrives but novices are scarce, or are otherwise unlikely
to participate, the likelihood of a bubble decreases. The history of
market democratization is interesting in its own right. Although we
only sketch it briefly here, it gives us important clues as to when we
should expect influxes of novices, noise traders, or however you wish
to call them.

Market Democratization

Today, many stocks can be had for the price of a Happy Meal at Mc-
Donalds, and the average stock can be acquired for the cost of an
entree in a midpriced restaurant.[23] So from a cost perspective, it is
not surprising that approximately half of US households own stocks.
About 40% of those, or 20% of American households, have not only
signed up for their company-sponsored 401(k) or invested in a mutual
fund but also have gone the extra mile and purchased the stock of a
specific company. In other words, in 2015 there were approximately
24 million households set up to purchase stocks.[24] It is no wonder. Purchasing stocks has never been easier. Establishing a trading account is
no more difficult than opening a bank account, and trades themselves
are very inexpensive. According to the Bureau of Labor Statistics, the
average US worker earns enough to buy the average-priced share in
just fifty minutes. For a day's wages, a worker can choose all but the
priciest 1% of currently traded shares.

Although we wish we knew how many people were investing and when—and most important, when we might have seen changes in this number—before the 1950s this information was never recorded systematically. However, we can calculate how much work—as in paid labor—was needed to enter the market over time. We do that in Figure 3.1. On the vertical axis of Figure 3.1, we show the number of months of work it would take to earn enough money to purchase a single share of the average priced stock on the New York Stock Exchange over time. The horizontal axis lists the years. At the beginning of our series in the early nineteenth century, it took about five months of work to purchase the average share. By the latter half of the 1800s it took only a couple of months to earn enough to purchase the average share. By the 1920s only 0.4 months of labor was required. And merely 0.015 months was needed by the end (1995), or less than one hour!

This change has been revolutionary. In 1817, the first year in which we can observe both wages and stock prices, the average stock price on the New York Stock Exchange was $106. That's about $1,500 in 2015 dollars. But keep in mind that relative to today, most people were quite poor in the United States. Having $1,500 in 1817 was much, much rarer than it is today. At the typical monthly wage of $22, it took an average manufacturing worker five months to earn enough money to purchase a single share of the average security.[25] In 1850, "only" four months' wages purchased the average share, and it was never less than one month for the rest of the nineteenth century. So, we can gather that there were not a lot of novices joining in. Just to make sure that investing was really out of reach, shares were traded in minimum lots of one hundred shares. That is, if an unskilled laborer started saving every penny of his or her wages in 1850, it would not be until 1866 that he or she would have earned enough to trade the average lot on the New York Stock Exchange. It was possible to trade smaller "odd lots" on the rival (and long defunct) Consolidated Exchange, but for all practical purposes, the stock exchange was a playground for the very rich for most of the nineteenth century.

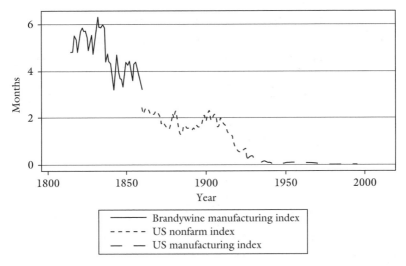

FIGURE 3.1   Months of labor to purchase average NYSE share, 1817–1999
Sources: Data through November 1925 are taken from the Yale NYSE database; Rose
Razaghian, "Financial Credibility in the United States: The Impact of Institutions,
1789–1860," *Yale School of Management,* July 29, 2013, https://som.yale.edu/faculty
-research/our-centers-initiatives/international-center-finance/data/historical
-newyork. Average prices from December 1925 to 1999 are calculated on the basis
of data from *CRSP US Stock Database,* Center for Research in Security Prices (CRSP),
Booth School of Business, University of Chicago. The average unskilled wage in Brandywine County, Pennsylvania, is used to calculate monthly wages from 1817 to 1860,
the US nonfarm index is used from 1861 to 1928, and the US manufacturing index
from 1929 to 1999. Robert A. Margo, "Daily and Monthly Wages in the Philadelphia
and Brandywine Regions: 1785–1860," table Ba4219-4223; "Hourly and Weekly
Earnings of Production Workers in Manufacturing: 1909–1995," table Ba4361-4366;
"Annual Earnings in Selected Industries and Occupations: 1890–1926," table Ba4320-
4334, in *Historical Statistics of the United States, Earliest Times to the Present: Millennial Edition,*
ed. Susan B. Carter, Scott Sigmund Gartner, Michael R. Haines, Alan L. Olmstead,
Richard Sutch, and Gavin Wright (New York: Cambridge University Press, 2006).
Note: The y-axis is the amount of labor, measured in months, that the average worker
would need to work in order to buy the average priced share traded on the New York
Stock Exchange.

The first three decades of the twentieth century witnessed profound change in the time it took to earn enough money to invest. Initially, share prices remained relatively high, but urbanization, public
education, and the Second Industrial Revolution increased earnings
and wealth. As a result, workers earned significantly more.

To better see the trend since the 1920s, we introduce a new figure (Figure 3.2) so that we can rescale the y-axis to days instead of
months. By 1925, the average worker could enter the stock market for
twelve days' wages, and many fewer for professional classes. In the late
1920s, average share prices appear to have declined significantly. Either nominal values were kept low to encourage trading or the flurry
of public offerings led to cheaper stocks on the market.[26]

Following the Crash of 1929, relative purchasing power remained
stagnant, falling slightly with wages in the hard, early years of the
Great Depression before recovering with the economy in the late
1930s. Federally imposed wage controls limited income growth during
World War II. As share prices rose, stock purchasing power declined.

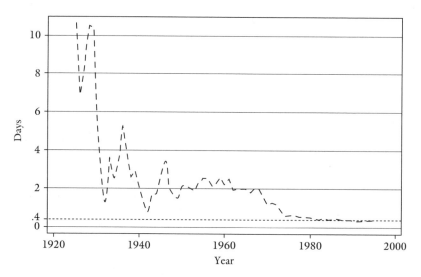

FIGURE 3.2   Days of labor to purchase average NYSE share, 1920–1996
Sources: Average prices for December 1925–1999 are calculated on the basis of data
from *CRSP US Stock Database*, Center for Research in Security Prices (CRSP), Booth
School of Business, University of Chicago. Wage data: Robert A. Margo," Hourly and
Weekly Earnings of Production Workers in Manufacturing: 1909–1995," table Ba4361-
4366, in *Historical Statistics of the United States, Earliest Times to the Present: Millennial Edition,*
ed. Susan B. Carter, Scott Sigmund Gartner, Michael R. Haines, Alan L. Olmstead,
Richard Sutch, and Gavin Wright (New York: Cambridge University Press, 2006).
Note: The y-axis is the amount of labor, measured in days, the average worker would
need to work in order to buy the average share traded on the New York Stock Exchange.

Even as the overall economy recovered strength in the 1950s, market democratization stalled at approximately two days' work to purchase an average share. It would take the information technology revolution until the 1980s to bring the average share price down from two days' work to less than an hour.

Overall, the basic trend is evident. The market has become much more accessible. Of course, average share prices are a function of supply and demand, as well as fluctuations in wages. Nevertheless, they paint a long-run aggregate picture. Although with sharp declines, the cost of shares should focus our attention on particular periods, we need richer information to understand when there were novices. We need to uncover when the conditions were right to see an influx of new investors. It is a story that repeats itself over and over again. As a market heats up, and as access to technology improves, a fraction of those for whom investing was on the margin of affordability began to invest. Over time, this margin shifted, so that less and less affluent people were able to access financial markets. From the 1960s we have reasonably accurate data on the number of investors. For the early part of the period we investigate, though, we do not. For this reason, we use the historical record to guess the periods when the largest influxes of novices occurred.

The Nineteenth Century: 1800–1904

"Be it known that I, CHARLES GOODYEAR, of the city
of New York, in the State of New York, have
invented certain new and useful Improvements in
the Manner of Preparing Fabrics of Caoutchoue
or India-Rubber; and I do hereby declare that the
following is a full and exact description thereof."
JUNE 15, 1844, PREAMBLE OF US PATENT 3,633
(VULCANIZED RUBBER)

Investors invest in corporations. So to understand the development of the stock market and the setting in which we study bubbles, we have to understand how corporations changed throughout our time period.

Today, we show our students how to incorporate a company as part of an undergraduate assignment. We do not teach it in detail, because it is not a difficult task for anyone, including college students. When our period of study begins, however, in 1844, it would have been difficult for Mr. Goodyear to set up a company to commercialize his rubber process. At the time, incorporation in New York State was still governed by the inaccurately named General Incorporation Act of 1811, which applied only to companies producing textiles, metal, or glass. All others seeking to incorporate needed a special act of the New York State Legislature. Getting the legislature to allow one to incorporate through a special act did have advantages. Such enterprises were not limited to capitalizations less than $100,000, they could have more than five founding partners, and they did not need to seek renewal after twenty years.[27] Goodyear, however, had a backdoor. First, he started production in a textile factory he and his brothers had set up prior to his invention in Springfield, Massachusetts. He also licensed his invention to a company in Providence, Rhode Island. It appears that, in practice, once a corporation was chartered, it could change its purpose—at least on the margins, in this case from the production of textile products to rubber products.

In New York, a more general act went into effect in 1848, although it took until the 1870s before most companies were chartered under the law. It is surprising to learn that many of the largest firms of the nineteenth century were not corporations at all. Standard Oil was set up as a trust, and Carnegie's steel as a limited partnership. Not only was corporate law not well established, but the secondary market for shares was underdeveloped. Mary O'Sullivan, perhaps the preeminent expert on capital markets in the period, notes that the market for industrial securities was very limited until the end of the century. Individuals did invest in railroad bonds to support the connection of their local towns to the emerging rail network. Shares of some of these railroad lines were then floated on the New York Stock Exchange.[28] However, there was little room for experimental capitalism on public markets. Importantly, there was not a general expectation of selling shares as a means for investors to earn a profit; rather, the expectation was that shares would yield dividends in the same way that bonds earned interest. For example, investors in early automobile companies expected dividends, not to be able to sell their shares.[29]

Incorporation became easier and easier as states struggled to balance shareholder and public protections with facilitating business. This culminated in Delaware's general incorporation laws in 1893. These laws were the most management-friendly in the union and, conversely, the least protective of shareholder rights. Because it is the management of a company that decides where to incorporate, this "last-mover" act by the Delaware legislature led to a general preference of incorporation in Delaware that persists to this day.[30] General incorporation removed a choke hold on the supply of new firms, but it did not lead to a general democratization of investment. In fact, if anything the race to the bottom reduced shareholder protections.

While general incorporation was emerging, one of the most profound changes in capital markets was also occurring. So much so that it is difficult to overstate how qualitatively different trading was in 1890 from 1860. One might even claim that this change in market technology was the most important transformation to financial markets that ever occurred—rivaled perhaps only more recently by electronic trading.

A fundamental assumption of Econ 101 is that everybody easily can and does know prevailing prices. This prevents people from arbitraging prices. As a solution to difficulties in communicating prices, trading in the NYSE was done by members in twice-daily auctions. (Yes, for you economics geeks: a Walrasian auctioneer actually existed in lower Manhattan in the 1800s.) Although over-the-counter (OTC) trades happened outside the exchange in the street, some estimate that the volume of trades on the OTC market was much larger.[31] To facilitate the trades, trading was done using pencil and paper, and information traveled via couriers. To get the prevailing prices paid by insiders, individuals would listen literally with their ears on the doors of the exchange, and information would then pass to the messengers out into the street where OTC trading took place. This began to change with the first telegraph line in 1844—the same year as Goodyear's patent.[32]

The telegraph led to a revolutionary change in how capital markets were organized. For the first time it was possible to make trades from across the country—and across the ocean, for that matter. The trades were not blind as the telegraph also conveyed prices to potential traders. However, conveying prices via telegraph was imperfect and slow. Then, twenty-some years later, in 1867, an invention appeared that even more profoundly changed capital markets: the stock ticker. The stock ticker utilized telegraph lines to convey market prices, at least if you could afford access to the lines. Now, investors could gather remotely and follow the market in (Victorian) real time. Just three years later, in 1870, the president of telegraph giant Western Union privately predicted that stock-ticker traffic would soon dominate the telegraph business.[33] So important was the impact of stock tickers that, in 1871, the New York Stock Exchange abandoned its twice-daily auctions in favor of continuous trading and assimilated the OTC trading from the street. Only four years after its invention, there were around seven hundred machines installed in New York City in "brokers' offices, banks, hotels, restaurants, and even in saloons and cigar stores."[34] After Western Union acquired the ticker service provider in 1871, it expanded the service over its national network. In 1873, service was offered in twenty cities, and by 1879 there were 1,574 tickers in service—two-thirds of them in New York.[35] At this point, in 1874, Edison improved the ticker with the invention of the "quadruplex," which enabled Western Union to quadruple its capacity without upgrading telegraph lines. By 1886, Western Union was operating two thousand ticker machines, and rival Commercial Telegraph Company was operating another nine hundred in major cities around the country. The arrival of the ticker changed how decisions were made because for the first time it was possible to reliably aggregate information. The Dow Jones Index was first published in 1884, and soon a "science" of stock prices emerged.[36]

The ticker was a great instrument of democratization. In 1871 the *Chicago Tribune* made it arcanely (and perhaps optimistically) clear that "no broker is necessary, any person, man or woman, boy or girl, white, black, yellow or bronze can deal directly."[37] Financial historian

David Hochfelder describes how the ticker and quadruplex enabled the emergence of "bucket shops" where such small traders would speculate.[38] From the 1870s until they were outlawed in 1914, bucket shops occupied storefronts and served a broad swath of the urban population that received up-to-date prices with stock tickers. The bucket shops made trading affordable by enabling investors to make much smaller trades. While the NYSE required minimum trades of one hundred shares—or trades in the hundreds or thousands of dollars—bucket-shop transactions were much smaller, usually $10–$50. This was still a large sum of money—$50 was almost a month's wages for an unskilled laborer. However, bucket shops typically encouraged customers to buy on margin. With a typical 5% margin requirement, $50 stocks could be had for $3, which was a little more than a day's wages in 1870 for a skilled worker and two days' wages for an unskilled laborer.[39] Never mind that prices might then be manipulated and margins called so as to shake down clients. The bucket shops proliferated.[40]

The restrictive policies of the NYSE led to the emergence of competition. In particular, the Curb Exchange emerged in the 1880s and is central to our story. It was called "the Curb" because trading literally took place outdoors, rain or shine. Stocks deemed too risky or unworthy of the backing of the Big Board were traded on the curb. Note that the over-the-counter market existed through the 1880s outside the NYSE and traded the same securities as the Big Board. It was assimilated into the NYSE with the movement to continuous trading. The Curb exchange was a completely different animal. The Curb's leadership was careful to allow trading only in smaller, more speculative securities that were not listed on the NYSE; thereby, the Curb had a more symbiotic, tense relationship with the Big Board. This was further tempered by a lack of will on the part of the Big Board to rein in the Curb's actions: some estimates indicate that 80% of the Curb's business came from NYSE members.[41] In the 1880s the majority of Curb activity involved the trading of highly speculative mining stocks.

The emergence of the new exchanges and new organization of the NYSE with the telegraph and the stock ticker came at a time when the railroads and industrialization associated with the steam engine were driving the economy. Booming economies tend to lead to higher wages, more disposable income, and potentially new investors. This period is no exception. From 1879 to 1891 wages increased by 33%, from around $30 to $40 a month! The market reflected this. The brand new Dow Jones Index increased from 62 in 1884 to 78 in 1890. The new communication technologies and their rapid application to trading, together with the expanding economy and rising wages, suggest that there would have been more demand and access to stocks.

This suggests we should have seen more novices in the 1880s. But this is insufficient to conclude that the 1880s were ripe for market speculation in new technologies. Critically, the telegraph and ticker changed how trading occurred and who was doing it; at the same time, what was being traded was also changing. Contemporary reporters were struggling to make sense of this change:

> Last spring, when the market was in the dumps and London was constantly selling, it was suddenly turned and made intensely active by a movement in the industrial stocks. These stocks are beginning to come forward again. Public attention is turning to them, because it is getting to be recognized that as between a high-priced railroad stock of uncertain dividend, and an industrial stock, there is usually a good deal more money in the latter, while the risk is not appreciably greater . . . If investors did not want these industrial stocks the creation of them would not be going on . . . but they do want them, because there is more money in them, as a class, than in any other securities now in the public market.[42]

This quote is the first use of the word *industrials* in the context of investments in the *New York Times*. Six years earlier, in 1885, 81% of Big Board listings were railroad stocks—the industry accounted for one-twelfth of the US economy! Railroads were well suited to trading because they were easy to evaluate: metrics were clear and comparable across different routes. In contrast, industrials are heterogeneous, and to this date new industrial stocks befuddle investors. In 1885, there was only a sprinkling of industrials on the Big Board, and the few industrial securities that were traded initially appeared in the Unlisted Department, which included lower-status stocks that were not formally accepted on the exchange.[43] O'Sullivan points out that the industrial securities were not necessarily what we would today call start-ups, but even established industrial concerns were an enigma to investors who did not have a clear way to know what a share of an industrial should be worth. In the 1800s there was no accepted way to evaluate firms, no rules that governed disclosure, no generally accepted accounting practices (GAAP), and trading was unregulated. There was no common way to think about "growth" stocks—indeed, the idea of growth stocks did not emerge until the 1960s (see discussion in Chapter 5). But the new industrials still attracted investors because they were filled with wonder and generated cash. With the development of the telephone and telegraph—and the rise of alternative markets—the stage was set in the early 1890s for the impact of the new investors. History does not disappoint. Following the recession of 1890–1893 and the Panic of 1893, when the Dow Jones average bottomed out at 33 from its 1890 high of about 70, we see a general rise in security prices. That all this newness might be associated with speculative episodes is not surprising. As noted in Chapter 2, in 1900, perhaps foreshadowing Tesla Inc., the equivalent of ten billion of today's (2015) dollars were committed to new electric vehicle start-ups floated on the Curb market. Most of this value was eventually lost.[44] Contemporary observers took notice: "In 1903 the financial writer Sereno Pratt claimed that there was 'no better proof . . . of the universality of speculation' than the ubiquity of the ticker."[45]

We are unable to say much with specificity, but our best guess is that the emergence of new trading technologies in the 1880s together with the bucket shops led to an influx of new investors. Eventually, in the 1890s the supply of industrial stocks also increased, attracting more investors, especially after the 1893–1897 recession. The emergence of the Curb market during the period and the sharp increase in industrial stocks point to a rise of a new investor class during the last two decades of the nineteenth century—a trend that likely accelerated at the very end of the century.[46] Based on 1930s work by Harvard economist Gardiner Means, we estimate that between five hundred thousand and one million people, or between 1 in 15 and 1 in 7.5 households, were investing at the onset of the twentieth century. On the basis of our analysis of profound changes in the institutions and technology of trading, we believe that many fewer were investing just thirty years earlier. In particular, we expect the greatest increases to have occurred with the diffusion of the ticker between 1885 through the Panic of 1893, and then after 1897 as the economy began to grow again. Nevertheless, we should be cautious with this statement, as inside observers believed that the prices on the NYSE market during the period were the aggregation of opinions of a "few hundred" informed men.[47]

The Great Democratization: 1900–1929

In the period leading up to 1900 we see the most profound changes in the organization of trading activity in history. But the period 1800–1904 only set the stage; the play hadn't really begun. It wasn't until the 1920s that democratization accelerated in a meaningful way. Additional regulatory, organizational, and technological advances were needed for that next big leap. At least four additional factors led to continued and, in the 1920s, accelerated market democratization: the continued rise of industrials, the spread of the telephone, the emergence of national brokerage houses (in particular Merrill Lynch), a wide-scale marketing campaign by the New York Stock Exchange, and perhaps blue-sky laws to make trading and traded companies more transparent to shareholders.

The rise of industrials was swift, although it was certainly hampered by the Panic of 1907 and most likely that of 1893 as well. In 1900, NYSE unlisted stocks would command about 33% of the value of the market and 80% by the 1920s. The decade of the 1920s was set for speculation in industrial securities. This story is echoed on the Curb: in 1911 half of all listings were oil or industrials; by 1920, the number had reached 80%. Like the NYSE, the number of companies traded on the Curb increased immensely. For every company traded on the exchange in 1900, there were thirty in 1930—the majority of this increase occurring after World War I.[48] Many of these were directly relevant to our study: shares of firms commercializing radio, airplanes, and other new technologies all began trading on the Curb, moving to the NYSE only when they had become sufficiently large. Several oil-related innovations appear on our list, and the Standard Oil trusts all were listed there, apparently because J. D. Rockefeller wished to avoid disclosure requirements that had been initiated on the Big Board.

While throughout the period the technology of investing made the markets much more accessible, and also disposable income increased, most of the rise in participation came after World War I. But in a surprising way, war policy itself may have attracted people to the markets. The Wilson administration chose to finance the war in part through the direct sale of so-called Liberty bonds to the general public. For many whose mode of savings was putting their money in a jar, or perhaps opening a bank account, this was the first time they had owned an intangible financial asset as an investment. The phenomenon was widespread. Estimates suggest that up to 25% of the population purchased the bonds.[49] Then, throughout the 1920s there was an ideological and business movement to enhance access to capital markets and create what became to be known as "citizens' capitalism." The primary vehicle was to sell shares to employees and customers—and literally millions of individuals became shareholders through these programs, more than five hundred thousand in AT&T alone![50] There were hundreds of such programs operating throughout the first three decades of the 1900s.

New technology played an important enabling role. In addition to the telegraph and associated ticker-related innovations, the telephone also contributed to the process of market democratization. We already discussed one of the most valuable business franchises to emerge from Western Capitalism in the nineteenth century, Alexander Graham Bell's American Telephone & Telegraph. The telephone had a profound impact on communication, so it is not surprising that it also influenced how investors accessed financial markets. Telephone, telegraph, and ticker—in conjunction with the spread of local brokerage houses—allowed individuals to trade stocks on the NYSE from anywhere in the country.

During the 1920s members of the New York Stock Exchange opened up brokerage houses across the United States (and the world). By 1900, NYSE members had brokerage offices throughout the city and country, 370 of them to be exact. By 1914, there were 414, but after the war the Big Board greatly expanded its reach. There were 663 in 1920, then 1,053 in 1928 and 1,200 in 1930. The market leader of this movement was Charles Merrill, and he led through the expansion of his firm, Merrill Lynch. Merrill Lynch leveraged ideas about familiarity discussed earlier in the chapter. The brokerage represented consumer-facing companies and promoted their shares to its customers. As described by financial journalist Joe Nocera, Merrill Lynch's "small customers were investing in the same stores they were shopping in." Charles Merrill both promoted chain retailers' shares and supported their businesses directly.[51] New investors were investing in businesses they knew because they were customers of those businesses. By the mid-1920s, it was possible to sit in one's home, place a phone call to the local brokerage office, and have a trade executed on Wall Street. Finally, in 1928, the NYSE embarked on an aggressive public relations campaign aimed at popularizing the "people's market."[52] As the market was reaching its peak, the Big Board embarked on a media campaign to attract new investors, otherwise known as novices.

What is fascinating about this period was that investors were flocking to the markets even though they remained exceptionally opaque institutions. Insider trading and price manipulation were not illegal. The list of ploys that were permitted is astonishing: for example, one common practice was to send simultaneous buy and sell trades to the same broker to create a fictitious price. As the demand for and success of industrials increased, and interest in investing spread to more and more parts of the population, the resulting squeeze of investors by insiders proved politically unsustainable. In the 1910s, a series of securities regulations were enacted that sought to protect minority shareholders in almost every US state.[53] The pressure caused the NYSE to act to preempt government intervention. But the exchange moved unevenly, initially banning only the most egregious practices. In 1913, the practice of buying and selling simultaneously was banned, although using customers' funds to manipulate prices to members' advantage was only "condemned." Only in 1917 did the NYSE enjoin its members from buying tomorrow's headlines from hungry newspaper reporters, and it took another year after that for the exchange to forbid the deliberate circulation of rumors intended to move prices. Given the range of predatory practices to which the unsuspecting investor could be subjected, it is hardly surprising that many potential novice market players opted not to participate. There is little evidence that these protections were enforced, and the legal obligations of corporations toward their shareholders were being undermined by a race to the bottom in the laws of general incorporation.[54]

Despite the questionable market reforms and remaining opaqueness, the conditions had been set and market capitalism exploded. Regional exchanges opened in Detroit, Cleveland, San Francisco, Chicago, and Los Angeles. Besides the aforementioned New York Curb Exchange, similar exchanges emerged near other regional exchanges. O'Sullivan reports that the number of traded securities increased significantly from 1880 through 1930. The number of stocks traded across all US exchanges increased from 916 in 1900 to 1,340 in 1915 and 2,659 in 1930.[55]

These changes were met with increases in investors. Gardiner C. Means's estimates from 1900 (mentioned earlier) were based on the total number of "book stockholders," or the sum of the number of people holding each individual stock. This overcounts the total number of individual owners because the same person might hold positions in more than one company, in which case that person would be counted twice. But this method is good for examining trends, as the total number of individual investors must be highly correlated with the number of book stockholders, a number that quadrupled between 1900 and 1930. Specifically, the number of reported book owners increased from 4.4 million in 1900 to 7.5 million in 1913, and then to 12 million in 1920 and 18 million in 1928. Means estimated the total number of individuals by dividing book owners by 4 and triangulated with income tax records. Between four million and six million individuals owned shares in corporations in 1927, perhaps three million to five million of them in public corporations. And based on income-tax records, there are reasons to believe that the "few hundred men" controlling the market in 1900 were being diluted. From 1916 to 1921 the top twenty-five thousand highest-earning Americans saw their ownership share of corporate America decrease from 57% to 37%. During the same period, individuals who didn't make the top hundred thousand highest earners saw their ownership share rise from 24% to 44%. But perhaps the most remarkable change occurred at the end of the 1920s. Between 1927 and 1930 the number of individuals owning stock almost doubled. Means estimates that ten million people owned stock by 1930. Ownership of corporate America became more diversified across class as well. Means opined that the shift was of "almost revolutionary proportions, and of great social significance."[56]

There are often brakes on investors' ability to engage in speculative activity, and one of the most common is limiting their ability to buy stocks on margin. Indeed, a central theme of any historical reckoning of the striking frothiness of the late 1920s is the degree to which investors bought stocks on margin. When investors buy on margin, they pay a fraction of the cost of the purchase and borrow the rest of the money using the value of whatever shares they buy as collateral. Lenders bet that the value of the securities will remain sufficiently high to cover their loans. This leverage can greatly magnify the effect of investor optimism, as smaller amounts of new investment can be used to drive up prices. Across most histories and studies of bubbles, such leverage is highlighted as an important factor in driving up prices. Buying on margin was common throughout the early twentieth century (and a subject of some of the reforms instituted by the NYSE during the 1910s), but in the 1920s it reached an unprecedented scale.[57] What is particularly surprising, and to our knowledge has not been noted by prior scholars, is the extent to which margin loans were made by novices in 1928 and 1929. We depict this in Figure 3.3: from 1927 through the crash and into 1930, the predominant source of funds was not the New York city banks (which we would expect to have the highest level of expertise) or the outside banks (which we might expect to be informed, though not quite as much as the local New York city banks), but the nebulous "others." Just over half of these funds came from outside corporations, which sought to park idle funds in the hands of investors who were paying interest rates well above 10%, while the rest came from abroad, both from individuals and from investment trusts. From 1926 through 1930, New York banks loaned $25 million on margin ($342 million in 2016 dollars), and out-of-state banks loaned $16 million ($218 million in 2016 dollars), but other lenders loaned more than $48 million, equivalent to $641 million in 2016, so more than both other groups combined. Not only were novices investing, we can also conclude that stock market speculation in the late 1920s was also backed by a new and likely inexperienced class of margin lenders. The democratization of investment had worked on more than one level. Money markets allowed

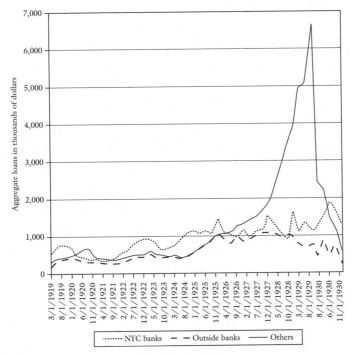

FIGURE 3.3   Margin loans by lender, 1919–1930
Source: Board of Governors of the Federal Reserve System (US), *Banking and Monetary Statistics, 1914–1943* (Board of Governors of the Federal Reserve System, Washington, DC, 1943), 494, table 139.

industrial firms to park idle capital in the hands of market speculators, even as the firms themselves were ill equipped to understand the risks involved in the practice.

The Great Kibosh and the Resurrection: 1930–1980

The Great Depression put the kibosh on market democratization for decades. The conservatism of individuals scarred by the events of the 1930s helped depress ownership levels to a fraction of the population until the 1950s.[58] That is, despite the series of reforms in the 1930s that successfully increased market transparency—including the creation of the Securities and Exchange Commission—market participation did not increase for thirty years. At this point, the memory of the great crash was fading, and a new generation of investors began looking at the stock market. The introduction of mutual funds helped: these bundled offerings mitigated some of the psychological biases described earlier and allowed investors to delegate decision making to expert fund managers while simultaneously diversifying holdings. Around the same time, Merrill Lynch instigated a brokerage house campaign aimed at making stock investing more accessible to ordinary people.[59] The history of this period includes important additional changes: growing incomes and decreasing transactions costs made stocks more affordable to all, and perhaps most important, the standardization and regulation afforded by the Securities and Exchange Commission may have increased investor confidence. By the mid-1950s, the number of new investors again began to increase.[60] Fortunately, and thanks in no small measure to the regulatory reforms of the 1930s, for the post–World War II period, we have much better data on the number of shareholders, and this allows us to skip over some of the historical details and identify the arrival of novices based on specific trends in the data. There are several estimates of the number of shareholders, the most optimistic of which is that put forth by the NYSE. Their fact books estimate that in 1952, there were six million shareholders; about 4% of the US population owned stock. By 1956, some estimates suggest that this number had increased by one-third.[61] By 1965, the number increased to twenty million, or 10%

of the population.[62] That is, the 1960s witnessed a very sharp increase in the number of individual investors investing in the stock market. By 1972, this number may have been as high as thirty-two million people, although it declined following the oil crisis to twenty-five million in 1975.

This pattern is mirrored in our time series of stock affordability in Figure 3.2. Following World War II, average share prices continued to decline, wages rose, and odd-lot stock trading was increasingly available. By the 1950s, almost any manufacturing worker could afford to purchase an average priced stock with a couple of days' wages, and this remained fairly constant until the 1970s. While not cheap, stocks were now in the realm of affordable investments for much of the population. It was in the 1970s that the cost of a share decreased to less than a day's labor. In short, we most likely did not see many new novices throughout the 1940s and 1950s, and we then witnessed a sharp increase in the late 1950s and in particular in the early 1960s. The windows of bubble opportunity for the technologies on our list were all closed by the end of the 1970s, so we stop our historical account here. We briefly consider the impact of changes since, such as the impact of discount brokerage firms like Charles Schwab and then, later, internet trading in Chapter 5.

Novices make mistakes, and these mistakes impact markets. In this chapter we've explored why this happens and considered when novices entered the market. They entered for a variety of factors—and there can be little doubt that rising prices enticed new investors and falling prices discouraged them. But underlying this cyclical pattern is a history of profound changes in how price and trading information is communicated, how investor behavior is regulated, how much it costs to invest, and how stock market investing integrates into the social fabric of society. Understanding these changes allows us to identify periods in which we should expect more novices—and hence a greater likelihood of price fluctuations and bubbles. In particular, we have identified distinct periods where an influx of novices might have influenced markets. The 1890s, the 1920s, an increase in the 1950s and a bigger one during the go-go years of the 1960s. It was during these periods that we might expect more "noise traders" than before. This is when we might expect more bubbles. If our theory is correct, we should be more likely to see market speculation and bubbles in periods when there were more novices in the market. Moreover, speculation should be most concentrated in technologies novices believe they understand and with which they have some familiarity. These are assumptions we test in Chapter 4.

Chapter 4

WHEN ARE THERE NOT BUBBLES?

Applying the Framework

It is now time to put our framework to the test. In Chapter 2 we described how narratives feed on uncertainty and, when extant, produce conditions that can lead to bubbles. In Chapter 3 we described how novices are more likely to buy into narratives about opportunity and explored how the supply of novices has varied with the development of institutions that facilitate trading and the startling decline in the cost of investing. We now consider whether these factors have any predictive power. When technologies lend themselves to better stories, are we then more likely to see a bubble?

Bear with us for the next few paragraphs. We wish to go though and describe the core of our exercise. It's a bit tedious, and a bit technical (we put most of the more obscure technical details in the notes and online Appendix, at http://www.sup.org/bubblesandcrashes). But we hope to be transparent so that you can judge for yourself whether you think our approach is reasonable. If you are not interested in the details or measurement, skip ahead to the section on the automatic watch.

We systematically evaluated every technology in our list to understand the levels of the types of uncertainty described in Chapter 2. We evaluated the stage of the technology at the time of industry emergence, its complexity, and the degree to which successful commercialization was understood to require the complementary capabilities of existing firms, or whether it was thought to be disruptive to existing value chains by making other technologies obsolete. We also evaluated the extent and effectiveness of intellectual property protections, whether there was uncertainty regarding the type of business model that would lead to success, and whether there were indeed different bets about successful commercialization strategies. To make things as comparable as possible, we developed a strict scheme to map vague historical attributes into numerical rankings. To these measures, we added factors that we predicted would lead to a narrative, somewhat independently of the strict levels of uncertainty, including whether the technology was consumer facing (and therefore likely to be accessible and available); whether its capabilities were surprising, and whether it was likely to be of broad, collective interest; and, relatedly, whether its capabilities were concrete and obvious. Finally, we asked whether there were novices investing in the window of bubble opportunity. This meant asking whether high levels of uncertainty in each technology and its potential commercialization paths coincided with periods of excess novices in the market identified in Chapter 3: in the 1890s, the late 1920s, or between 1960 and 1973. This strategy enabled us to score each technology on a scale of 0 to 8, where 0 is least likely to lead to a boom and bust episode and 8 is most likely. You can see this in Figure 4.1 later in the chapter, where we put the sum of the bubble risk-factor score on the horizontal x-axis. Technologies on the extreme right are the 8s, and those to the left have lower scores. Our model predicts that these "low-scoring" technologies will be less likely to be associated with market speculation.

To illustrate the power of the framework, we work through several examples on our list: the automatic watch, nylon, sulfa drugs (the first antibiotics), and movable type. We further develop the stories of the jet engine, the automobile, and aviation, which we explored in earlier chapters. Each example is invoked to describe a different pathway of events, narratives, and outcomes. At the end, we turn to the chart to discuss the correlations between the factors and our measure of speculation so you can understand how well the model works in aggregate.

The Automatic Watch: How Significant a Technology?

One of the authors, Brent, treasures a family heirloom, his Grandpa Joe's automatic watch. The watch was a gift from his father's medical practice to his grandfather in 1967. His grandfather had been volunteering in the practice to keep busy after Brent's grandmother had suddenly passed away, and the practice gave him the watch as a gift of appreciation. It was a stylish, expensive object for a frugal and abstemious man. Brent's grandfather wore this watch until he died almost twenty-five years later. This choice of gift for an older man in the mid-1960s hints at the rather peculiar inclusion of the automatic watch on our list of major technological innovations. This was a sophisticated object of the day, and many of the researchers who were studying Kondratiev long waves in the 1970s and whose efforts produced our underlying sample of technologies likely sported automatic watches. The technology itself was long in development, with related patents spanning centuries. Englishman John Harwood took out English and Swiss patents for a self-winding watch and entered the market in 1928. At the end of the day, style aside, the self-winding watch was a marginal improvement over a watch that one had to wind. Nice, but not nearly as profound as, say, insulin or flight. Uncertainty regarding the size of the market was not particularly high. So this technology has low uncertainty, and our model suggests that an associated boom and bust was unlikely.

Looking at other factors, it does not get much better for those hoping for a speculative episode. As an incremental luxury good, the automatic watch did not have the characteristics necessary for an emergent narrative. Although it is simple and concrete, it is neither particularly emotional nor unexpected to the general public. Or if it was, the reflected narratives of the day did not convey those emotions. In fact, almost no narrative emerged. In the *New York Times*, the innovative, patented Harwood automatic watch was mentioned twice—in advertisements for the Harwood company. If you are curious, it was sold at Saks Fifth Avenue. In fact, the automatic watch received a middling narrative score of 1 on our 0–2 scale but produced no observable narrative at all. All the factors that we evaluate are measures of the potential for an event (i.e., could a story about the technology be told?), not a declaration that the event did occur.

Although it is true that the narrative emerged in the 1960s—a time when there were many new investors, or novices, in the stock market—investors had no way to invest! Mr. Harwood, the British founder of the eponymous company, was a watch repairman. As is true today, expertise in the production of mechanical watches rested in Switzerland, so Harwood worked with the Swiss to produce his watch. Rolex quickly followed, as did other Swiss watchmakers. These manufacturers were private at the time. There was no opportunity for a public pure-play investment by which investors might have speculated. The automatic watch is a great example of a technology that was exceptionally unlikely to produce a speculative investment bubble.

When we aggregated the factors, the automatic watch scored a 4. There was no pure play, no boom and bust, and no bubble.

Phototype Printing: Technological Disruption Without Pure-Play Investment

In 1951, Albro T. Gaul's *The Wonderful World of Insects* was published in New York by Rinehart and Company. This introductory text to the world of entomology included dozens of sketches. A beautiful book, it was not noteworthy because of its content. Its significance, instead, was stated on the final page of the book, "*The Wonderful World of Insects* derives added significance from the manner it which it was composed. It is the first volume composed with the revolutionary Higonnet-Moyroud photographic type-composing machine. Absolutely no type, in the conventional [hot metal] sense, was used in the preparation of this book."[1]

Though a vast improvement on Gutenberg's original movable type, the prevailing, midcentury hot-metal technique was still a messy, inefficient industrial process. Production was difficult, with high fixed costs and multiple complementarities at work. As a result, three firms dominated the printing machine market. Of these, the American firm Mergenthaler controlled 70% of the market. The new photographic typesetting technique was invented by two French electrical engineers:

René Higonnet and Louis Moyroud. After they were unable to generate interest for their invention in France, they teamed up with the struggling Lithomat Corporation of New York to produce the Lumitype Photon. So promising was the new technology that Lithomat soon dropped other pursuits and renamed the company "Photon." The technology spread slowly, and it was not until the late 1960s that half of new machines were no longer based on the previously dominant molten-lead process. The new technology was important because machines could be placed in office environments. They were smaller, quieter, and, perhaps most important, did not use the not-very-office-friendly material molten lead. The technology is interesting because until the invention of phototypesetting, printers used mechanical impressions. After *The Wonderful World of Insects*, it took Mergenthaler eight years to offer its own phototype machine, and the company never recovered its former dominance. But Mergenthaler adapted better than its other competitor Intertype, which never successfully made the jump to the new technological paradigm and eventually closed shop in 1984. Companies such as Photon maintained strong competitive positions.[2] The slow pace of adoption of the new phototype machines, together with a commanding position in fonts, allowed Mergenthaler to survive. In the late 1960s, Mergenthaler produced its first digital phototypesetting machine. Although much of the market was ceded to new entrants, Mergenthaler regained a leadership position and took a 30% share of the market. The destruction of the value of Mergenthaler's and other incumbents' complementary assets in metallurgy and the production of molten lead machines, together with the long lag between the emergence of the first phototype product and mass adoption in the market, suggests considerable uncertainty.

A search of the press at the time reveals that there was discussion of these new generation machines and competition in the market. However, there was no way for an investor to directly participate. In 1963, Mergenthaler had merged with Electra-Autolite, which produced auto and electrical equipment. Even without the complication of diversification, an investor seeking to own a piece of the new phototype industry confronted the problem that Mergenthaler was also an incumbent manufacturer whose revenues continued to be derived from the legacy technology that phototype aimed to replace. The investor would have needed to balance the value-creating effect of Mergenthaler's entry into the phototype market with the value-destroying effect of phototype on the firm's legacy, molten-lead, Linotype business, thus diminishing the upside of such an investment play.

Without a pure play, no investment narrative developed. While the importance of the new machines was reported in the news, including documentation of Mergenthaler's entry and investment in the new technology, contemporaneous reports indicate that this was a minor news item. Perhaps we should not be surprised: the market for printing equipment is important, but individual consumers and investors did not buy printing equipment. It was a back-end technology, the output of which was exactly like that generated with molten-lead typesetting machines. This does not make for a story of general public interest. The technology was not simple; and while the technology represented a major change for publishing houses, the printing revolution generated little emotion outside the industry. It is not a coincidence that the technological advance embodied in *The Wonderful World of Insects* was printed as a note at the back of the book. Printing technology did not engage the public. This lack of stickiness inhibited the construction of a narrative, much less the emergence of a speculative narrative that could have led to a broad financial bubble. Phototype's score is high on dimensions of uncertainty, and it was commercialized at a time when there were novice investors in the market. However, the technology does not serve well as a subject for narrative. To summarize, phototype scored a factor score of 6 due to high uncertainty and the presence of novices. However, there was no narrative and no way to invest in the technology directly. Hence, no boom and bust, and no bubble.

From Antibiotics to Hosiery: Popular Narratives Without Investment

In December 1936, Franklin Delano Roosevelt Jr., a twenty-two-year old "Harvard crewman" and the second youngest child of President and Eleanor Roosevelt, was diagnosed with a streptococcal throat infection that developed into acute septicemia. Fearing the worst, his mother, Eleanor, rushed to his bedside, where she joined his fiancée, Ethel du Pont.[3] Even a few years earlier, the young man would almost certainly have died, but his physician administered a new sulfanilamide-based (sulfa) drug, and Roosevelt made a miraculous recovery. The story was widely reported in the press and drew attention to the existence and presumed effectiveness of the drug. An article in the *New York Times* reported that the company that produced the version of sulfanilamide that saved young Roosevelt received hundreds of inquiries from potential patients.[4]

Unlike the discovery of insulin—which affected only those suffering from diabetes—the introduction of sulfa drugs offered the first truly broad spectrum treatment of the bacterial infections that plague everyone. And while penicillin is often mentioned as the first antibiotic, that title properly belongs to sulfanilamide.

The first sulfa drug, a chemical named sulfamidochrysoïdine, was patented in Germany in late 1932. More correctly, sulfanilamide was the active agent, and sulfamidochrysoïdine was the mixture that allowed safe delivery of the active agent. The drug resulted from an exhaustive search at Bayer laboratories to figure out whether any known synthetic dyes had antibiotic properties. The active ingredient, sulfanilamide, a red or pinkish dye, also successfully cured bacteria-infected mice. In February 1935, Gerhard Domagk published results showing effectiveness in humans. Within two months the drug was introduced under the brand name Prontosil. At the time, most doctors believed that bacterial infections could not be treated with "chemotherapeutic agents" like Prontosil.[5] However, FDR Jr.'s miraculous recovery changed the narrative among physicians and reversed prevailing beliefs about such treatments.

In most of the other cases of medical innovation in our sample, patent claims limited the ability of potential competitors to enter the new market. Sulfanilamide was different because it had been invented and patented decades earlier for its properties as a dye, and the original 1909 patent had expired. Thus, once the active ingredient was

understood, any competent chemist could synthesize a vehicle to deliver sulfanilamide. As such, many firms rushed to enter the lightly regulated market for synthetic chemotherapies. Entry was easy because
sulfa drugs were available over the counter (i.e., without a prescription
from a licensed medical expert). Medical authorities worried about
the misuse of the new drugs, especially to self-medicate for treatment
of potentially embarrassing conditions like gonorrhea.[6] These fears
proved well founded when a Tennessee-based pharmaceutical company, S. E. Massengill, sold an untested, liquid version called "Elixir
of Sulfanilamide." The catastrophic elixir killed more than one hundred patients and led directly to the passage of the Food, Drug, and
Cosmetic Act of 1938, which put the US Food and Drug Administration in the position of overseeing the safety and effectiveness of all
medications sold in the United States.[7] Little more than a year after
the public learned about the effectiveness of sulfa medications, the
cost of entry increased substantially.

Either way, uncertainty was high because the therapeutic possi-
bilities of the new class of drugs were poorly understood. From 1938
onward, new uses of sulfanilamide or close chemical variants were
discovered; headlines from 1938 and 1939 in the *New York Times* were
triumphant: "meningitis deaths 'unbelievably' cut," "pneumonia
curbed," "drug checks tubercle bacilli," "agencies hail mortality drop
in birth cases," "rheumatic fever yields."[8]

With war raging across Europe, in October 1939, the German scientist Gerhard Domagk was awarded the Nobel Prize. But even if we
were to ignore the Nobel Prize, sulfa drugs were the most important
advance in chemical therapeutics of the decade. In theory, any one of
these technological narratives might have coordinated beliefs about
the opportunities for the new drug class. The technology had all the
trappings of a compelling story. The idea was simple and concrete
and had many of the attributes that, according to the Heath brothers,
make ideas sticky.

The narrative never sparked an investment bubble. It is possible
that the outbreak of the war killed this possibility, but we do not believe that to be the case. There was a miraculous drug narrative. What

was lacking was a parallel investment narrative. While the Elixir of Sulfanilamide debacle closed any window that might have existed for small pure-play firms to enter the market, it seems that from the outset larger chemical companies held an advantage in the development and marketing of chemical therapeutics. We observe some information about entry: none of the firms reported by the Council on Pharmacy and Chemistry in early 1937 to have submitted sulfa compounds for inclusion in the council's list of "New and Nonofficial Remedies" was a pure-play investment opportunity. All—Calco Chemical Company, Lederle Laboratories (American Cyanamid), Eli Lilly and Company, Merck and Company, E. R. Squibb and Sons, Winthrop Chemical Company (Sterling Labs), and Parke, Davis and Company—were either diversified or private.[9] Not only were there no public stocks likely to tightly track the fortunes of the new sulfa drug business, once the Food, Drug, and Cosmetic Act of 1938 was passed, it became more difficult for an entrepreneur to start one. Given the new regulatory environment and the technical expertise necessary to safely develop, market, and deliver a new sulfa drug, it was difficult to construct a story in which small start-ups might compete with these large companies. Moreover, the existing firms already possessed valuable, and ultimately necessary, complementary assets in the marketing and distribution of chemotherapies. For example, Eli Lilly had experience in the production of insulin. Thus, not only was there no pure-play investment opportunity: the prevailing market structure limited the ability of entrepreneurs to plausibly concoct a narrative that would support one. As a result, no speculative narratives emerged. For example, in 1941 the *Wall Street Journal* had a feature article about American Cyanamid, but the headline proclaimed: "New Products in Its Calcium Field." Sulfadiazine—American Cyanamid's sulfa product—was not mentioned until the ninth paragraph.[10] Similarly, on the occasions the company was mentioned in the *Wall Street Journal*, its position in the rubber business was always featured more prominently than its nascent sulfa drug business.[11] We might add that during this period there were not novices in the market; the memory of the Great Depression was still fresh in investors' minds. By May 1943 the promise of sulfa drugs was eclipsed by the "medical magic" of penicillin.[12] Attention had turned elsewhere.[13]

In our coding, sulfa drugs scored a 5 on factors for a bubble: the technology was not tightly controlled, uncertainty was high, and a variety of narratives were constructed. However, because no pure-play investments were available, no boom and bust episode could form, and hence no bubble.

Narratives emerge around somewhat less consequential products than antibiotics. When nylon hosiery was first offered for sale in October 1939—in a limited market test in Wilmington, Delaware—consumer response was unambiguous: "Customers were lined up three deep at the counters."[14] Later that week, DuPont vice president Charles Stine officially introduced the miracle fiber to considerable fanfare. Speaking at a gathering of three thousand members of a women's club to celebrate the New York World's Fair, Stine promised that nylon could be spun into "filaments as strong as steel, as fine as a spider's web, yet more elastic than any of the common natural fibers." The audience erupted into applause.[15] Although whispers of nylon had been circulating in the business press for a year or more, a large-scale rollout of synthetic stockings was still several months away. DuPont sought to manage both supply and demand, distributing as much nylon fabric as its first factory could produce while simultaneously warning consumers about DuPont's inability to meet expectations: "Most stores laid elaborate plans to restrict the sale as far as possible, and some set a maximum of two pairs to a customer."[16] Think: new iPhone! Initial demand did not disappoint. Stock-outs were common, and DuPont was unable to replenish the supply chain for almost two months. By the time the hosiery market reached a semblance of equilibrium the following spring, merchants were selling more than six million pairs of nylons per month, and the new fabric accounted for over 15% of overall hosiery sales by volume.[17]

To be sure, the introduction of nylon was "a four star success."[18] But the stock of DuPont barely budged. Should we have expected otherwise? Perhaps not. Since the company's founding in 1802 as a gunpowder manufacturer, DuPont had developed into a diversified chemical company. Despite nylon claiming a 15% share of the hosiery market, DuPont was not a pure-play investment in nylon. This would change over time, although DuPont would never become a true pure play in any single product. Writing about the history of DuPont, historians of technology David Hounshell and John Smith conclude that DuPont "was by the 1950s, in many respects, a fibers company that had some other businesses on the side."[19] But in 1940, DuPont was still very much a diversified firm.

Alternately, would investors have been tempted to fund competitors? As director of DuPont's chemical department, Charles Stine had overseen the introduction of the scientific research and development strategy. The firm had invested tens of millions of 1930-era dollars to bring nylon to market and could boast a strong portfolio of product and process patents related to nylon.[20] Despite the hoopla, no one could tell a story, or imagine a future, in which a nylon start-up challenged DuPont and took center stage.

The lack of a pure-play investment opportunity meant that investors could not invest only in nylon. By the same token, we cannot assemble an index that accurately tracks the technology—there were no nylon start-ups whose value might multiply exponentially as they tracked the new industry; there were no stories to tell about pioneering entrepreneurs who would revolutionize the materials with which we clothe ourselves.

This example illustrates a key point: the existence of pure plays in new technology industries and speculative narratives about these industries are codetermined. By this, we mean that they are caused by the same thing. The existence of pure plays is influenced by the nature of the technology and who is likely to control the technology based on legacy capabilities, intellectual property protection, and other factors. The availability of narratives is influenced by the same factors. Start-up stories are more interesting than profits or products in particular divisions of existing firms, and—all else equal—publicly traded start-ups are the most interesting of all. Start-ups are more likely to form when entrepreneurs can tell a story about how a new technology makes existing firms' capabilities obsolete.

The flip side of this argument is that when start-ups or pure-play companies are developing a new technology, the other factors that we expect will be associated with market speculation are also likely to be present. It is for this reason that the propensity to see speculation in industries with pure-play entrants is so high. The same forces that encourage speculation simultaneously encourage the formation of pure-play ventures.

Without a pure-play investment option and with total factors at 1, nylon did not experience either a boom and bust or a bubble.

Jet Engine: A Pure Play

The jet engine completely transformed the air transportation and the defense industries. The first applications were defense related and secret. As the veil of secrecy was lifted in the 1950s, the potential for the technology became clear. By 1955, the stock market was already six years into a bull market, and while the Korean War had ended, in the language of President Eisenhower, the "military-industrial complex" was ascendant. Jet fighters and bombers, such as Boeing's B-52 were in great demand by the Department of Defense. Reflecting the business opportunities that the expanded defense spending created, E. F. Hutton published a "missile index."[21] The Cold War and its offshoot, the aviation arms race, made consistent headlines throughout 1955.

The existence of successful military applications reduced uncertainty about whether the technology would eventually make its way into passenger travel. And perhaps more important, the constant stream of military orders and the arms race were real purchases that affected the bottom lines of companies in the industry. In 1955 and 1956, Douglas Aircraft announced plans for a commercial jet, although in October of the same year it was understood that Boeing and Douglas would compete to get a technology to market, and passenger jet travel was still a few years off.[22] However, what did not emerge was a bubble narrative similar to what was observed earlier in aviation and radio. Although the technological uncertainty was still high, perhaps not much different from the uncertainty that existed in propeller-based planes at the time of Charles Lindbergh's historic 1927 flight, the business uncertainty was completely different. Airlines were an established business that the jet plane would complement and enhance. It was expected that existing manufacturers would produce commercial jetliners.[23] Indeed, the public markets were sufficiently skeptical that Boeing's massive $1 billion ($9 billion in 2017) development of the 707 was financed by a consortium of banks.[24] The more modest uncertainty dampened the frothiest tendencies in the market and constrained the prospects for entrepreneurial narratives.

In 1955, our aerospace and defense index hits a frothiness of 2.94. Our use of the index is generous: this was not strictly a pure-play index, and it reflects, in part, the general emergence of the military-industrial complex. Nevertheless, the performance of several of the companies in the index is relatively closely tied to the jet. The aerospace index fell from its peak, recovered within a decade, and never lost more than 50% of its value. Recall that the frothiness measure reflects deviations from the underlying market trend; because the trend was relatively stable, even a comparatively modest collapse translates into high frothiness. Our analysis of the contemporary press accounts attributes these stock movements to the Cold War narrative. This narrative lacks the speculative fervor that we document in the cases of the radio, airplane, and automobile. We find few stories about investors flocking to the stock market.

Although we are unable to know precisely who was purchasing stocks in the aerospace index that we study, and the share of novices in the market had increased significantly during the 1950s, most of these investors were investing via new mutual funds, and the popular stocks in investment clubs were blue chips. Therefore, it is unlikely that these movements were driven by novices, so we classify this episode as a boom and bust but not a bubble.[25] This is a judgment call derived from a reading of historical accounts about the makeup of investors in a class of stocks; if we are wrong, this episode could be correctly classified as a bubble. To summarize, the total factors for the jet engine was 6, with medium levels of uncertainty and a good foundation for a narrative but a lack of novices. The boom and bust appears.

Commercial Aviation: A Broad Bubble

In April 1925, Henry Ford and his son Edsel invested in Stout Aircraft. Ford was to build the engines, and Stout was developing the flying "Flivver." The Flivver was to be an all-metal aircraft, an advance over the existing wood "aeroplanes." Recycling earnings from the Model T, Ford provided land, infrastructure, and production know-how necessary to manufacture the airplanes.[26] At the time, the Flivver was what today we would call "vaporware," a promised but not yet existing product. At the time, Stout had produced a few planes that Ford was using to ferry mail between its operations in Detroit and Chicago.[27] The aviation industry appeared ready to take off after the industry emerged from a post–World War I nosedive during which leaders such as Curtiss-Wright resorted to selling appliances to keep afloat. The rush was on.

By the mid-1920s the technology had advanced sufficiently, and investors were enthusiastically buying the few available aviation stocks such as Curtiss and Fokker. When Ford invested, Curtiss was trading on the Curb exchange at $17 per share. When Lindbergh flew across the Atlantic in May 1927, Curtiss was trading at $34 per share. Lindbergh's flight, as discussed in Chapter 3, coordinated and propelled both public and investor imaginations in an ongoing narrative. One year later, in June 1928, Curtiss was trading at $125 as investors tried to buy a piece of the three hundred companies in the aviation industry. Savvy observers understood that it was not difficult to start manufacturing airplanes; demand might outstrip supply in the fall of 1928, but that was unlikely to persist once announced investments in production capacity began to come online.[28] However, the story proved irresistible. Human flight had sparked the popular imagination from the dawn of time: "The glamor and romance of man's conquest of the air is a big help. So are these venturesome undertakings of the airman which are recorded on page one. . . . [The small investor] reaches the conclusion that 'somebody's going to make a lot of money out of aviation.' He wants to get in on the ground floor."[29] Wright Aeronautical's declaration of a 100% dividend reinforced this narrative. Wright was then selling at $280 per share. It was *real*: airmail miles flown were up 40% over 1928. Forty companies were carrying either mail or humans, and no fewer than twenty-eight had announced plans to produce, together, ten thousand planes. Attracted by the apparent success of the airframe manufacturers, firms in adjacent sectors sought to enter. Automobile manufacturers leveraged their expertise in internal combustion engines in the new market; General Motors invested in Fokker and purchased aviation engine manufacturer Allison Engineering, Packard was experimenting with a diesel engine, and Henry Ford also announced an engine-manufacturing program. The scale was completely different: at the time Ford and GM together manufactured almost three million cars per year. Aviation was a much smaller business. Even large aircraft such as the Flivver were small, propeller-driven models that could carry no more than a dozen people. It was so easy to enter that by 1930, 124 firms would raise over $300 million through initial public offerings ($4 billion in 2017 dollars). The market was frothy, peaking at a frothiness of 3.32 in 1929, about 17% more than the overall market. 96% of this value was erased by 1932, whereas the general market would drop "only" 80%.

The crash was driven by the reality of the commercial aviation business. Between Lindbergh's flight and 1930, eight thousand non-military aircraft were sold. Only six hundred or so went to what we would now call airlines, and a similar number were exported. Perhaps 40% were sold to private users for recreation or business purposes. The remainder went to pilots and aviation schools. That is, a large share of early production was reinvested in building pilot capacity for future production. At the time, profitability in the industry was entirely supported by the US Postal Service. Air traffic handled approximately 1% of the long-distance passenger market; the rest was dominated by rail. In 1929, revenue for passengers was $0.65 per ton-mile, and for mail, $5 per ton-mile. The implication is that by weight, an airline could earn fifteen times more ferrying post than people. Flying people was "sexy" but not sustainable without mail.[30]

The bubble in aviation is perhaps the canonical example of bubbles in our story. Only radio is as dramatic. First, it rests on a very sticky story. Aviation demanded attention—and received it after the

Lindbergh flight. Airplanes were simple, visible, and concrete. Aviation was so exciting: how would there not be money to make? The leap from Lindbergh to profitability was not discussed in any detail, and in the late 1920s, the market had become a place where novices were investing.

The realities of the new industry gave rise to speculative narratives, or bids, around the fortunes of an almost-limitless number of firms. Barriers to entry were low, so many firms could and did enter. As we document elsewhere, even Ford's hypothesized advantages in the production of internal combustion engines and manufacturing capabilities did not pan out.[31] Several narratives allowed investors to entertain the possibility of riches from companies developing businesses in the manufacture, operations, and perhaps flight training parts of the industry.[32] The existence of these pure-play bets reflected technological, competitive, business model, and value chain uncertainty. Just as it was unclear whether profits would be made in the production of content, radio sets, or broadcasting, in aviation it was unclear whether profits would be made in the production of airplanes, flying passengers, or training pilots. The resulting pure-play aviation companies became protagonists in stories of interest to technological enthusiasts and, with some overlap, investors. As it turned out, growth in the commercial aviation industry was very slow, and until Douglas developed the DC-3 in 1936, profitability relied on the subsidies provided by the US Postal Service.[33] Investors who invested at the peak of the aviation index would not return their principal until the mid- to late 1950s.[34] Our model predicts this reality. Uncertainty is high across the board; the technology has characteristics that facilitate narratives; it appears at a time when there were many novices in the market, and there were pure plays. It is not surprising, therefore, that the aviation index was very frothy at 3.75; nor is it surprising that this index lost almost the entirety of its value.

Wankel Motor: A Narrow Bubble

In a sense, the internal combustion engine is a ridiculous technology. Fuel is mixed with air and ignited causing a violent explosion.

The force of this explosion is harnessed to move a piston about 2.5 inches—at best, half the length of the book or e-reader you're holding. At this point, an explosion in an adjacent cylinder occurs, and this energy is used to stop the piston on a dime and move it in precisely the opposite direction. The engine is horribly inefficient—in a modern car, about 75% of the energy from these explosions is wasted: converted to heat instead of forward motion. The internal combustion's saving grace is that the high density of energy stored in gasoline makes for great portability. The eponymously named "Wankel," or rotary, engine was considered a solution to this problem. The Wankel engine uses controlled explosions to turn the axle, much like pushing a merry-go-round. In theory, it is much more efficient, simpler, vibrates less and is more compact.[35]

Writing about the future of the automobile in 1972, journalist Jan Norbye described the road ahead: "Chances are good that in a couple of years you can buy a Ford rotary, or a Chevrolet rotary, or a Hornet rotary from your local dealer."[36] Given the economic and cultural importance of the automobile, the potential to make the internal combustion engine less ridiculous sparked public imagination, even when there was doubt how such a project might be integrated into motor vehicles. First, in 1959 speculation occurred in the Swedish company NSU (where Wankel was working). US-based Curtiss-Wright had secretly licensed the rotary engine technology from NSU. When Curtiss-Wright realized that the secret project was well known in the engineering world, the company publicized its efforts in a coordinated media campaign, taking out full-page ads in several newspapers. NSU's strategy of country-level exclusive licenses fueled a narrative about the Wankel's potential to revolutionize "everything." Citroën, Alfa Romeo, and small automaker Toyo Goygo (Mazda) sought to differentiate their vehicles by developing rotary engine cars in 1965. At the time, NSU itself was already producing a sports car in West Germany.[37] A significant bubble in NSU stock (several hundred percent) and about 50% in Curtiss-Wright ensued.[38] Optimism and investment continued throughout the 1960s. By 1969, Mercedes announced a new Wankel-powered sports car that could go from zero to sixty miles per hour in 4.6 seconds. Wankel had "captured the attention of the automotive world,"[39] and the "little engine [was] a big performer," with the potential for "revolutionizing the worldwide auto industry."[40] The narrative was compelling. The engine "weighs a third less and has forty percent fewer moving parts than other internal combustion engines yet can deliver the same horsepower so smoothly one cannot hear the engine running in traffic."[41] The promise of the engine, in particular its small size, led to speculation that the engine could sit in other parts of the car, freeing designers to reimagine its basic structure. Although production levels in Europe were low, and persistent problems with the rotary seals remained unresolved, delays in the US rollout were attributed to the less threatening problem that the Wankel produced more emissions than a standard internal combustion motor. That is, the idea that environmental regulation was holding up the Wankel business steered the narrative away from the very real technological problems with the engine.[42] Instead, the European experience was seen as evidence that the technology was "proven." The articles under the above-mentioned headlines reported that Curtiss-Wright had licensed the rights to the Wankel to General Motors. General Motors expected to bring the technology to market within a decade. Ford and Chrysler were rumored to be following suit. The big three automakers were not attractive investment targets, as the Wankel would make up only a fraction of their portfolio. Instead, speculation on the Wankel focused on Curtiss-Wright.[43] The stock had moved from 10 in 1971 to 52 by June 1972. The narrative was intoxicating. For example, on June 10, shares in Heinicke Instruments were driven up 73% on the rumor that it was acquiring an outboard motor company that had a licensing agreement with Curtiss-Wright.[44] On July 4, *Fortune* magazine ran a feature article on the Wankel motor and reported that some analysts predicted that by 1980 a majority of automobiles would use Wankels.[45] However, the environmental story was giving way to the underlying reality of technological roadblocks. Throughout July a series of conflicting reports of GM's technological challenges with the Wankel led to a 25% decline in Curtiss-Wright stock.[46] In late August 1972, GM's announcement that it would produce the Wankel in "limited quantities" was front-page news.[47] In April 1973, victory was claimed, even though details about problems in the rotary seals were leaking out.[48] These reports generated additional speculative activity in Curtiss-Wright and some machine tool companies.

It was not to be. In the end, sealing the rotating cylinder proved too difficult; the promised advantages of the Wankel motor could not be realized.[49] By the end of 1974, GM had stopped licensing payments to Curtiss-Wright. But even before the GM decision was announced, Curtiss-Wright declared that it would withhold dividends, and the stock lost 87% of its value. The stock had been frothy too, with peak frothiness greater than 5 when market frothiness was 1.4. Speculators underestimated the likelihood of technological failure. By any measure, there was a boom and bust in Curtiss-Wright stock, all associated with the Wankel engine. Further, given that the Wankel story occurred when many novices were entering the market, we view this event as a bubble.

The Wankel motor illustrates several of the criteria that we predict will be associated with a bubble. Two types of Wankel motor stories emerged. The first type discussed the likelihood that the general public will buy cars with rotary engines. These stories are of general interest to readers of newspapers who often own cars; the title of Norbye's article makes this clear: "A Wankel in Your Future." The second type of article was targeted toward investors. This technology demonstrates both the existence of bubbles and the emergence of narrative. Investors were primarily interested in the investment opportunities that were mapped to the fortunes of the rotary engine. Therefore, the volume of narrative—and indeed its contagion—was, in part, a function of whether there was a possibility for investors to bet on a pure play.

In the case of the Wankel motor, the narrative that emerged was very optimistic. The appeal of the story relied on the fact that the engine is the core component in the automobile and the automobile played a central role in American life. Thus, even though the engine is not consumer facing, it would have affected products that most people owned and, at least in terms of use, understood.

It was exceptional for the public to have access to a stock that tracked an essential, embedded component of the automobile. For decades, the automobile industry had been vertically integrated. This opportunity was an artifact of the intellectual property regime surrounding the Wankel motor. If Curtiss-Wright had developed the technology internally and sold it, NSU would have sued. Therefore, Curtiss-Wright found it advantageous to license the technology from NSU. Curtiss-Wright then built up a portfolio—more accurately, a thicket—of more than one hundred related patents to enhance their intellectual property claims. GM did not need Curtiss-Wright's expertise to build the engine. In fact, GM was developing the rotary engine internally and simply paying Curtiss-Wright to avoid a legal dispute. But it was going to be very difficult for any engine manufacturer in North America to use a rotary engine without a license from Curtiss-Wright. The result of this, and what is exceptional in this case, is that the strength of the Curtiss-Wright patent portfolio allowed Curtiss-Wright to overcome the fact that it did not have the capabilities to vertically integrate and produce automobiles or, for that matter, any of the other products such as outboard motors, motorcycles, or snow blowers that might use a rotary engine. The centrality of the automobile in American life, together with the investment opportunity, made the Wankel story doubly interesting. Thus, despite the high uncertainty and ambiguity about the future success of the technology, uncertainty about control of the technology was low, and a narrative emerged around Curtiss-Wright: investors came to believe it was inevitable that the Wankel would fundamentally change a central product in many Americans' lives and that Curtiss-Wright would profit from it.

The stories of Curtiss-Wright in the 1960s and early 1970s and Bell Telephone in the 1880s are similar in that in each case, as a result of intellectual property rights, investing in the new technology implied investment in a single firm. While we see a bubble in Curtiss-Wright, we do not see nearly the same stock movements in Bell. There are two reasons for this difference. The first is that investment was much less democratized in 1883 than it was by 1973. Whereas in 1883 a worker would have needed to save up for two months to purchase a single share, in 1973 it would have only taken a few hours to earn enough to purchase a share of Curtiss-Wright. In 1883, there were few novices, or noise traders, with the capability to speculate in Bell Telephone.

The other factor is no less important: whereas Bell Telephone eventually succeeded, the Wankel never achieved its imagined potential. Despite optimistic predictions, the market share of the rotary engine in passenger automobiles remained tiny. This observation is at the center of the debate over the definition of a bubble. If the bet pays off, in hindsight, it looks like a pretty good bet. Who is to say that the investors were not making reasoned, "rational" decisions? This question is, of course, fundamentally unanswerable. If rational explanations were correct, we would expect the discourse influencing investors to have reflected reasoned thinking about the new technology, its potential, the probability of success, as well as the likely risks. Investors in the Wankel would have been subject to long descriptions of the technical issues associated with the rotary seals of these engines, as well as emergent problems in Europe. This was not the case. Instead, reporting was superficial, suffused with hyped-up language that stoked an unwarranted narrative of inevitability.

Thus, the Wankel engine scored a 4. Control uncertainty was low, technological uncertainty low, but narrative rank was high and there was a pure play. And the timing coincided with the presence of novices. Curtiss-Wright stock was frothy, peaking at 5.06 and falling 88%. By our criteria, it was a bubble.

Transistor: A Broad Bubble with a New Set of Novices

With a total factor score of 7 out of 8 in our model, the transistor is a prime candidate for a bubble. Its first mention in the bowels of the *New York Times* in December 1947 suggested that the new technology might be used to make "hearing aids for the deaf."[50] Transistors have two capabilities: they can amplify signals, and they can turn them on and off. It is this second capability that sits at the heart of computers, whereas the first is the foundation of the early hearing aids. That is, the transistor—the ur-general-purpose technology that powered the digital age—was first recognized primarily as an analog device.

The market for products that used transistors had characteristics of uncertainty that amplified narratives. There was considerable competitive uncertainty. With the exception of IBM, incumbent vacuum-tube firms were not able to make the transition to electronics; accordingly, new entrants dominated the industry. The early market was driven by defense applications, and by the mid-1950s electronic hearing aids appeared on the consumer market. But hearing aids have limited resonance with the public. Nevertheless, the transistor had a consumer-facing killer app: the transistor radio. Though expensive at $50, hundreds of thousands of radios were sold through 1957. Importantly, the transistor created an entry opportunity for new firms that might have been struggling to compete in the manufacture of vacuum-tube-based technologies. New applications such as the photocopier also appeared. Defense applications and the digital functions of the transistor sparked the beginning of Moore's law: exponential miniaturization of digital functionality. This variety of applications and new firms founded to explore them led to a host of narratives, embedded in an overarching story about the new electronic age.

By the early 1960s, with the advent of the integrated circuit, the market was in the throes of the "'tronics" boom:[51] "Dozens of companies now have 'electronics' in one form or another woven into their corporate names. To mention just a few: Electro-Sonic Laboratories, Electronic Assistance Corp., Electro Nuclear Systems, Electronics Inc., Electronized Chemical Corp., Electrosolids Corp., Electronic Nuclear Co., Electronic Missiles Co., and Electronisonic Laboratories. . . . There are so many of them that customers are always getting confused in placing their orders."[52]

No longer was investment logic centered on dividends, a direct measure of profitability. Instead, the focus was on "value," which meant capital appreciation. The greater-fool theory now had a narrative: buy today and someone will pay more for it tomorrow, especially if some version of the word *electronics* is in the company name.[53] Important businesses emerged during this period, including household names, such as Texas Instruments, Xerox, and Polaroid, but many over-the-counter issues, such as the names above (our favorite is Electronisonic) are long forgotten. Our index, which unfortunately misses the small, over-the-counter firms that we expect to be most frothy, has peak frothiness in late 1961 of 2.75.[54] In part reflecting the fact that the bigger players comprise the index, the measured decline is not extreme (only 30%), although this was more than the decline in the general market (21%).

The emergence of the "value" narrative implied that profits were no longer necessary to encourage investment. Facilitating this narrative, the Great Depression was more than twenty years in the past, and there were many novice investors in the market.[55] A brief correction in 1961 was attributed to oversupply of semiconductors, although clearly the overpromise of everything electronic contributed to the decline as well. Technological and production improvements to chips resulted in increased competition, a decline in profitability of these early firms, and the shuttering of many.[56] Our model predicts these events reasonably well. Supported by the concrete example of the transistor radio, high uncertainty helped move an obscure, mysterious technology into the public imagination.[57] We record a middle-level narrative score, and the timing of these events does coincide with the arrival of novice investors. Finally, there were pure plays. By our criteria, a bubble occurred in the transistor, and our theory predicts it.

How Is the Theory Doing?

In Figure 4.1, we summarize our analysis, which is based on Table A.1 in the Appendix. The figure aggregates the factors in the model on the horizontal x-axis, and on the y-axis it reports the percentage decline in value from the index value at peak frothiness to the low point in the subsequent decline. Each index is based on the aggregate movements of stock prices of companies associated with each technology.

The non-pure-play technologies scattered along the bottom are those for which there was no investment vehicle, or those for which the investment vehicle was heavily diluted in the sense that the technology represented a single product line in a diversified company. For

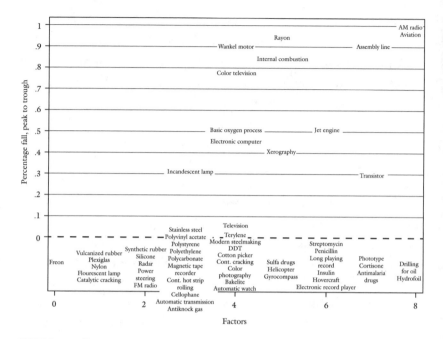

FIGURE 4.1   Factors versus percentage fall of indices, Original 58 technologies
Sources: Factor scores are calculations detailed in the Appendix. Scores are in
Table A.1. Sources for stock indices are detailed in Table A.3.
Notes: Percentage fall, shown on the y-axis, is the decline from the index value at peak
frothiness to the lowest point within the following seven years. The x-axis is the factors
predicted to lead to speculation. The scale is 0–8. The predicted likelihood of speculation is higher as we move to the right. Per discussion in the text, no pure-play investment opportunities existed for those technologies listed below the dashed line.

these non–pure plays, we cannot observe a frothiness score or a market decline. In the figure, they are stacked for readability around zero,
but it is not the case that those at the top of the stacks are frothier in
any way than those at the bottom.

Intriguingly, consistent with our discussion of nylon, sulfa drugs,
and the Wankel engine, narratives and conditions for narratives are
associated with the existence of a pure play. In cases where new technologies complemented capabilities of existing industry players—as
in the case of most drugs and chemicals, for example—pure plays
do not emerge, which further confounds potential emergent narratives. Across all fifty-eight technologies, our uncertainty factors (sum

of technology and business uncertainty, together with control uncertainty) are correlated with the emergence of a pure play at 0.34, a correlation high enough to be interesting. Speculation requires pure plays, and pure plays are defined by the way new technologies complement existing firm capabilities. Existing firms tend to have diversified across a range of markets, and new technologies that complement those already in use are likely to become part of the portfolios of diversified firms. Indeed, some technologies on our list, such as nylon, emerged as part of the research and development efforts of an already-diversified firm. We should not be surprised, therefore, that investors were unable to map their investments directly onto the fortunes of many new technologies.

Conditional on there being a pure play, frothiness increases with the factors. However, our ability to test this statistically is weak. There are only fifteen technologies for which we observe frothiness: the pairwise correlation between the factors and frothiness is 0.4, and a similar correlation (0.45) is found between factors and the percentage decline from peak to trough.[58] Fifteen is not a large sample, so our ability to say that this is not a chance correlation is diminished. Therefore, we must weigh the entirety of the information we have available, which includes the historical narrative, in our assessment of the framework.

Six technologies do not experience bubbles during the window of bubble opportunity: the incandescent lamp, the electronic computer, the television, the basic oxygen process for steelmaking, and the telephone. The incandescent lamp was frothy—greater than 2—but it declined less than the general market index. Television stocks performed very well throughout the 1950s. Television production was dominated by RCA, which was also in the business of radio. Our index excludes RCA and is comprised of pure-play television manufacturers. The market did a fairly good job evaluating these stocks, as compared to its evaluation of radio. This is not surprising because there was little question that the television business model would mirror that of the radio industry. The basic oxygen process completely changed the way steel was made; until its introduction, steel was made in large open hearths. However, the large capital investments associated with the new and old technologies implied that the transition spanned decades, and hence, even though our steel-sector index does a good job representing the affected firms, none of the indexed firms was ever truly a pure play. The stocks are better viewed as a balanced portfolio of both the new and the old steelmaking technologies.

The Bubbles That Weren't

Our favorite part of the graph is that it allows us to explore a world that wasn't—what social scientists like to call "counterfactuals." We can imagine what we might have seen had there been investment vehicles for the technologies on the bottom of the figure, those for which there was no pure-play investment vehicle. For example, drilling for oil checks all the boxes, scoring a full 8 on factors that are likely to lead to bubbles. But we are unable to measure broad-based market speculation in drilling for oil. This technology was first employed by "Colonel" Edwin Drake in western Pennsylvania. Drilling for oil was revolutionary, as it provided a much-cheaper source of energy and light than whale oil. The discovery of oil together with a means to extract it generated considerable popular excitement and thousands journeyed to see the new opportunity. There were purportedly several hundred emergent oil companies, and historical records indicate that shares were traded with patterns we would associate with a bubble.[59] The popular press created cartoons describing the speculative losses many oil investors experienced. However, these stocks were not traded on the New York Stock Exchange, and we were unable to locate records of stock trades and prices from the period. As such, we were unable to reconstruct an index for them and cannot measure frothiness. Perhaps the best interpretation of this is not a bubble that wasn't, but a bubble that wasn't measured.

We might have also expected a cortisone bubble. The technology of cortisone had all the trappings necessary for a narrative: a Nobel prize was awarded, and Merck had rights to the technology—although its position was quickly eroded as close substitutes such as prednisone and prednisolone were synthesized. However, there were no pure plays. We suspect that had there been, we would have observed a bubble in the late 1950s or early 1960s.

In fact, given our expectation that industry structure interacts with the formation of narratives, we believe that had the industry structure allowed pure plays for these non-index technologies, the factor scores would have been higher. We would have given them higher narrative scores. This would have shifted these technologies to the right, implying a greater likelihood of speculation.

To sum up, for each of these technologies we evaluated whether at the time of introduction there was uncertainty along a variety of dimensions. As we have seen in the earlier cases, how the new technologies fit into the industry structures at the time and the degree to which the capabilities of existing firms were important and helpful in bringing these new technologies to market is critical in the emergence of a speculative narrative and associated bubbles in the stock market. We evaluated not only the technological uncertainty at the time of introduction but also the degree to which the technology relied on extant firms' existing sales, marketing, and production capabilities. This is often highly related to the degree to which the new technology is a component in a broader value-delivery system. When new technologies produce entirely new value chains, or mostly new value chains, they are often disruptive to those firms that have invested in the current ones (and are also likely to become objects of speculative narratives). We also consider the extent to which the technology is likely to engage the popular imagination by hinging on or becoming part of a particularly sticky idea. Cures for illness and manned flight make for better dinner conversation than do improvements in the process of steel production or the use of chemicals instead of heat to separate benzene from crude oil. Speculative bubbles are rare when there are not new value chains or when commercialization will rely heavily on assets of existing firms, even when the new technology captures the public's imagination.

Of course, there must be a vehicle for speculation. And the existence of this vehicle—the pure play—can help reinforce the narrative and allow for greater speculation. Similarly, the lack of a pure play suggests that the narrative around certain technologies would have been even greater if the public also had reason to discuss how to get a piece of the action. However, the existence of a pure play does not guarantee a narrative.

Our framework is imperfect. Measurement is imprecise. For example, we believe we undermeasure the boom and bust in the case of the transistor, because we are unable to pick up all over-the-counter companies. The overall exercise is ambitious. We are trying to compare uncertainty and the attractiveness of narratives across technologies and times that are inherently different. Our measures of market activity, frothiness, and percentage decline also have limitations. And perhaps most important, history does not provide many major technologies that have pure-play investment opportunities. We cannot construct a large sample to wash out errors in measurement in our data. We devote the next chapter to evaluating whether the framework helps explain booms, busts, and bubbles in technologies that originated more recently. But even if the framework does a decent job explaining new technologies, it is a framework, a theory—not a law.

Our framework focuses attention on particular attributes of new opportunities. It provides a way to interpret the past and guides questions about the future. Perhaps our most important lesson is that answering these questions requires an understanding of the particular characteristics of a given technology, an understanding of the capabilities needed to commercialize it, and an understanding of the historical moment of its arrival.

Chapter 5

RECENT AND FUTURE BUBBLES

IN 2008, *FORBES* MAGAZINE, based on expert opinion from the Wharton School at the University of Pennsylvania, published a list of the thirty technologies that had changed life most dramatically during the previous thirty years.[1] We call this list the Wharton 30. This list, in Appendix Table A.2, includes nineteen information technology technologies, eight of which are internet infrastructure or direct internet applications, seven health-care-related technologies, three energy technologies, and a single business model innovation. Can our framework be used to predict which of the thirty technologies generated a bubble? For example, casual observers understand that there was an internet bubble in the late 1990s, but would our model have predicted it? Should we have expected the alternative energy bubble that crashed in 2008? What about the absence of a bubble in LCD display technology, on which you may be reading these words?

We examined these thirty technologies with the same empirical rigor as the first fifty-eight, which we call the Original 58. Statistics gives us only one part of the picture. We were able to construct indices for only sixteen or, as we shall see, perhaps seventeen of the thirty technologies. But nevertheless, here is what we found: the model predicts reasonably well which technologies will have a pure play:

the correlation between the quantified factors that we introduced in Chapter 4 and the existence of a pure play is 0.4. Another way to look at it is that these factors averaged 5.9 for those technologies with associated pure plays and 4.1 for those technologies without. But we were surprised to observe that bubbles occur in most of the pure-play technologies. Moreover, at first glance, the factors do not predict the decline very well. But just as with the first fifty-eight, there are relatively few observations. Sixteen technologies had specific, traceable, pure-play indices. The correlation between both the frothiness and the percentage of index decline and the factors for these technologies is about 0.3. That is, the model performs similarly for the Wharton 30 as it did for the Original 58. Nevertheless, we are quite fearful of seeing patterns that are not really there, or, as we like to say, "scientific apophenia." Formally, scientific apophenia is "the assigning of inferential meaning when limited statistical power should have prevented such a conclusion or when the data are actually random."[2] This is not some far-fetched problem; one of us has written a paper describing and measuring the extent of exactly this problem.

In the context of the Original 58, we are concerned with the peculiar economic history of the twentieth century. Many of the speculative episodes center on the Roaring Twenties and the Great Depression. What if we are mistaking coincidences of history associated with these events for meaningful, more general social processes?[3] To resolve this problem, we need to take our model to other settings to determine whether the basic framework has general predictive power. If we found the first result by chance, it is unlikely that chance will repeat itself. If we can satisfy ourselves that our model is useful, then we will feel more confident applying the model to current and even future scenarios.

To make matters worse, it is possible that we were correct about the more distant past, but we still may find that the model is irrelevant in more recent times. Scientists call this a problem of *external validity*. Does the theory apply in settings that are different from the one from which it was generated? In our case, there are reasons to think that it may not. For example, what if investors make better decisions now than in the past? Investors and other market participants may have learned from the investment missteps of the past and become less prone to making decisions that lead to speculative episodes; there may have been a secular increase in the rate of technological innovation in recent decades due to increased investments in basic and applied research. Investors would then have been exposed to a greater number of new technologies and have developed better tools for evaluating them. More frequent exposure to technological innovations might have led to more experienced pools of investors, fewer novices, and less speculation. Similarly, financial innovations may have led to more efficient capital markets in which contrarian or short positions can be more easily taken. Call it learning, inoculation, or innovation—the net effect would be similar: contemporary financial markets would be less susceptible to speculative activity. Better financial market regulation may also have reduced the likelihood of speculation in uncertain technological innovations. Advances in any or all of these areas would reduce bubbles generally and thereby reduce the predictive power of our theory.

In contrast, financial markets may now be more vulnerable to speculation. The growth of the high-tech public relations industry pumping out "narratives" may counteract investor sophistication. In addition, increasingly sophisticated public and private financial markets may have led to a greater number of pure plays.[4] The ideology of the value of tying pay to performance has led to the emergence of tracking stocks that capture the performance of specific parts of multidivisional firms. These forces allow pure plays for investors, even if a subsidiary is owned by a diversified firm. Indeed, we find that there are more pure plays in the Wharton 30 than in the Original 58! Finally, it is possible that the democratization experienced during the past forty years when the Wharton 30 was commercialized is more profound than what happened earlier.

But there is an additional, methodological problem. Given that we may not have sufficient historical perspective to evaluate the Wharton technologies and the fact that there are many plausible interpretations, we are in danger of choosing an interpretation that best fits the model. We cannot answer the types of questions we ask in this book with a randomized controlled trial so as to replicate the exercise in Chapter 4.[5] Instead, we must pick and choose the aspects of the Wharton 30's histories we believe are relevant to our story. That is, we need to make these judgments as we are learning the story of each technology, including whether or not a bubble occurred. To meaning-fully interpret history, one has to, well, understand the history. But the histories of several of the Wharton 30 are yet unfinished. Neverthe-less, the exercise is useful. Although it does not, indeed cannot, prove our theory, it allows us to triangulate, to learn a bit more. The irony is not lost on us: a central argument of our book is that understanding booms, busts, and bubbles requires a deep appreciation of the his-torical contexts in which technologies appear, but this is difficult to do when the history is still playing out.

We hope we have injected you with a hefty dose of skepticism. But now, we forge ahead. Will we become a bit more certain looking at the Wharton 30? How does our model fare? Can we use it to project into the future?

The Internet: Bubble with a Wake

The internet comprises many technologies. The Wharton experts list internet, broadband, and www (browser and html) as the most impor-tant invention of the period between 1978 and 2008. However, other internet-related technologies make a good showing in their list, too. The enabling technology for the internet, PCs and laptop comput-ers, comes in second. The internet's original killer app, e-mail, ranks fourth, and microprocessors that enable PCs and laptops seventh. Fiber optics, used to carry internet signals around the world quickly and efficiently, rank eighth. Open-source software and services (e.g., Linux) would be much more difficult to use without the communi-cation infrastructure afforded by the internet, and Wikipedia would not make sense without it. Coming in fifteenth is online shopping, e-commerce, and auctions (e.g., eBay). Sixteenth is media file compres-sion (e.g., jpeg, mpeg, mp3), which developed as a result of attempts to maximize internet bandwidth, and finally, twentieth is social network-ing via the internet, a clear derivative of our top-placed technology. That makes eight of the thirty technologies on the list internet related.

Importantly, although the internet complemented existing compa-nies' capabilities, it also was hypothesized that it would make firms obsolete. There are some sectors in which this turned out to be cor-rect in a relatively short time frame (Amazon.com quickly affected booksellers) and others in which it has not (Webvan did not disrupt traditional grocers). It was unknown in the late 1990s precisely which businesses were in trouble. Moreover, there was considerable variation in the scale necessary to achieve success. There was significant tech-nological and business model uncertainty. No less important were the numerous attempts to monopolize the gateways to internet traffic. For example, an early internet success story, America Online (AOL), was one of many internet portal plays in the early internet. Nobody knew who would profit from the new technology.

The internet arrived at a time that interest in the stock market was spreading. Moreover, one of the bellwether applications of the internet—online stock trading—substantially accelerated its democra-tization. Discount brokers such as E*Trade, Ameritrade, and even the established discount broker Charles Schwab made it easier for indi-viduals to invest in mutual funds and individual stocks. New investors entered the market. The adoption of online trading was remarkable and fast.[6] For example, at Charles Schwab, online trades accounted for 20% of the market in 1995. By 2000, that share was 80%, where it remained even after the market crash.[7] These early adopters traded speculatively—being 2.5 to 5 times more likely to trade on margin than old-fashioned, call-your-broker-to-make-a-trade investors. Im-portantly for our story, online traders focused their trades more on technology stocks, traded more frequently, and underperformed the market.[8] The price of transactions decreased as well. Whereas com-mission costs for broker-assisted trades ran into the hundreds of dol-lars, the new online brokers executed trades for as little as $8.[9]

Although we lack an overall census of trading behavior, we do have very suggestive evidence that the effects were widespread. For example, the ease of trading on the web doubled trading frequency and portfolio turnover in the 401(k)s of two large companies, and the increase was more pronounced in young, white, wealthy men—a demographic particularly interested in tech.[10] We know that wealthier people are more likely to hold stock. However, during this period, all else being equal, those who owned a $2,000 computer were 33% more likely to hold stocks than those who didn't. This is a large number. We would see the same difference if the potential investor had $27,000 more income![11] However, it was not just that traders were emancipated from their brokers. Some investors were trading the old-fashioned way and soliciting advice from their stockbrokers. But even these professionals were largely inexperienced. In 2000, more than one hundred thousand financial professionals—half of the profession that includes financial planners, advisers, and brokers—had entered the profession since 1990.[12] They had missed the 1987 historic market crash. The infiltration of novices was not restricted to stock market investors and their advisers. The venture capital market was filled with novices. From 1990 to 1995, the share of investments made by venture capitalists who had been practicing for less than five years hovered at about one in ten. It then increased about 8% every year so that by the year 2000, 40% of venture capital investments were by investors who had made their first investment since 1995, that is, during and just before the boom.[13] Thus, at almost every level of the investment chain, there were many actors who were relatively inexperienced.

These novices, from individual investors and financial professionals to venture capitalists and entrepreneurs, were taken in by a particular set of beliefs about the "new economy" that was being ushered in by the internet. The idea of "get big fast" propelled the investment frenzy: "Tossing aside just about every experience-honed tenet of business to build businesses in a methodical fashion, internet businesses . . . adopted a grow-at-any-cost, without-any-revenue, claim-as-much-market-real-estate-before-anyone-else-moves-in approach to business. This mentality [came] . . . to be known as 'Get Big Fast.'"[14]

"Get big fast" was a belief that there were significant first-mover advantages in internet business domains and that, therefore, the key to success was to preempt others in particular internet niches.[15] In theory, first movers would lock in consumers or users and would then enjoy secure, defensible rent streams for long periods of time. Indeed, this belief played out in a few cases, such as eBay and Google.[16] But in many spaces, it failed miserably. To see this clearly, it is helpful to revisit the story that we told to introduce the book, that of Toby Lenk, CEO of the ill-fated eToys.com. In 1998 Lenk was confident: "There is all this talk about [competitors] Toys 'R' Us and Wal-Mart, blah blah blah. We have first mover advantage, we have defined a new area on the Web for children. We are creating a new way of doing things. I am the grizzled veteran at this thing."[17] Lenk had a Harvard MBA and had worked at Disney in strategic planning. Perhaps he was a veteran in business compared to other younger internet entrepreneurs. However, a mere three years into the commercialization of the internet, there were no veterans of e-commerce, "grizzled" or otherwise. This did not prevent him and his investors from supporting a massive infrastructure investment. As Lenk reflected after his $850 million paper fortune had evaporated: "We had the capacity for $500 million in revenue but came to a stop at $200 million. That's hard to survive."[18] Lenk's bet on getting big fast turned out to be wrong. At the time, though, he was not a contrarian thinker. "It was the whole land-grab mentality," Lenk observed. "Grow, grow, grow. Grab market share and worry about the rest later. When you're in that cycle, and less capable people are doing IPOs, it's like an arms race. If you turn down the gun and put it on the table, all you're doing is letting other people pick it up and shoot you. I made the decisions and I take full responsibility. But there were a lot of amazing forces at work."[19]

The ideas behind "get big fast" had taken root by 1995. But it is the Netscape initial public offering, or IPO, that is considered the event that brought the internet-as-an-investment-opportunity to the general public's attention. The IPO itself was remarkable. At the last minute, the offering price was doubled from $14 to $28, and shares moved as high as $75 during the first day of trading before closing at $58.25. Overnight, the yet-unprofitable company that produced the gateway to the internet was worth $2.9 billion! The event was etched into the public's memory and the term *Netscape moment* has since been used as shorthand for an event that signals the inflection point of new industry development.[20] The investor interest in the Netscape IPO did not come out of thin air. Rather, the media had been drumming up interest, describing the revolutionary qualities of the internet. The IPO happened at a time when technology was making the internet more accessible to the public through the Mosaic and then Netscape browsers, which is to say that the internet made information about the internet more accessible. The somewhat unprecedented success of the IPO sparked the public's imagination and "confirmed" that the media hype was real. Before the Netscape IPO on August 9, the *New York Times* published articles with the words *internet* and either *stock* or *share* at a rate of 0.8 articles a day. After August 9 that rate increased to 1.5.

The increased media attention fed the "get big fast" frenzy. Before long, success was defined in terms of website traffic ("eyeballs") and top-line revenue, as opposed to a traditional and important measure— at least in terms of solvency—profit. When Jupiter Research projected that top-line aggregate (revenue) sales figures for online sales in 1998 would reach $2.3 billion, *Fortune* magazine confused revenue for profit, reporting that "the $2.3 [billion] figure sent a message: Companies are making money out there in cyberspace."[21]

The hype extended throughout the internet entrepreneurial eco-system. Approximately 50,000 firms were formed to commercialize the internet.[22] About 24,000 of these raised $256 billion from inves-tors between 1996 and 2002. A subset of these, around 8,500 compa-nies, received the lion's share of private equity investment in the form of $217 billion of venture capital financing.[23] The NASDAQ, the Curb market of the 1990s (home to most internet stocks), rose 500% between 1995 and 2000. There were 245 internet-related IPOs from 1996 through the third quarter of 2000, and 195 offerings of these oc-curred during the frenzied period of 1999 and 2000. Ironically, a be-lief that becoming profitable from the "get big fast" strategy took time prolonged the frenzy by extending the window of the bubble oppor-tunity. The market was patient during the 1998 holiday season when ecommerce businesses were struggling to deliver gifts on time and efficiently. But by the 1999 holiday season, investors expected profits.[24]

The failure to deliver profits helped trigger the crash in e-commerce stocks and closed the internet IPO window.[25] From its peak in March 2000 to its nadir in September 2002, TheStreet.com's e-commerce index dropped 87%. The general decline of the NASDAQ was a less extreme, though still precipitous, 76% (5,132 to 1,185); the S&P 500 fell a mere 48% (1,527 to 800). That is, the leading technology on the Wharton 30 list experienced a major boom and bust. Given the strong evidence of the role of novice investors, it was a bubble. The internet had a value of 8 in our factor scoring. There was no intellectual property protection to speak of, and there was so much business model uncertainty that it inspired books about internet business models![26] The technology had all the components of a sticky story, and there were pure plays that drove the narrative—*hundreds of them!* Novices were in the market, and we have strong evidence that many directed their investments to the internet. The market was frothy—the internet index registers at 4.29—and the internet index lost 84% of its value.

What is particularly fascinating about the narrative frenzy surrounding the internet is that it swept up technologies that were not all that exciting to the general public or that were relatively mature in terms of the nature of their industry structure. The internet proved a killer app for PCs, which is an important consumer-facing product. But it also swept up more mundane Wharton 30 technologies, including fiber optics, open-source software, and media file compression. Speculation in the PC industry in the latter part of the 1990s is a reflection of the convergence of a maturing PC industry and the burgeoning internet and networking technology sectors. The internet led investors to believe that there would be increasing demand for computer hardware, including personal computers and laptops, computer chips, and internet backbone equipment. Uncertainty about the rate of adoption of the internet—and precisely how it would manifest in hardware purchases—created excitement and increased demand uncertainty. The business model for PCs was well understood, and much of the uncertainty around platforms had been resolved at this point; Microsoft, together with Intel, was dominant. There were no arguments that PC manufacturers needed to "get big fast" to dominate hardware markets; Microsoft was already big enough to be subject to a Department of Justice antitrust investigation. Thus, our model would predict that, although there might be a bubble in the PC space, with a factors score of 5, it should be less pronounced than the internet index, or that of e-commerce for that matter. And it was: the frothiness of the PC index crested at 3.65 in January 1999, and then 80% of its value washed away.

Relative to the internet, fiber optics peaked late, with its factors scoring a modest 4. The underlying story around fiber optics—that is, transmitting bits through glass—is not sexy. Fiber was not sold to individuals, and the intellectual property surrounding the fiber technology was well protected. The technology was also not new; its first prominent application was at the 1980 Lake Placid Winter Olympics. In fact, one could make a strong argument that the window of bubble opportunity had long closed by the late 1990s. But a narrative took off, and a fiber boom and bust ensued. Corning, a glass company, had become the darling of Wall Street. Given this, the business opportunities were in laying fiber and surrounding technologies. There were many small concerns, but in terms of public pure plays, the index was powered by two new companies: Qwest Communications, which went public in 1997, and Global Crossing, which went public in 1998. In retrospect, both industry players and investors ignored the basic economics of fixed and marginal cost pricing associated with transmitting bits. Once the fiber is ready for use, the cost of using the fiber is zero. If there is overcapacity and competition, which there was, fiber companies will reduce their prices to marginal cost—and indeed, this is what happened. The new-economy internet narrative drowned out the prospect of overcapacity and competition, which economists have understood since the 1800s. Fiber will power the internet! In fact, we observe a bubble only because the internet narrative created demand for Qwest and Global Crossing in the first place. So we are left with an insight: narratives can create pure plays, and pure plays allow for the creation of bubbles. But without the speculative narrative, there is no pure play, and hence nothing to measure. That is, we observe the index only because there was a bubble! Sure, an investor could have invested in Corning back in 1945—but considering this a pure-play investment made sense only under the presumption that fiber optics would become a major part of Corning's business. And that happened only once the internet narrative took hold.

The telecom bust was both surprising and severe—driven by an exceptional narrative and fraud.[27] The peak frothiness was 3.48—less than that of the internet. But the crash was greater: the sector lost 97% of its value. Should we interpret this as a strike against our theory? Fiber optics scores a 4 if we view the window as occurring in the 1980s, and a 5 in the 1990s because more novices were present. The middling factor score is due to Corning's strong patent position, although there was some business model uncertainty. Fiber itself is a boring back-end technology. Alone, it makes for a terrible narrative. It is possible to understand what happened in this market only when one understands that fiber is on the list *because* it is an internet-supporting technology. Indeed, the fiber narrative was a subplot of the internet narrative in the same way that the rubber narrative in the 1900s was a subplot of the automobile narrative. If we are to view fiber as part of the internet story, then it is incorrect to score fiber as a stand-alone technology. Instead, it should have the same score as the internet it-self—an 8. Bubbles happen when fundamentals are ignored—and that is what happened here. Investors were not investing in fiber; they were investing in the backbone of the internet.

The areas of open-source software and media file compression are similar. Neither technology is that interesting to the general public. Open-source software is about giving software away for free. Media file compression is a series of algorithms that allow for efficient storage and streaming of information. By themselves, they make for terrible narratives—except to people who are programming and compression algorithm geeks. However, just like fiber optics, the stories of each of these technologies were swept up in the internet narrative. Red Hat, which gave away the Linux operating system for free and sold services to help customers use it, was a hot tech stock during the tech bubble in 2000. Media file compression had stronger complementarities with the internet. The media file compression index comprises companies such as NetRadio and Broadcast.com, which sought to stream video or audio over the internet. So a correct understanding of the technology requires a broad assessment of, again, the opportunity of the internet. When the internet narrative began to crest, it brought up these technologies in its wake.

In Figure 5.1 below, we consider the fiber optics window as having closed in the early 1990s; that is, there is no boom and bust in fiber optics because there were no pure plays until the late 1990s. However, we might reasonably think of the window as having closed later, after 2000. But then it also makes sense to reinterpret its factor score to reflect the fact that investors were considering how the technology was being used for the internet. In this case, we would score it as a 7 or 8. As it happens, the model is equally predictive either way in terms of the correlations we describe in the opening paragraphs of the chapter. But if we ignore the convergence by keeping the score as a 5 and using the extended window, the model does not perform as well. Similarly, if we score open source and media file compression as stand-alone technologies, they score a modest 5 each. There is a strong argument that we should consider media file compression an internet technology. Streaming music and video was sticky, disruptive, and subject to high levels of uncertainty. So we scored it an 8. Open source is trickier. We score it an 8 because it was understood in the context of the internet—to reflect the technological convergence. These are judgment calls—and the correlation between the factors and the frothiness as well as the percentage fall are sensitive to these judgments. If you would like to experiment with these assumptions yourself, you can find the data at the book's website (http://www.sup.org/bubblesandcrashes).

Either way, our model performed reasonably well in that it correctly predicted a bubble in internet technologies but not in the early history of fiber optics. We think we deserve a gold star! But the judgment calls we make are not ironclad. So we give half a gold star to false positives, to maintain a healthy degree of skepticism.

Score: Our model, 1.0; False positives, 0.5

Personal Computers and Laptops: Investors Get It Right

PCs and laptops are rated as the number-two innovation on the Wharton 30, and we just saw that they were the object of market speculation during the late 1990s.[28] However, here we focus on the early days of the industry, before the internet tidal wave swept up the stock prices of PC manufacturers. At first, personal computers were the domain of a small group of hard-core hobbyists. With the introduction of the "trinity" (Apple II, Commodore PET, and Tandy TRS-80) in 1977, the industry began developing. Home computer sales increased as a result of the curiosity of early adopters, Radio Shack's nationwide store network, and eventually gaming. However, the best gaming PC, the Apple II, was very much a luxury item. It was difficult to use, programs were loaded onto tape, and it cost more than $1,300—equivalent to $5,000 today.[29] The Apple II really began to gain market share with the introduction of VisiCalc, a spreadsheet program. At that point, it became more than a toy. Indeed, some were buying a $2,000 Apple II solely to run the $100 program, which did not run on other platforms.[30] With the introduction of the IBM PC in 1981, the later introduction of the PCjr in 1984, and the development of a suite of useful programs—most important, spreadsheet and word-processing software—personal computers started to reach a larger market. When Lotus 1-2-3, the new spreadsheet program that took advantage of the PCs greater computing power was introduced in January 1983, VisiCalc sales evaporated overnight.

The excitement over the PC was strong. Although it is consumer facing, early sales were mostly for businesses, driven by the spreadsheet application. Early spreadsheet software, given the nature of its functionality, caught the imagination of people in finance and potential investors. The term *personal computer* was mentioned in 0.37% of *New York Times* articles at the peak of the first PC bubble in 1983. This was the more than any other item on the Wharton list, with the small exception of *internet*, which was mentioned in 7.5% of articles in 2000.[31] To the extent that popular media reporting reflects public interest, the PC created interest, but the internet created a frenzy.

The PC excitement produced an expected entrepreneurial response: competitive entry. Similar to the history of television described in Chapter 4, and despite growing demand, a crash was precipitated by excessive competition in the PC market and the emergent dominance of Microsoft and Intel, at the time referred to as the "Wintel" monopoly. First, IBM entered with its highly successful PC in 1981. Compaq produced the first IBM clone a year later, undercutting IBM's price. This triggered a struggle between IBM and its clones for market dominance. The battle, and missteps of the presumptive winner, IBM, reflected the significant uncertainty with which part of the value chain would lead to great profits (e.g., hardware assembly, software, microprocessor) and precisely how to extract rents from each part of the value chain.[32] Early bets by IBM and early speculative betting on Commodore and, for that matter, Apple, reflected considerable uncertainty in the ways companies would earn profits.[33]

These events were set in an opportune macroeconomic period. There was a strong bull market between 1981 and 1983; the Nasdaq more than doubled during this period. As our model would predict, the movements of PC stocks were more dramatic. Adjusting for stock splits, Commodore International's price rose from $0.88 to $90 from 1975 to 1980. An additional stock split was timed with the expected introduction of a lower-priced computer that would compete with Tandy and Apple and was designed, according to the company's chairman, to bring the "stock back within the range of the average investor."[34] In November 1980, Apple's IPO was one of the most anticipated IPOs in then-recent memory.[35] The only pure-play PC makers that one could invest in the early 1980s were Commodore, Apple (which had its IPO in November 1980), Compaq (which had its IPO in December 1983), Atari, Digital Equipment, Altair, and Prime Computer. This PC index increased 163-fold from 1977 through 1983! This, of course, dwarfed movements in the NASDAQ. The optimism implied by the index was misplaced—at least temporarily. The index declined by more than two-thirds from 167 to 49 by mid-1985. Eventually, with the exception of Apple's Macintosh, the IBM PC and its clones dominated the market and knocked out competing platforms such as the TRS-80 and Commodore. The battle between these computer companies only scratches the surface of activity. The number of companies making computers had increased from 8 in 1981 to 47 in early 1985; microcomputer software companies had increased from 34 to 280; the number of disk-drive manufacturers increased from 11 to 54; and LAN networking companies increased from 9 to 61. Competition, along with the quick domination of the PC market by IBM, strangled profits, or, according to William Hambrecht, the chairman of an investment banking firm specializing in technology, "What we're going through is a large-scale hangover from a speculative orgy."[36]

It was a hangover, but the index was not frothy at all. In fact, the frothiness peaked at 0.3 (you read that correctly). The reason is that the further entry of players such as Dell and Gateway into the market, combined with the relative success of Apple, reinvigorated the index. Computers were a huge and profitable market. By February 1987 the index had recovered; though volatile, it never dipped below 300. An investor aggressively rebalancing his or her index would have done exceptionally well.

To summarize, in the 1980s, the PC had some of the characteristics we might think of as likely to lead a boom and bust cycle or a bubble. Competitive uncertainty was high, as was business model and value chain uncertainty. In addition, the PC made for a good story; it was consumer facing and captured the public imagination. There was not, however, a cohort of novice investors. The introduction of the three computers in 1978 (Apple II, TRS-80, and Commodore PET) seemed to have triggered broader interest. What we do not see during this period is a secular increase in the entry of new investors. During the 1970s and 1980s the share of households holding stocks (outside of retirement accounts) is relatively constant.[37] Thus, there is not a source of novice investors that would likely have been feeding the bubble. Our model gave PCs a factors score of 7, and the decline was 71%. However, this was a short-term event—the index recovered—and is not something we would consider a bubble. We'll call this a draw and give ourselves half a gold star in support, and false positives half a gold star.

Score: Our model, 1.5; False positives, 1.0

Liquid Crystal Displays: Controlled Disruption

Liquid crystal displays, or LCDs, changed the way we interact with information in fundamental ways. Not only have LCDs made our TVs flatter, lighter, and brighter; they also have enabled the mobile phone revolution. Take a moment to look at your immediate surroundings. Chances are good that you are either reading this text on an LCD screen or are about to stop reading to check your e-mail on an LCD screen—or both! LCDs have become ubiquitous and have enabled the development of many multibillion-dollar product categories, such as laptop computers, GPS devices, portable game devices, tablets, and smartphones. Surely a technology this revolutionary should have sparked an investment frenzy. Was there a bubble in LCDs? Would our model predict one?

The story of the modern LCD dates to the mid-1960s, when research was fueling dreams of video display screens that would be light enough to hang on walls and in cars. Over the course of the following decades, the promise of affordable, mass-market video displays was always just over the horizon. As the industry pioneer Larry Weber says, "For thirty years, we could say we will have wall-hanging televisions in ten years."[38] Because the technology was potentially revolutionary (with a large, consumer-facing product market) and highly uncertain (always ten years away), liquid crystal display technology was clearly a candidate for speculation.

The technology moved from science experiment to nascent industry in the late 1980s and grew to scale in the 1990s, in conjunction with the rise of the laptop or notebook computer. In the course of the same interview, Weber said, "Now [1996], I can say 'next year.'" By 2000, the traditional cathode ray tube (CRT) technology was clearly in decline, and flat-panel displays using LCD technology were poised to dominate the industry. Sales soared, rising from $3.17 billion in 1990 to $29.5 billion in 2000. At the same time, the average price for a standard product (10.4-inch display) fell from $3,000 in 1991 to $230 at the end of 2000. The 10.4-inch was the largest standard display in production in 1991, but by 2000, it had become among the smallest. The promise of early LCD science was delivered during the 1990s.

Were investors in LCDs equally rewarded? The pace of technological change in the 1990s was extraordinary, faster than in microprocessors and other technologies supposedly driven by Moore's law.[39] Large-scale, high-throughput facilities were required. With each new generation of technology, entry costs increased, reaching $1 billion for an advanced "generation 4" manufacturing facility. Entrants into this maelstrom "did not enter an industry so much as they entered a knowledge stream," with critics calculating "the cost of entry as a plunge into the infinite."[40] Yet despite high entry costs, from 1991 to 1996, "at least twenty-five high-volume fabrication lines were started to produce the most advanced FPDs [flat-panel displays]."[41] More than 80% were built in Japan, where major industrial conglomerates like Hitachi, Sharp, NEC, Fujitsu, and Matsushita competed fiercely. Later in the period, Korean industrial chaebols like LG and Samsung also entered the market. Many of these firms showed strong stock performance during the 1990s, in line with relevant market indices, and shares also declined in the early 2000s, but there was not an LCD bubble.

Should we have seen one? LCD production was not the province of start-ups: as described in *Popular Science* in 1997, "the technology is fiendishly difficult to scale up," requiring careful coordination of multiple, complex production processes.[42] Only large manufacturers were able to enter at sufficient scale, and because the producers were multinational conglomerates, investors were not able to invest specifically in the LCD industry. Later, even as LCDs became more affordable and were incorporated into an ever-increasing array of products, the displays were usually embedded in more complex technological assemblages such as laptop computers, DVD players, and other portable electronics (e.g., GPS, games). Although the final products of the electronics industry were consumer facing, the firms producing the displays were relatively undifferentiated and therefore less likely to attract speculative interest. There is some evidence of popular interest; that is, there was a technological narrative. But there was no accompanying investment narrative.[43] General media did not amplify the initial crossover report in the *New York Times*; nor did public markets respond. In fact, the low score in technological and business uncertainty is consistent with the absence of a pure play. For there to have been a bubble in LCDs, the technology would have needed to be swept up in a convergent technological narrative like we saw in the case of fiber optics and the internet. LCDs scored a 3 on our factor scale. There was low control uncertainty and moderate technological uncertainty—which declined with the emergence of the industry in the 1990s—but these did not support a good narrative. Even though there were novice investors, the model does not predict a pure play—and there were none. Therefore, there was no boom and bust, and no bubble.

Score: Our model, 2.5; False positives, 1.0

Laparoscopic Surgery: Lack of Narrative

Laparoscopy, ranked tenth on the Wharton list, is a technique of creating a small incision and visually examining interior parts of the body through a fiber-optic instrument. Laparoscopy is used in myriad diagnostic and surgical techniques.[44] Laparoscopic surgery is slowly revolutionizing surgical practice. The central advantage of laparoscopy is that it is less invasive than traditional surgery and therefore provides for a patient's quicker recovery. The idea that smaller incisions lead to quicker recoveries was recognized by 1925. Early applications were mostly diagnostic and because light is needed to see inside the body, the heat given off by 1920s incandescent lights was problematic. In the 1950s the use of fiberglass to transmit a distal light source opened a new era of endoscopy. However, it took many decades before laparoscopy made a significant impact in surgical procedures. The first laparoscopic appendectomy was completed in 1981. A more complicated procedure, the laparoscopic removal of a gallbladder, followed in March 1987. Importantly, the use of a video camera in the procedure allowed for taping and viewing at specialized meetings of gastrointestinal surgeons in 1989. A picture is worth a thousand words: the documentation of this event led to an overflowing lecture hall at the meetings of the American College of Surgeons in San Francisco in 1990. Laparoscopic surgery was popular—at least among surgeons. Within a few years laparoscopic techniques had been applied to a host of other—mostly gastrointestinal—procedures.[45]

Would our theory predict the development of a boom and bust or a bubble? The first requirement is that there be uncertainty about the value of the innovation and, in particular, which company would benefit from its commercialization. There was clearly uncertainty about the precise future for laparoscopic surgery. Was there a general emergent narrative? Of the seven *New York Times* articles mentioning the term *laparoscopic surgery* in 1993, two were focused on concerns about the efficacy of the technique, and two on its benefits—including a story about virtual reality. One was about a medical students who died in a car crash, and one on the declining fortunes of American Surgical, a company that produced surgical equipment and profited in part from laparoscopic surgery.[46] The narrative of inevitability, though, did not appear. In 1995, there were ten articles in the *New York Times*.[47] In the following decade there were thirty-seven. Although laparoscopy was mentioned, it was often in passing. A story about the removal of polyps from Plácido Domingo's colon mentioned the use of laparoscopic techniques. There were several articles about laparoscopically removing an ovarian cyst from then-chief of the Environmental Protection Agency, Christine Todd Whitman, or its use in the removal of a rare tumor from Dan Quayle's appendix. The rather astounding fact that 80% of gallbladder surgeries were completed using laparoscopic techniques was only an incidental part of the narrative. The fact that celebrities received laparoscopic treatment might have coordinated beliefs—just as in the case of the secretary of state's daughter's treatment for diabetes, or the president's son's use of sulfa drugs (both cases described in Chapter 4). But laparoscopic surgery is hardly a consumer-facing technology. The sales process is complex, whereby the expert surgeon might recommend the technique to a patient—and a third party, a health insurance company, tends to cover the costs. Most individuals will never have need for the technology— as most people never undergo surgeries that require such techniques. While the advantages of this technique over traditional surgery are important, they do not rise to the dramatic, widespread potential of insulin (resurrection!) or a cure for disease. It was not the case that appendicitis was formerly fatal and now cured. Rather, the treatment (appendectomy) had become a bit better.

There was also the potential for pure plays with laparoscopy. The medical device industry was a hotbed of start-ups and attracted significant venture capital funding.[48] While events in this space were dwarfed by the activity in the internet sector, there was room for investment. The timing of the development of laparoscopic techniques coincides, more or less, with the development of the internet, and there was a wave of investment in medical devices that followed the internet boom and bust episode (though the fall-off in investment was not nearly as sharp for medical devices as it was for the internet). So there was certainly democratization. However, while one could invest in medical device giants such as Johnson & Johnson, and American Surgical was a major player, there were no pure-play stocks on the public market. So while democratization was at a temporal peak, there were few vehicles for popular investment. Inexperienced investors did not have an avenue to speculate.

Laparoscopic surgery has a factor score of 3 on our scale of 0 to 8. While the uncertainty regarding the relative efficacy of the technology was somewhat high, in the 1990s there was little uncertainty about the type of firm that would control and earn money from the technology, there were no pure plays, and the technology itself did not make for a great narrative. In short, our model does not predict that the conditions were fertile for a bubble—nor does it predict public pure plays.

Score: Our model, 3.5; False positives, 1.0

At this point, and in light of the more general analysis summarized in Figure 5.1 and the online Appendix (see http://www.sup.org/bubbles andcrashes), we will call this a victory for our model. The model fares well in the new, post-1980 economy. The presence or absence of specific factors is correlated with increased or decreased likelihood of speculative activity in both recent technologies and older ones. However, having followed our argument this far, you should not be surprised that we caution you not to overinterpret our findings.

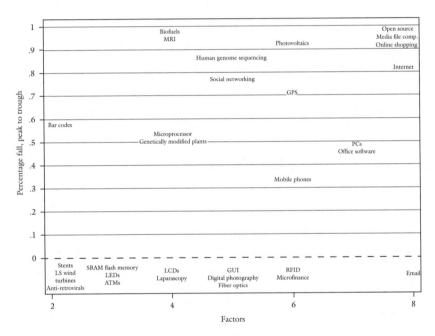

FIGURE 5.1   Factors versus percentage fall of indices, Wharton 30
Sources: Factor scores are calculated detailed in the Appendix. Scores are in Table A.2. Sources for stock indices are detailed in Table A.3. Knowledge@ Wharton, "Top 30 Innovations of the Last 30 Years," Forbes.com, February 19, 2009, https://www .forbes.com/2009/02/19/innovation-internet-health-entrepreneurs-technology _wharton.html.
Notes: Percentage fall, shown on the y-axis, is the decline from the index value at peak frothiness to the lowest point within the following seven years. The x-axis includes the factors predicted to lead to speculation. The scale is 0–8. The predicted likelihood of speculation is higher as we move to the right. Per discussion in the text, no pure-play investment opportunities existed for those technologies listed below the dashed line.

Throughout this exercise we have made judgment calls for the sake of our empirical analysis. Specifically, as we saw with fiber optics and the internet or with LCDs, our model cannot predict which technologies will converge and which interdependencies will arise. That understanding can come only from investigating the historical context of each technology and its uses. The application of our framework to the set of more contemporary Wharton technologies shows that the model is generalizable to some extent. But the history of these technologies is still unfolding.[49]

We expect and hope that our analysis will be reinterpreted as the future unfolds. This may lead to different assessments of the variables that we have used to characterize the technologies in our sample. To facilitate this process, you will find our data, coding, and historical analysis online at the Stanford University Press website. Check it out. If you come to a better alternative explanation, then we have successfully moved the conversation forward.

Future Bubbles and Non-Bubbles

In the concluding pages of this chapter, we apply the model beyond the confines of technologies that are already known to have been significant and outside the domain of technological innovation. We first consider housing, one of the largest and most costly bubbles in the long history of such episodes. We then apply our model to the case of Tesla and the electric vehicle.

Housing

The housing bubble that burst in the United States in 2007 sparked the largest economic calamity since the Great Depression. Our framework has much to offer in understanding these events and leads us to focus on two questions: First, why did lenders lend to subprime borrowers, and why did borrowers take loans that they were unlikely to be able to repay? Second, why did investors purchase mortgage-backed securities even though they understood them very poorly?

Housing markets are interesting because there is no fundamental uncertainty in the technology of housing or in the market structure of new home construction or home sales in general. Rather, the narrative that sustains housing bubbles is that prices will not fall. However, mortgage-backed securities were new, or at least unfamiliar to most. Their pricing required models of future home prices, which all used past price trends to predict the future ones. We learned in Chapter 3 that narratives based on past events are often misleading, and that, together with a host of incentive problems, created the housing bubble.

The housing market during this period had (and still has) three central types of participants. First, borrowers take out mortgages to buy homes. Second, originators, usually banks and mortgage companies, lend the money to the borrowers. If originators hold the loans they originate, they will lose money in case of default. Originators do not like defaults, so they have strong incentives to ensure that the borrowers to whom they lend will be able to repay the loans. Starting in the 1980s, originators often bundled mortgages together as "mortgage-backed" securities and then sold them to the third party of interest, investors on capital markets.[50] On the one hand, the securitization of mortgages encouraged lending and allows a greater share of the public access to credit at lower cost. On the other hand, this system relied on an investor's ability to judge the quality of the loans. For that to work, either the originators needed the will and ability to certify the quality of loans, or a third party needed to do this. Unfortunately (for most of us), a series of practices and deregulatory events that began in the 1970s eroded incentives to ensure loan quality.[51] Put simply, there were insufficient incentives on the part of the originators to evaluate borrowers' ability to repay loans and insufficient incentives on the part of third party certifiers, credit-rating agencies, to make sure that they were not overstating the quality of the loans. These failures encouraged originators to create risky loans that could be easily sold to naive investors.[52]

The housing market was rife with investor inexperience. For example, one criteria we used in Chapter 3 to define a novice was someone who had never experienced a bear market. Credit-rating agencies seemed to consider our definition explicitly. They ignored the bursting of the housing bubble in the late 1980s by integrating into their mathematical models only the history of defaults that had occurred since 1992.[53] Credit-rating agencies did not simply behave like novices; they codified their naïveté by putting it explicitly into their mathematical formulas! Not all loans were securitized. Bankers who held on to the securities likely made the same mistake.[54] Some buyers of mortgage-backed securities did see through the credit-rating problems. However, it appears that there were enough inexperienced traders who did not; originators exploited this to dump the lowest-quality loans on them.[55]

Inexperience was rife in the borrower's market as well. In 2007, 51% of first-time home buyers were between the ages of twenty-four and thirty-five, and an additional 20% were between the ages of thirty-six and forty-five. That is, in 2007, half of the first-time homeowners' market comprised people who were at most seventeen years of age at the time of the previous real-estate crash, and 70% were under the age of twenty-seven.[56] This inexperience made it more likely that they would hold the belief that housing prices would indefinitely increase.

We can learn more by looking at how prices varied across geographic regions, which we do in Figure 5.2. In some markets, such as Dallas, it was more difficult for home buyers to get loans. This constrained the demand for housing and kept price variations relatively modest. This was not true in other cities. For example, prices in Boston and San Francisco remained relatively in line with each other from 2000 through 2004. In both cities the supply of housing is severely constrained, which leads to an inelastic housing supply, which gives a sense of real scarcity and "justifies" increasing housing prices. Cities with more elastic housing supply, such as Phoenix and Las Vegas, experienced more modest price increases. Then, in 2003, these rapidly growing cities began seeing dramatic increases in prices, perhaps the result of home builders' somewhat sluggish initial response to increased market demand. Given these circumstances, it is understandable that first-time home buyers might have failed to an-

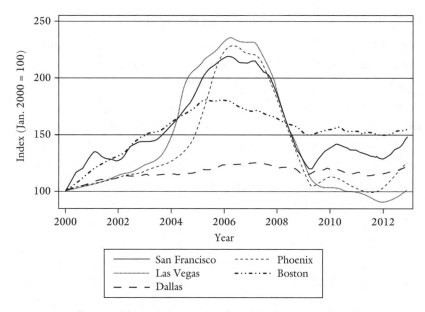

FIGURE 5.2   Geographic variation across five cities in seasonally adjusted housing prices, 2000–2012
Source: S&P Dow Jones Indices LLC, S&P/Case-Shiller Home Price Indices [SFXRSA, LVXRSA, PHXRSA, BOXRSA, DAXRSA] retrieved from FRED, Federal Reserve Bank of St. Louis, https://fred.stlouisfed.org/series, August 15, 2014.

ticipate the response of the construction industry to extreme increases in home prices. Mortgage originators and buyers of mortgage-backed securities probably should have known better.[57]

It is important to note that the housing bubble would likely not have occurred at all, or would have been much smaller, absent the myriad incentive problems in the mortgage origination market. This point is well documented in the finance literature and in the federal government's own inquiry.[58] However, our claim is that it would also have been unlikely had the level of inexperienced investors not risen to the levels it had by 2007.

We are no longer keeping score, as housing is not one of the Original 58 or one of the Wharton 30, but if we were:

Score: Our model, 4.5; False positives, 1.0

Tesla and the Electric Car

Tesla Motors, the electric car manufacturer led by PayPal entrepreneur and itinerant futurist Elon Musk, was founded in 2003 and had a successful, if unspectacular, IPO in 2010. During its first two and a half years as a public company, Tesla shares seesawed around their initial offering price. Then, in early 2013, the company announced its first quarterly profit, and the price of Tesla shares increased dramatically. As of this writing, Tesla's valuation gyrates around $50 billion, on par with General Motors and Ford.

Many hundreds of posts on internet fora have argued the merits and demerits of Tesla's valuation, and far be it from us to second guess the value of any specific stock. Although the electric vehicle is not one of the Wharton 30 (perhaps, in part, because the history of the electric vehicle goes back to the 1890s), we can still ask whether our model can explain some of the recent activity in Tesla shares.

First, is there uncertainty surrounding the future of the electric vehicle? Yes. For nearly a century, the future of the electric vehicle has been intertwined with the so-called better battery bugaboo, the fixation of scientists, engineers, and policy makers on the need for radical improvement in battery technology.[59] On numerous occasions, engineers and entrepreneurs have claimed that the advent of a super-battery was ready to disrupt the global vehicle market. Yet before the founding of Tesla, no new domestic manufacturer had successfully entered the automobile market since Walter Chrysler in 1924, and several attempts to reintroduce electric vehicles had failed. In reading press accounts of the rise of Tesla Motors, one might be forgiven for thinking that Elon Musk is the Übermensch, the modern Superman who has overcome the hundred-year history of the better battery bugaboo. Some aspects of the Tesla business model, such as the avoidance of privately owned dealerships, sidesteps traditional automotive distribution channels. Thus, to some degree, the fact that Musk succeeded in planting seeds of doubt in the minds of the critics of the electric car is testament to his success as an entrepreneur. Musk is a masterful storyteller. An individual investor might conclude, as many shareholders have, that Tesla will finally break the century-long hold of the internal combustion vehicle producers on the automotive market, even if other experts and short sellers believe otherwise.

Tesla's challenges in the electric vehicle market are profound— Tesla must not only sell an awesome car but also do so profitably.[60] Selling high-end luxury cars can be a good business, but Tesla is betting on bringing the electric vehicle (EV) to the masses. The problem is that the capabilities to design and produce vehicles are something incumbents are really good it, and they are already investing in and producing electric vehicles.

Is there a mechanism for would-be investors to speculate on the future of the electric vehicle? Yes, and here the story takes an interesting twist. Until several years ago, a number of private start-ups (and a few with successful IPOs) competed for EV investor's funds and faith. But following the failure of a host of EV and related start-ups, including Coda, Bright, Fisker, and A123, EV investors' only remaining pure-play EV choice has been Tesla. Despite the fact there are more Nissan Leafs and Chevrolet Volts on the road than Teslas, these vehicles represent tiny fractions of their parent companies' overall businesses, and lithium-ion battery cells, like LCD screens, are manufactured by global electronics conglomerates such as Panasonic and LG.[61] It is, therefore, possible that part of the enthusiasm for Tesla's shares is based on its unique status. Buyers of Tesla stock are buying more than a company; they are buying a technological narrative, a promise of a renewed, electrified transportation system. Whereas investors with a short interest in Tesla are betting against a firm, its supporters are investing in a social movement. In this respect, Tesla is more than a bellwether for the electric vehicle; it is a symbol of an alternative to a century-old industry and business model that many hold responsible for a host of social, economic, and environmental problems.

The Tesla narrative took off when Tesla announced its first profitable quarter in 2013. In retrospect, the numbers reported that day were not in conformance with generally accepted accounting principles (i.e., were non-GAAP) and included several unique, so-called onetime revenue sources. The profitable quarter, like many of Musk's accomplishments, was engineered to achieve a specific effect, and it seems to have worked. The resulting years-long run-up in the price of Tesla shares enabled Musk to prematurely retire debt the firm owed to the US Department of Energy's Advanced Technology Vehicle Manufacturing Program, with minimal dilution to Tesla shareholders—and personally, Musk emerged a multibillionaire.

More recently, Tesla has used its $5 billion battery "gigafactory," partially completed in Nevada, to extend the window of uncertainty created by the possibility of the firm successfully disrupting the existing auto transportation sector. Because it will take time for the impact of the gigafactory on the firm's prospects to be known with any certainty—and we can rest assured that any negative impact will be obfuscated—the decision to build the gigafactory can be seen not only as a daring strategic commitment by Musk but also as an attempt to further postpone the day of reckoning, that is, the day when uncertainty surrounding his promise to market an affordable, mass-produced EV with sufficient range will be resolved. Musk bought time, and partners like Nevada taxpayers and Panasonic shareholders who partnered with Tesla to pay for the gigafactory helped foot the bill.

The gigafactory is one of several, sequential narrative shifts that Musk has constructed. The latest are autonomous vehicles, solar panel production and installation, and electric trucks.

Should we expect a crash in Tesla shares? Our model would predict that this is a likely event: a consumer-facing technology, high uncertainty, and a skilled entrepreneur behind the curtain pulling the levers. We suspect that investors are ignoring a strong response from established automobile manufacturers entering the EV market and the way prices will fall in the face of this competition. We predict that Tesla shares will come down to earth. Call us when they do.

Chapter 6

POLICY IMPLICATIONS

What Should We Do About It?

On Black Monday—October 28, 1929—the Dow Jones index declined 13%. Black Tuesday—Tuesday, October 29, 1929—it declined a further 12%. The market was already well below its peak in September of 381. Two weeks before the start of the crash, when the market stood at 350, Yale professor Irving Fisher, whom we encountered in Chapter 3, proclaimed that the stock market was at "a permanently high plateau."[1] On October 23, when the market closed at 305, Fisher explained a drop in the market as "shaking out the lunatic fringe" and argued that security values were not "inflated."[2]

At the time, Irving Fisher was at the top of his field, an acknowledged expert on the concept of utility and the theory of interest. But his inability to perceive the fragility of the market peak that preceded the greatest economic catastrophe of modern capitalism destroyed his reputation. In the end, Fisher lacked an accurate mental model of trading behavior. Our model provides a concrete set of questions that Fisher might have used to arrive at a better set of predictions and thereby avoid his fall from grace. Arguably, a thoughtful business or economics major, armed with our model, would have done better than the illustrious Professor Fisher.

Our insights come from our understanding that market speculation is fundamentally a shared story: not a single story that we retell,
but an emergent set of narratives experienced by participants. The
narratives of the boom in 1929 were especially focused on the high-
technology industries of the day. Radio and aviation were miraculous
emergent technologies and also ways to get rich quickly. These narratives appealed to novice investors.[3] Understandings of when and
how narratives emerge and appeal would have been helpful to our
professor.

For example, if Fisher had asked whether there were many new,
inexperienced investors in the market, he might have been more suspi-
cious of the neoclassical orthodoxy he espoused. If Fisher had noticed
that the lack of entry barriers in new industries such as radio and
aviation allowed investors to construct hopeful stories for each of the
many firms listed on the exchanges, he might have been more cautious in his recommendations. If Fisher had paid closer attention to
the way the narrative of investment ignored the technical difficulties
in aviation or had engaged in a more careful analysis of the drivers
of profit in the radio industry, he might have moderated his predictions. If Fisher had asked whether events such at the Lindbergh transatlantic flight might have generated optimistic beliefs, reinforcing an
inevitability investment narrative that appealed to naive investors, he
might have drawn different conclusions. He gave his final statement
before a room full of bankers. Instead of making a bold proclamation,
he would have been better served using his audience to understand
where the funds for margin loans were coming from.

Hindsight is 20/20. But these questions that we suggest that Professor Fisher might have asked are questions we should all ask about
our own investments. Our analysis leads directly to a series of questions that investors and related stakeholders can and should ask to
better understand if perhaps, this time, the market they are interested
in, or invested in, is in the throes of a bubble. The questions are all
designed to focus our attention on whether investors are likely to develop optimistic beliefs about a class of securities and whether those
beliefs are fueled by a runaway investment narrative. We consider

questions across a range of categories outlined by our theory: story, use, naïfs, pure play, competition, business model, narrative accelerator, leverage. We note that these categories are slightly different from our retrospective factors. We needed to adapt our model to be useful in divining the future as opposed to the past. The questions and categories are overlapping by design. While we expect these questions to be asked when there is some suspicion that a class of market assets is frothy, we can also ask them prospectively: Are a particular set of assets likely to generate a bubble if an associated technological innovation shows promise?

Using the Framework

Story
Is it a good story, and is the story solid?
Does the new technology spark the imagination? Is the idea behind it sticky? In 1878, the *Cleveland Herald* witnessed the trial of electric light at the Union Steel Screw Company: "Without the slightest manual interference, the lamps flashed out their lights in all its magnificence. The rooms were flooded with a pure white light like the light of the sun. . . . "[4] This account—and the larger narrative of electric light—fits the model well. The Heath brothers, whose model we introduced in Chapter 4, coined an acronym to summarize their approach—SUCCESS: Light is *simple*. It's brilliance and quality were *unexpected* and *concrete*, and the newspaper's report was *credible*. The production of light was part of an *emotional story*. Electric lighting was a *sticky* idea.

Use
Stories become compelling if the protagonist is something we use.
Is the investment target producing something you or investors use? If you are attracted to the investment because you use the technology and you think it is "cool," ask yourself whether there are likely to be many other potential investors in the same situation. If so, this excitement is likely to not only be priced into the stock already; it will

also be harder for contrarian opinions to break through discussions. Also, you may prefer the narrative that supports your consumption decision. If you drive a Tesla, you may love your car, which makes it easier to believe that Tesla will make money selling that kind of car. If you use and rely on Twitter, you may believe that Twitter will make money. Do people with iPhones hold Apple stock? Do Amazon Prime members hold Amazon stock?

Naïfs
Naïfs are more likely to buy into narratives of inevitability.
Are many investors naive?

Are many investors naive, in the sense that they are new to investing or, alternatively, new to investing in a particular domain? In the run-up to the dot-com bubble the share of investments made by new VCs moved from 10% to 40%.[5] In 2000, 50% of finance professionals had been in the industry fewer than ten years. That is, they had never experienced a bear market. This matters: experienced money managers invested less heavily in technology stocks. Inexperienced day traders were circumventing professional advice and were the most likely to trade speculatively in internet stocks. Users of the new internet technology were more likely to invest on margin. On December 31, 1999, three months before the crash, margin debt as a percentage of customer assets for traders on E*Trade was 9.6%. This was more than seven times the 1.3% rate of investors at Merrill Lynch.[6] During the boom, more experienced investors were less susceptible to froth.

Pure Play
Is there a pure play? Is that pure play credible?

Of course, if there is no pure-play investment opportunity, there will be no bubble. But sometimes, we might believe that there are pure plays and ignore the resilience of incumbents, underestimating their capabilities. That is, disruption makes for a good story. For example, if you believe that Tesla will dominate the electric vehicle market through competitive pricing of the Model 3, you should also believe that Tesla will easily replicate the supply chain and related production efficiencies that have been honed and perfected at Toyota, Honda, Ford, or General Motors over decades. If you own Tesla stock but do not have a good sense of what goes into developing those supply chain and production efficiencies, and whether Tesla has assembled a team that is capable of developing them—or an understanding of the risk profile of such developments—then you are making an uninformed bet. If you are relying on analysts' or friends' recommendations, are these insiders thinking about these issues?

Competition
Does the narrative ignore future competition and potential downward pressure on prices?

Will many firms compete for dominance in the market? Conditional on finding customers and successfully selling to them, will the surviving firms be able to make money at market prices? If so, why? Do they have strong intellectual property rights? Do they have technological or production capabilities that are hard to replicate? Perhaps they have key sales relationships or a strong brand position? If so, these structural features will limit the number of alternative stories that can be woven around potential winners. If the competitive landscape is unclear, then the probability of a bubble is higher because future margins might be low as a result of competition; the effect of competition on margins is often overlooked.

Consider that Uber and Lyft provide almost identical services—and prices for their services are unsustainably low. Perhaps if one competitor exits, the other will be able to raise prices. But by how much will the competitor be able to do so before users substitute other forms of transportation? In well-functioning markets with free entry, the ability to price competitively is limited by the degree to which companies are able to differentiate their products. If there is little reason to believe that a single company will dominate a particular market or provide a solution that does not have clear substitutes, then there is little reason to believe that they will generate long-run profits relative to their activities, because over time margins will fall.

Business Model

Are there multiple competing ideas about how people will make money? Are there multiple competing business models?

If you hear a variety of stories and theories about who might profit from a particular innovation, this suggests that there are many competing narratives that might appeal to different investors. Are they all told with an air of inevitability and urgency? For example, for many years, Bell was the only game in town—especially after the company managed to keep out both Western Union and, later, everyone else with an exceptionally expansive patent ruling. Radio was different. Although eventually RCA was able to dominate the market, it was unable to restrict entry into the production of radios; nor was it able to restrict entry into broadcast and production of radio shows. This left multiple areas for investing, as it was unclear which would be the core profit driver. Automobiles have a similar history.

The fact that in radio the business model that would lead to profits was unclear allowed for much more experimentation in different parts of the value chain: the production of radios, broadcast, production of content, and so on. Different business models allow entrepreneurs and their investors to weave stories around their favorite ideas. Greater variation increases the likelihood that a narrative will appeal to a potential investor. Today, we see a range of different business models in the nascent self-driving vehicle market. Will the first applications be in small communities? Trucking? Cities? Local delivery? Will these be features of existing cars that people own, or will self-driving cars be owned by mobility companies and rented out as a service? Will the vehicles look like driverless cars or something totally different (rolling lockboxes or electric drones)? Most important, is it all inevitable? And when will it happen? Autonomous vehicles are coming, inevitably, and quickly!

Narrative Accelerator

Has the narrative been coordinated by some big event?

Does (or did) the technology of interest have a Lindbergh moment? In 1848, President James K. Polk pronounced in his address to Congress, "The explorations already made warrant the belief that the supply is very large and that gold is found at various places in an extensive district of country."[7] This is just a small excerpt from six full paragraphs describing the findings in California. In 1848, California was a distant, dangerous, and difficult place to get to. Polk lent his credibility to rumors, making the opportunity appear more certain than it was. And while there really was gold in California, there was not sufficient gold to allow every prospector to make money. For most prospectors, the gold rush was a gold bust. Asking whether a specific event coordinated beliefs and attention and thereby sparked a narrative is worthwhile.

By all accounts, President Polk did not give credibility to the gold rumors for personal gain; he thought he was right. However, when a particular story line is propelled by entrepreneurs and investors who will gain by the narrative, be skeptical. On the one hand, the power of the narrative can create real effects and changes. A successful narrative can be self-fulfilling. On the other hand, the power of words is not limitless, and often, compelling narratives fail to make money and end in failure.

To the extent that would-be investors feed on a single source of information (i.e., Facebook "news"), these individuals will be vulnerable to "coordination" either by chance or by deliberate deception. Therefore, our recommendations in this area can be associated with those like author Clay Johnson who call for a more deliberate and varied "information diet" in which you carefully consider multiple sources and types of information. Consuming a varied and healthy information diet—in addition to making you a more interesting person—is likely to minimize the risk of unwittingly falling victim to belief coordination. This leads to the natural question: are beliefs being driven from broad sources of information, or are beliefs being driven by few sources?

Leverage
Is there too much leverage?

"*Please God, just one more bubble*" reads an apocryphal bumper sticker reportedly sighted in Silicon Valley.[8] The idea behind the bumper sticker is that the entrepreneur or investor will be able to invest early and get out prior to the crash. That is, hopeful investors believe they will be able to shift the risk to follow-on investors. Leverage works the same way. Leverage fuels speculation by allowing speculators to earn higher returns while not assuming the entirety of the risk associated with their speculation. Fortunately, leveraged bubbles are also harder to generate because they require not simply that an investor is overoptimistic about the value of an asset but also a that a lender or series of lenders are willing to embrace the same narrative. This can happen for two complementary reasons. First, the lender may be as overoptimistic as the speculator. We expect lenders to be the grown-ups—there is a reason that the stereotype of bankers is that they are conservative and boring. They are supposed to be the more experienced actors in the room. But this is not necessarily the case. Thus, we should ask what expertise the lenders have and on what experience that expertise is based. The second problem is that loans and equity funds are often issued through intermediaries, and the intermediaries often have different incentives from those of the lenders themselves. Venture capitalists invest other people's money. Bankers, by definition, do this as well. A failed bank does not imply that the banker or the decision maker will go bankrupt him or herself, or even lose his or her job! Bonuses tied to originations are not generally clawed back if and when loans fail. This moral hazard problem was rampant during the events that led to the 2008 crisis.[9] If the intermediaries are compensated on the basis of loans originated but are not exposed to the default risk associated with these loans, then we should expect lenders to fuel speculation. Asking how lenders make decisions and how they are rewarded is crucial to understanding whether someone is artificially inflating a bubble.

Putting It Together

We can now tally up the answers to these questions. If the answer is affirmative across all six categories, we should be very concerned that we are in a bubble. If one comes to the conclusion that the answer is no across more of these categories, the fear of the god of froth should decline. When only one or two categories are affirmative, it would appear unlikely.

- **Story:** Is the story particularly compelling or sticky?
- **Use:** Is the story about something that you are familiar with in terms of use or imagination but in an area that you fail to understand the business well?
- **Naïfs:** Are there other naive investors in the market? Who is investing in this technology?
- **Pure play:** Is there a stock that is believed to track the fortunes of the technology directly?
- **Competition:** Does the narrative ignore future competition?
- **Business model:** Are there a variety of stories about how money will be made commercializing the new technology?
- **Narrative accelerator:** Did something or somebody turbocharge the narrative?
- **Leverage:** Are investments significantly leveraged? Do intermediaries play a large role?

We do not have an algorithm. We have a set of conditions that are likely to be associated with market speculation. Their presence does not strictly imply that a bubble is occurring, and their absence does not strictly imply that it does not. There is no such thing as a sure thing in fair investing.

Should We Care?

Bubbles are neither good nor bad, nor are they neutral.

Before the oil boom in Texas, the University of Texas occupied a "one room shack so rickety that class had to be stopped when the wind howled through the structure."[10] The university was financed by meager grazing leases on its vast tracts of state-granted land until 1923. At this point New York investors financed oil exploration and black gold was found. The *New York Times* proclaimed that soon thereafter the university's endowment rivaled that of Harvard.[11] If we stretch things a bit, we can claim that the rise of the University of Texas is due to Wall Street financiers. Take that, Texas!

Mel Kranzberg—not from Texas—was a historian of technology, one of the founders of the Society for the History of Technology, and a professor at Case Western Reserve and Georgia Tech from the 1950s through the 1980s. Kranzberg is known, among other things, for his six laws of technology. The first is "technology is neither good nor bad nor is it neutral."[12] We began this subsection with a transposition of Kranzberg's law. Kranzberg was making the point that we cannot know the ramifications of innovation—and that innovation can simultaneously be good for some and bad for others—but rarely will it be neutral. Bubbles are investment frenzies. They stimulate innovation and investment that may be used to build out infrastructure. It may even be true that investments and innovations that occur during frothy times are systematically different from those in other times. For example, the Harvard Business School economist Ramana Nanda and the MIT Sloan economist Matthew Rhodes-Kropf suggest that during boom times, venture capitalists fund start-ups that are more likely to fail.[13] This is not surprising in and of itself—but they also point out that some of these succeed, and when they do, they are more highly valued, and their patents are more likely to be inputs into more innovation. Venture capitalists have an appetite for transformative businesses during a boom but less so during a bust. The reason, they argue, is that the VCs believe they will be able to sell off more speculative businesses to the public in boom times but not in bust times. The implication is clear: frothy times will lead to greater and bolder risks, and this appetite for risk is good for society as a whole because some of these investments will pay off and create futures that would not have happened absent the bubble. There is more evidence to support this idea. MIT economists Jorge Guzman and Scott Stern observe that start-ups founded during boom times are of higher growth potential than those founded during recessions.[14] Bubbles might be good!

In contrast, when bubbles pop, the costs can be substantial and can spark recessions and calamities. The Great Depression is the result of a popped speculative bubble made worse by poor policy decisions—not to mention being a major cause of the rise of fascism in Europe and World War II. The Great Recession in 2008 led millions to lose their jobs, and its aftermath is still playing out today. More modestly, the bursting of the dot-com bubble in 2000 led to a recession, an almost complete shutdown of the IPO market, and a reaction among high-tech investors. Job losses can be devastating to individual lives; to the extent that reigning in excessive speculation will avoid these costs, we should work hard to avoid bubbles or at least mitigate their harms to the most vulnerable among us.

Policies governing investments often fail to take into account the role of narratives in investment decisions. New IPO prospectuses may advertise the prospects of new issues in colorful and hopeful language. IPO road shows are about telling stories! The Securities and Exchange Commission requires that risks be articulated, and they are . . . in dry, often boilerplate language that varies little from offering to offering. The required risks and warnings are designed to not invoke stories, just like the risks read at breakneck speed on TV drug advertisements to a backdrop of beautiful healthy people. Any policy should recognize how narratives are manipulated to generate stories of inevitability. Policies should not only mitigate the risks associated with market speculation in terms of the likelihood of its occurrence but also shift the costs of speculative crashes to those who are most able to bear these costs. We have many policies in place that try to protect the most vulnerable participants in the financial system, although in our observations, these policies tend to come under assault by those who are most able to bear the costs of failure.

Our theory suggests that bubbles are less likely when the questions we have articulated are answered in the negative. Our policy recommendations are directly tied to these. There is already an extensive literature on policy and financial bubbles. For a thoughtful review of financial regulation and bubbles, we recommend Erik Gerding's excellent book *Law, Bubbles, and Financial Regulation*.[15] In particular, the role of leverage has been extensively studied in the context of market speculation, so we avoid policy recommendations directly related to leverage here. Instead, our focus is on the other question categories, as they are more unique to our framework.

Story and Use

We certainly do not recommend policies that limit what products people use, the stories they tell, or the extent of their imagination. However, policies to educate individuals about how their day-to-day consumption choices may bias their investment assessments would be very helpful. Policies that educate individuals about how they construct narratives to justify their investment decisions would likely inform potential investors. To wit, investors would be unwise to buy Twitter or Facebook stock on the basis of the extent of Twitter or Facebook users in their extended social network.

Naïfs

We live in a capitalist society; we encourage investment in securities through investment retirement accounts, but we do not require basic financial literacy in our education system. Students learn Shakespeare (which we applaud), but it is helpful to remind would-be investors that all that glitters is not gold. And we are more likely to notice glitter when it is dangled right before our eyes. It is astounding that several hundred years into financial capitalism, and one hundred years since the New York Stock Exchange worked to democratize markets, policies that encourage the pursuit of financial literacy including a fair understanding of the risks and rewards of investment are not widespread or universal. There may not be an easy fix. Experimental evidence does suggest that experienced traders often get caught up in the froth and become sophisticated only after experiencing a crash. We often hear kernels of wisdom about the importance of experience, such as "Smart money is just dumb money that's been through a crash." The underlying insight there is consistent with our theory. Experienced investors are less likely to throw money at random narratives. But policy makers (and educators, for that matter) might ask: Can we create experiential exercises that awaken the same critical sensibilities necessary to exercise expert judgment when evaluating proffered narratives?

We propose that a series of questions aimed at helping investors identify whether they are in a bubble might be helpful. Experimental work on bubbles has tried to highlight various aspects of a market but has not sought to get investors to contemplate a series of questions designed to identify when bubbles are likely. The questions we have proposed are designed to get investors to think critically about why they believe a particular narrative, and we expect they will indeed dissuade some investors. We do know that we ourselves will ask these questions of markets that we perceive to be frothy. With some luck, we will avoid getting caught in the next bubble.

But given that behavioral studies have shown that the risk and hazards of bubbles are not internalized except by experience, perhaps we can look for ways to inoculate investors. As entrepreneurship professors, we teach entrepreneurship by forcing our students to become entrepreneurs during a semester. Students are required to pursue real businesses and earn money.[16] (We often have to repeat this instruction several times as many students hear our words but fail to internalize what we are asking of them because it diverges from what is normally expected of students in most classes.) Following this experience, some students become more attracted to the idea of entrepreneurship. Others are repelled. Both are excellent outcomes, as the cost of the experiment (the class) is much less than quitting a paying job and launching a business. However, learning comes only through real, hands-on experience; only then, do the students feel the ambiguity and lack of control that entrepreneurs need to cope with when starting their own businesses. The good thing about doing this experiment in a classroom at a university is that failure is not particularly costly. Egos might be bruised a bit—no one likes to fail—but students gain a visceral experience of what it is like to be an entrepreneur.

Similarly, in financial literacy classes we might engineer experiences where students see bubbles firsthand and have something riding on it (perhaps grades). Instead of having student contests where stocks are tracked and those who pick the "best" ones over a short period are rewarded, which teaches precisely the wrong lesson about the "skill" of stock picking, it might be better to have students participate in low-stakes simulated markets and have them experience bubble narratives firsthand. Such an experience, coupled with lessons about how bubbles are formed and why they happen, may help future investors become more sophisticated before they enter the market in the first place.

One might interpret government policy in a similar way. Efforts to restrict investing on the basis of income or wealth can ensure that the costs of failure and experimentation are associated with the capacity to absorb losses. For example, the 2015 crowdfunding regulations restrict investors with incomes or net worth less than $100,000 from investing more than the greater of $2,000 or 5% of their incomes or net worth in any twelve-month period. Wealthier investors may not invest more than 10% of their income in any given year. Purchasing stock in new ventures is incredibly risky, and these guidelines should restrict someone from investing their life savings in a new firm. We also strongly recommend learning more about crowdfunding and the risks of small business in general. In particular, understanding the base risk rate of new firms (fewer than 50% survive five years) should be something that every investor should understand.

For high-growth entrepreneurship, the private sector seems to do a reasonable job at educating novice entrepreneurs. The incentives to do this are clear: investors wish to ensure that they earn returns on their investment and therefore have experimented with a variety of models to enhance the competence of entrepreneurs. This is done through mentoring by venture capitalists and angel investors, and via more direct training programs now seen in venture accelerators such as Y Combinator and Techstars. However, equity investors achieve returns or "exits" by selling the story of their investments to willing buyers. It is up to the buyers, be they corporations or public investors, to analyze their narratives carefully.

Finally, we note that policies that encourage disclosure are laudable and good, but only insofar as the disclosures and facts are then worked into narratives—or perhaps more correctly, into counternarratives. Facts without stories are just noise.

Pure Play and Competition

As professors of entrepreneurship, we often hear our students pitch new venture concepts: "It's an untapped market," they will often say. Or, "There are no competitors." This conclusion is inevitably wrong. Scholars have shown that most entrepreneurs underestimate the threat of competition, even from something as predictable as entry.[17] Intrepid and ultimately successful entrepreneurs frequently own up to having underestimated the challenges associated with their ventures and admit that had they known then what they know now, they may not have taken the leap. Without being too self-serving, we do believe that educating entrepreneurs and investors about the realities of the venture creation process (what we do!) should go some way toward mitigating the risks associated with naive assessments of competition. However, recent reforms of US securities regulations intended to encourage investment in start-ups may have the opposite, if unintended, effect of drawing attention to novel ideas at the expense of due diligence of potential competitive threats.

More generally, we encourage policy makers to take a dynamic view of technology markets. When barriers to entry are low in new technology markets, we should expect that there will be excessive entry. This will have the effect of driving down profits and increasing exit rates—patterns that have been documented extensively across many industries including autos, radio, television, aviation, rubber, and more.[18] Make no mistake, extensive competition leads to large-scale business model experimentation and is often very good for consumers, but it will depress security prices, and investors and policy makers need to be aware. The inability to foresee entry is common and pervasive.

The flip side of this argument is that the industrial organization of many industries effectively precludes market speculation in the technologies they incubate. For example, it was difficult to spark a bubble in the LCD industry because it was difficult to make an investment that tracked that industry directly. So while many policy recommendations suggest different ways to limit or gum up trading, the most successful "policy" has been the haphazard way that the commercialization of new technologies is organized in various industries.

Business Model

Business model proliferation is a direct result of underlying uncertainty about how a given technology or innovation will be commercialized. As a result, we often see increased entry when it is unclear how to make money from a new technology. As we write, this is precisely what we are seeing in the context of autonomous vehicles, as different firms enter and sometimes exit different parts of the (changing) value chain. Over the course of the coming several years, most of these ventures will fail, resulting in real losses for real investors. We do not believe in a policy that would restrict such experimentation—in fact, quite the opposite. However, we do believe that monetary and fiscal policy makers need to be aware that this type of experimentation is systematically enacted by entrepreneurs offering the maximum number of potential narratives and justifications of how and why a technology will be successful and revolutionize its sector. The investors are betting that their vision will materialize, usually quickly. The skeptics may stay out, but they also generally have much weaker incentives to push their case. This may lead policy makers to look past the risks associated with a new field and themselves ignore underlying baseline failure rates and get caught up in the speculative fervor, as Alan Greenspan did in 2000 and Professor Fischer did in 1929.

Narrative Accelerator

Whereas the individual investor needs to ask whether an event has coordinated beliefs in a premature or overoptimistic way, policy makers need to recognize that they have the ability to coordinate beliefs. Like President Polk's speech about gold in California, public statements are magnified through media bullhorns. Robert Shiller argues that "the history of speculative bubbles begins roughly with the advent of newspapers."[19] Policy makers and the press alike should be aware of their role as agents of coordination that enhance narratives around particular technologies. President Coolidge urged investors and the public not to worry about margin loans at a time when margin loans represented about 18% the capitalization of listed stocks.[20] Such statements had real and serious economic consequences as they fueled chicanery associated with bubbles. Policy makers need to exercise great caution when commenting on markets that are filled with novice investors. Their words will be given undue weight and can spark large market movements.

Summary

We have thought about how our framework might inform the investment decisions of both individual investors and policy makers. We believe that policy can be improved by taking into account the role of narratives in generating financial bubbles, as well as the role public figures and events have in shaping those narratives, and allowing for the real effects of these stories.

We recommend that individual investors apply our framework by asking a series of questions about the investment context in which they are interested. Policy makers might develop and encourage investment training that allows safe failure, be that in the classroom or, as is already being implemented in some markets, through restricting the percentage of assets that can be invested in risky assets. Leaders and people in the public eye should take great care in their choice of words, as those words can coordinate beliefs that defy reality and potentially lead to bubbles. Those who hear these words should understand when they are uttered strategically in order to propel a narrative.

Sometimes, bubbles may spur productive experimentation that might otherwise not have happened, but such activity should not be funded by those who are least able to afford associated losses, and such investments should never be based on weak decision heuristics. These mistakes have been repeated countless times. That we get fooled is not surprising; narratives and stories are how we think. But with a better idea of how, when, and for whom these stories become costly, we can better avoid them.

APPENDIX: METHODS USED IN CODING TECHNOLOGIES

WE RESEARCHED EACH TECHNOLOGY in the historical and press records, producing historical accounts that answered a series of questions regarding each one of the factors articulated in Chapters 2 and 3. We then had two research assistants read through these documents and assign ratings as to the degree of uncertainty along each dimension. We code the technologies on a 1 to 9 scale, where scores of the scale are mapped to specific criteria regarding the type of uncertainty and the degree in which the technology was conducive to a narrative. This coding document, the codes, and the historical accounts are available via our online Appendix (http://www.sup.org/bubblesandcrashes).

We aggregate uncertainty to two dimensions: (1) control and (2) technology and business. We then rank the technologies along each dimension. For each dimension, the technology receives a score of 2 if it is in the top third of technologies, 1 if in the middle third, and 0 if in the bottom third. We similarly code and rank the narrative criteria such that each technology receives a score from 0 to 2 in terms of its susceptibility to narrative. Finally, we code the presence of novices based on the time period, where a score of 2 is given to technologies at risk during high-novice periods, 1 during periods with some novices, and 0 during periods with few novices. We add this to produce a scale from 0 to 8 for each technology.

Because we do not have a large sample (15 technologies of those analyzed in Chapter 4 that have corresponding indices and 17 of those analyzed in Chapter 5), there is not sufficient information in the data to reliably separate the effects of each factor. Hence, we aggregate the two uncertainty scores, the novice score, and the narrative scores to a single scale. This is the scale that appears in the figures in Chapters 4 and 5.

We did not code specifically for demand or for regulatory uncertainty in the main analysis, although we did experiment with a crude regulatory uncertainty score in Chapter 4. We found demand uncertainty too difficult to code reliably. However, we believe that demand uncertainty is most likely to appear when new technologies disrupt current value chains—that is, when technologies are doing completely new things or when they converge with another technology in an unpredictable way. Second, in practice, speculative episodes often occur when there is hype—that is, when the uncertainty is resolved but before it is clear whether a solution can be provided profitably. Thus, demand uncertainty is likely to be highly correlated with other types of uncertainty that we do measure (disruption, whether there is a clear business model, and whether it makes previous solutions obsolete, as well as narrative measures such as whether there is public interest). Because we must aggregate, and to the degree that the factors are correlated with one another, the marginal contribution of each new dimension is diminishing. Similarly, regulatory uncertainty was not measured directly; rather, it was factored into our measurement of who would control the technology. For example, for most of the pharmaceutical innovations regulation had a large effect on the existence of complementary assets—as few firms had the capabilities to work with the emergent Food and Drug Administration regulations—which thereby decreased uncertainty regarding who would control the technology.

Tables

TABLE A.1 List of 58 original technologies, factors predicted to generate a bubble, and whether we observe a bubble

| | | BUBBLE WINDOW | | UNCERTAINTY | | | | | | | | | | |
Technology	Invention	Start	End	Control uncertainty	Biz model/ tech/ disruption	Narrative score	Novices in market	Factor total	Bubble narrative in press	Bubble	Frothi- ness	Fall	Relative fall	Peak froth
1 Incandescent lamp	1879	1882	1910	Low	High	Medium	Low	3	No	No	2.19	0.29	0.87	4/1/1902
2 Television	1936	1949	1960	Medium	Medium	High	Low	4	No	No	0.57	0.03	1.49	3/1/1952
3 Electronic computer	1940	1951	1970	Low	High	Low	High	4	No	No	1.86	0.43	1.30	6/1/1968
4 Color television	1953	1954	1970	Medium	Low	Medium	High	4	Yes	Yes	2.29	0.76	2.08	11/1/1968
5 Basic oxygen process	1952	1964	1974	Medium	Medium	Low	High	4	No	No	1.14	0.49	4.46	10/1/1964
6 Wankel motor	1967	1967	1974	Low	Low	High	High	4	Yes	Yes	5.06	0.88	2.26	9/1/1972
7 Telephone	1877	1878	1890	Low	High	Medium	High	5	No	No	1.98	0.49	n/a	3/15/1883
8 Internal combustion	1860	1895	1922	High	High	Medium	Low	5	Yes	Yes	3.32	0.82	2.37	7/1/1919
9 Rayon	1890	1910	1930	Medium	Low	High	High	5	Yes	Yes	2.33	0.92	1.21	5/1/1928
10 Xerography	1942	1946	1970	Low	High	Medium	High	5	No	No	1.83	0.38	2.19	4/1/1966
11 Jet engine	1940	1952	1970	Medium	Medium	High	High	6	Yes	Yes	2.94	0.49	N/A	6/1/1955
12 Assembly line	1913	1913	1930	High	High	Medium	High	7	Yes	Yes	2.66	0.88	1.14	11/1/1928
13 Transistor	1948	1952	1960	High	High	Medium	High	7	Yes	Yes	2.75	0.27	1.22	12/1/1961
14 AM radio	1900	1900	1930	High	High	High	High	8	Yes	Yes	3.16	0.97	1.19	5/1/1929
15 Aviation	1910	1910	1935	High	High	High	High	8	Yes	Yes	3.75	0.94	1.19	5/1/1929
16 Freon	1930	1931	1945	Low	Low	Low	Low	0						
17 Vulcanized rubber	1840	1840	1870	Low	Medium	Low	Low	1						
18 Plexiglas	1933	1933	1940	Low	Low	Medium	Low	1						
19 Catalytic cracking	1935	1935	1940	Low	Medium	Low	Low	1						
20 Fluorescent lamp	1937	1938	1948	Low	Low	Medium	Low	1						

(continued)

TABLE A.1 (*continued*)

	Technology	Invention	BUBBLE WINDOW Start	End	UNCERTAINTY Control uncertainty	Biz model/ tech/ disruption	Narrative score	Novices in market	Factor total	Bubble narrative in press	Bubble	Frothi- ness	Fall	Relative fall	Peak froth
21	Nylon	1937	1940	1950	Low	Low	Medium	Low	1						
22	Power steering	1900	1926	1982	Low	Low	Low	High	2						
23	FM radio	1932	1932	1955	Low	Low	Low	High	2						
24	Synthetic rubber	1932	1935	1950	High	Low	Low	Low	2						
25	Silicone	1943	1943	1970	Low	Low	Low	High	2						
26	Radar	1945	1945	1960	Low	Low	Low	High	2						
27	Stainless steel	1912	1910	1925	Medium	Low	Low	High	3						
28	Continuous hot strip rolling	1914	1923	1933	Low	Medium	Low	High	3						
29	Antiknock gasoline	1935	1924	1955	Low	Low	Medium	High	3						
30	Cellophane	1917	1927	1935	Low	Low	Medium	High	3						
31	Automatic transmission	1939	1940	1950	Low	Medium	High	Low	3						
32	Polyethylene	1937	1940	1960	Medium	Low	Low	High	3						
33	Polystyrene	1930	1941	1950	Medium	Medium	Medium	Low	3						
34	Magnetic tape recorder	1899	1952	1962	Low	Low	Medium	High	3						
35	Polycarbonate	1955	1955	1970	Low	Medium	Low	High	3						
36	Polyvinyl acetate	1959	1959	1969	Medium	Low	Low	High	3						
37	Hydrofoil	1922	1960	1970	Medium	Low	Low	High	3						
38	Modern steelmaking	1855	1856	1890	Medium	Medium	Low	High	4						
39	Bakelite	1906	1909	1940	Low	Low	High	High	4						
40	Continuous cracking	1913	1919	1925	Medium	Medium	Low	High	4						
41	Automatic watch	1928	1928	1960	Medium	Low	Medium	High	4						

#	Technology								
42	Color photography	1935	1933	1945	Medium	Medium	High	Low	4
43	Cotton picker	1933	1941	1954	Low	High	High	Low	4
44	DDT	1939	1942	1960	Low	Low	High	High	4
45	Terylene	1949	1949	1959	Low	Low	High	High	4
46	Gyrocompass	1906	1909	1936	Medium	High	Low	High	5
47	Helicopter	1931	1936	1955	Low	High	Medium	High	5
48	Sulfa drugs	1932	1936	1939	Medium	High	High	Low	5
49	Insulin	1923	1923	1930	Low	High	High	High	6
50	Electric record player	1878	1935	1955	Medium	High	Medium	High	6
51	Penicillin	1942	1942	1950	High	High	High	Low	6
52	Streptomycin	1944	1945	1955	Medium	Medium	High	High	6
53	Long-playing record	1948	1948	1960	Medium	Medium	High	High	6
54	Hovercraft	1955	1955	1970	Medium	High	Medium	High	6
55	Antimalarial drugs	1930	1932	1965	High	High	Medium	High	7
56	Cortisone	1942	1948	1960	Medium	High	High	High	7
57	Phototype	1945	1952	1960	High	High	Medium	High	7
58	Drilling for oil	1859	1859	1880	High	High	High	High	8

Sources: See text for sources of list of technologies. Author calculations based on data from Table A.3 and various historical sources.

Notes: Technologies are divided into those that had strongly correlated stocks traded on public exchanges and those that did not. Within these groups, they are sorted according to the extent to which our theory predicts there should be a bubble. The year of invention is the first year a working prototype appeared. The bubble window begins with the first commercialization activities and ends when uncertainty was significantly reduced and/or the technology was subsumed by substitutes. We report the ratings on a scale of the uncertainty associated with each technology in terms of who would control the technology; the extent of uncertainty in how it will work and how money will be made (*Biz model/tech/disruption*), the degree in which it is susceptible to a narrative, and whether there were novices in the market. Each receives a score of 0 if Low, 1 if Medium, and 2 if High. We then sum this in *Factor total*. We report if we found a bubble narrative in the popular press, whether we detected a bubble, and if so, it's frothiness. We report how much it fell as a share of the peak, and how large this fall was relative to the market. Finally, we report when the peak froth occurred. We can report the stock market–related measures only if there were publicly traded pure plays on the market. The relative bubble calculation for "jet engine" is not meaningful because the denominator in this calculation, the SP index's value in April 1955, is near its lowest point through April 1962.

TABLE A.2 List of Wharton 30 technologies, factors predicted to generate a bubble, and whether we observe a bubble

	Technology	Bubble Window Start	Bubble Window End	Control uncertainty	Biz model/ tech/ disruption	Narrative score	Novices in market	Factor total	Bubble narrative in press	Bubble	Frothiness	Fall	Relative fall	Peak froth
1	Bar codes	1985	1996	0	0	0	1	2	No	No	2.32	0.60	2.09	8/1/1987
2	Biofuels	2001	2015	0	1	0	2	4	Yes	Yes	3.11	0.998	2.40	6/1/2006
3	Genetically modified plants	1995	2010	0	1	0	2	4	No	No	2.85	0.52	1.22	2/1/2008
4	MRI	1970	1990	1	1	0	1	4	Yes	Yes	2.77	0.96	38.83	6/1/1986
5	Microprocessor	1970	1996	1	1	0	1	4	Yes	Yes	2.04	0.54	1.88	9/1/1987
6	Human genome sequencing	1990	2010	0	2	0	2	5	Yes	Yes	4.35	0.88	1.94	3/1/2000
7	Social networking	2005	2015	1	1	0	2	5	Yes	Yes	2.17	0.79	1.86	2/1/2006
8	Open source	1975	2010	1	1	0	2	5	Yes	Yes	4.96	0.98	2.20	12/1/1999
9	Photovoltaics	1973	2010	0	1	2	2	6	Yes	Yes	3.43	0.94	1.89	12/1/2007
10	GPS	1989	2010	1	2	0	2	6	Yes	Yes	2.20	0.73	N/A	7/1/1995
11	Mobile phones	1985	1997	0	1	2	1	6	No	No	1.76	0.36	2.75	9/1/1989
12	PCs	1977	1996	1	2	2	1	7	Yes	No	0.56	0.47	1.97	11/1/1980
13	Office software	1983	1996	1	2	2	1	7	No	No	1.55	0.47	5.99	1/1/1984
14	Media file compression	1980	2010	1	2	2	2	8	Yes	Yes	4.17	0.98	2.14	3/1/2000
15	Online shopping	1993	2002	1	2	2	2	8	Yes	Yes	4.14	0.93	2.39	4/1/1999
16	Internet	1970	2005	1	2	2	2	8	Yes	Yes	4.29	0.84	1.84	3/1/2000

#								
17	Large-scale wind turbines	1770	1996	0	0	0	1	2
18	Anti-retrovirals	1983	1997	0	0	0	1	2
19	Stents	1986	1997	0	0	0	1	2
20	ATMs	1970	1990	1	0	0	1	3
21	SRAM flash memory	1960	1990	1	0	0	1	3
22	LEDs	1962	2010	1	0	0	1	3
23	Laparascopy	1990	2000	2	0	0	2	4
24	LCDs	1990	2000	1	0	0	2	4
25	GUI	1977	1996	2	1	0	1	5
26	Digital photography	1986	2010	0	2	0	2	5
27	Fiber optics	1980	2010	1	1	0	2	5
28	Microfinance	1980	2010	1	0	2	2	6
29	RFID	1970	2015	2	1	0	2	6
30	Email	1970	1996	2	2	2	1	8

Sources: Author calculations based on data from Table A.3 and various historical sources.

Notes: The relative bubble calculation for "GPS" is not meaningful because the denominator in this calculation, the SP index's value in July 1995, is near its lowest point through July 2002. See also notes to Table A.1.

TABLE A.3 Sources for index calculations

Technology	Source	Included firms for author-created indices with dates of inclusion
Major innovations		
Incandescent lamp	Cowles, Electrical Equipment, Series C, p. 196	Edison General Electric Feb 1890–May 1892; General Electric June 1892, Electric Storage Battery Feb 1905–Feb 1906
Television	CRSP	GENERAL ELECTRIC CO 02jan1948 31dec1949; STEWART WARNER CORP 04jan1954 31dec1975; WESTINGHOUSE ELECTRIC CORP 02jan1964 31dec1975; SPARKS WITHINGTON CO 03jan1949 30oct1956; SPARTON CORP 31oct1956 31dec1968; ZENITH RADIO CORP 02jan1951 31dec1953; AVCO MFG CORP 02jan1951 31dec1953; NOBLITT SPARKS INDUSTRIES INC 02jan1948 30jun1950; ARVIN INDUSTRIES INC 03jul1950 31dec1957; PHILCO CORP 03jan1950 31dec1953; SYLVANIA ELEC PRODS INC 02jan1948 06mar1959; CORNELL DUBILIER ELEC CORP 03jan1949 30dec1950; FARNSWORTH TELEVISION & RADIO 03jan1949 03may1949; F A R LIQUIDATING CORP 04may1949 08may1950; EMERSON RADIO & PHONOGRAPH CORP 02jan1947 01jun1966; ADMIRAL CORP 02jan1947 10apr1974; MOTOROLA INC 03jan1949 31dec1965; MAGNAVOX COMPANY 03jan1949 31dec1954; STROMBERG CARLSON CO 06jul1954 01jul1955; ANDREA RADIO CORP 02jan1975 31dec1975; GIANNINI CONTROLS CORP 02jul1962 17apr1967; CONRAC CORP 18apr1967 31dec1975; EASTERN STATES CORP 02jul1962 26jun1969; TELECTRO IND CORP 02jul1962 26may1967; PILOT RADIO TELEVISION CORP 29may1967 03aug1967; TELEVISION MANUFACTURERS AMER CO 03jan1967 29jan1970; T M A COMPANY 30jan1970 07may1970; TRAV LER INDS INC; PIONEER ELECTRONIC CORP 17sep1975 31dec1975

Electronic computer	CRSP	AMERICAN TELEPHONE & TELEG CO 31dec1925 20apr1994; A T & T CORP 21apr1994 21nov2005; GENERAL ELECTRIC CO 31dec1925 31dec2015; INTER-NATIONAL BUSINESS MACHS COR 31dec1925 31dec2015; AMERICAN TYPE FOUNDERS CO 31dec1925 16may1936 A T F INC 28jun1946 05feb1951; DAY-STROM INC 06feb1951 01feb1962; SCHLUMBERGER LTD 02feb1962 31dec2015; TEXAS INSTRUMENTS INC 01oct1953 31dec2015; PHILCO CORP 25nov1940 12dec1961; RAYTHEON MANUFACTURING CO 15sep1952 01may1959; RAY-THEON CO 04may1959 31dec2015; FAIRCHILD CAMERA & INSTR CORP 23oct1961 19jun1979; SONY CORP 17sep1970 31dec2015; NATIONAL SEMICON-DUCTOR CORP 20oct1970 26sep2011; FAIRCHILD SEMICONDUCTOR INTL INC 04aug1999 31dec2015
Color television	CRSP	*See* Television
Basic oxygen process	Standard & Poor's, Steel	
Wankel motor	CRSP	GENERAL MOTORS CORP 31dec1925 01jun2009; CURTISS WRIGHT CORP 22aug1929 31dec2015
Telephone	Boston Globe	Bell Telephone 22oct1881 06oct1889
Internal combustion	Cowles, Automobiles & Trucks, Series C, p. 240	
Rayon	Cowles, Rayon, Series C, p. 264	
Xerography	CRSP	XEROX CORP 11jul1961 31dec2015
Jet engine	Standard Statistics, Aerospace	

(continued)

TABLE A.3 *(continued)*

Technology	Source	Included firms for author-created indices with dates of inclusion
Assembly line	Cowles, Automobiles & Trucks, Series C, p. 240	
AM radio	Cowles, Radio, Phonograph & Musical Instruments, Series C, p. 259	
Aviation	Cowles, Airplane, Series C, p. 257	
Transistor	CRSP	AMERICAN TELEPHONE & TELEG CO 31dec1925 20apr1994; A T & T CORP 21apr1994 21nov2005; GENERAL ELECTRIC CO 31dec1925 31dec2015; INTERNATIONAL BUSINESS MACHS COR 31dec1925 31dec2015; AMERICAN TYPE FOUNDERS CO 31dec1925 16may1936; AMERICAN TYPE FOUNDERS INC 18may1936 27jun1946; A T F INC 28jun1946 05feb1951; DAYSTROM INC 06feb1951 01feb1962; SCHLUMBERGER LTD 02feb1962 31dec2015; TEXAS INSTRUMENTS INC 01oct1953 31dec2015; PHILCO CORP 25nov1940 12dec1961; RAYTHEON MANUFACTURING CO 15sep1952 01may1959; RAYTHEON CO 04may1959 31dec2015; FAIRCHILD CAMERA & INSTR CORP 23oct1961 19jun1979; SONY CORP 17sep1970 31dec2015; NATIONAL SEMICONDUCTOR CORP 20oct1970 26sep2011; FAIRCHILD SEMICONDUCTOR INTL INC 04aug1999 31dec2015

Wharton 30

Bar codes	CRSP	INTERFACE MECHANISMS 14aug1978 09jul1982; INTERMEC CORP 12jul1982 10sep1991; SYMBOL TECHNOLOGIES INC 04jun1979 10jan2007; TELXON CORP 21jul1983 04dec2000; ZEBRA TECHNOLOGIES CORP 15aug1991 29dec2017

Microprocessors	CRSP	ADVANCED MICRO DEVICES INC 14dec1972 29dec2017; CYRIX CORP 16jul1993 18nov1997; DIGITAL EQUIPMENT CORP 14nov1966 12jun1998; INTEL CORP 14dec1972 29dec2017; NATIONAL SEMICONDUCTOR CORP 20oct1970 26sep2011; TERADYNE INC 19oct1970 29dec2017; ZILOG INC 27feb1991 02mar1998; ZILOG INC 12mar2004 19feb2010
Genetically modified plants	CRSP	DOW CHEMICAL CO 26jun1937 30dec2016; MONSANTO CO 01apr1964 31mar2000; MONSANTO CO NEW 18oct2000 30dec2016; PHARMACIA CORP 03apr2000 16apr2003; SYNGENTA A G 14nov2000 30dec2016
Biofuels	CRSP	AVENTINE RENEWBL ENRGY HLDGS INC 29jun2006 27mar2009; COMMTRON CORP 08jul1986 19jun1992; DIVERSA CORP 14feb2000 20jun2007; RENEWABLE ENERGY GROUP INC 19jan2012 29dec2017; VERASUN ENERGY CORP 14jun2006 31oct2008; VERENIUM CORP 2 1jun2007 01nov2013
Human genome sequencing	CRSP	APPLERA CORP 30nov2000 01jul2008; APPLIED BIOSYSTEMS INC DEL 01jul2008 24nov2008; CELERA CORP 01jul2008 18may2011; E G & G INC 04apr1966 25oct1999; EDGERTON GERMES & GRIER INC 06jul1965 01apr1966; FOUNDATION MEDICINE INC 25sep2013 30dec2016; HUMAN GENOME SCIENCES INC 02dec1993 03aug2012; ILLUMINA INC 28jul2000 30dec2016; INCYTE CORP 17mar2003 30dec2016; INCYTE GENOMICS INC 15jun2000 14mar2003; INCYTE PHARMACEUTICALS INC 04nov1993 14jun2000; LYNX THERAPEUTICS INC 30dec1997 07mar2005; NATERA INC 02jul2015 30dec2016; P E CORP 28apr1999 29nov2000; PERKIN ELMER CORP 13dec1960 27apr1999; PERKINELMER INC 26oct1999 30dec2016; SEQUENOM INC 01feb2000 07sep2016; SOLEXA INC 08mar2005 29jan2007
GPS	CRSP	GARMIN LTD 08dec2000 30dec2016; TRIMBLE INC 03oct2016 30dec2016; TRIMBLE NAVIGATION LTD 20jul1990 30sep2016

(continued)

TABLE A.3 *(continued)*

Technology	Source	Included firms for author-created indices with dates of inclusion
Photovoltaics	CRSP	ASCENT SOLAR TECHNOLOGIES INC 10aug2006 24feb2016; CANADIAN SOLAR INC 09nov2006 30dec2016; CHINA SUNERGY CO LTD 17may2007 11mar2016; DAYSTAR TECHNOLOGIES INC 22mar2004 11apr2013; FIRST SOLAR INC 17nov2006 30dec2016; HANWHA Q CELLS CO LTD 09feb2015 30dec2016; HANWHA SOLARONE CO LTD 15feb2011 06feb2015; J A SOLAR-HOLDINGS CO LTD 07feb2007 30dec2016; L D K SOLAR CO LTD 01jun2007 21feb2014; RENESOLA LTD 29jan2008 30dec2016; SOLAR3D INC 04mar2015 29feb2016; SOLARCITY CORP 13dec2012 21nov2016; SOLARFUN POWER HOLDINGS CO LTD 20dec2006 14feb2011; SUNPOWER CORP 17nov2005 30dec2016; SUNRUN INC 05aug2015 30dec2016; SUNTECH POWER HOLD-INGS CO LTD 14dec2005 08nov2013; SUNWORKS INC 01mar2016 30dec2016; TRINA SOLAR LIMITED 19dec2006 30dec2016; VIVINT SOLAR INC 01oct2014 30dec2016; YINGLI GREEN ENERGY HLDG CO LTD 08jun2007 30dec2016
Mobile phones	Standard & Poor's, subindex Wireless Communication Services 50102010	ERICSSON 27feb2012 29dec2017; ERICSSON L M TELEPHONE CO 14dec1972 24feb2012; FLEET CALL INC 28jan1992 22jul1993; METROPCS COMMUNI-CATIONS INC 19apr2007 30apr2013; NEXTEL; COMMUNICATIONS INC 23jul1993 15aug2005; NOKIA CORP 24apr1995 29dec2017; QUALCOMM INC 13dec1991 29dec2017; RACAL TELECOM PLC 27oct1988 13sep1991; SPRINT CORP 27feb1992 12aug2005; SPRINT CORP NEW 12jul2013 29dec2017; SPRINT NEXTEL CORP 15aug2005 11jul2013; T MOBILE U S INC 01may2013 29dec2017; UNITED TELECOMMUNICATIONS INC 05jun1972 26feb1992; UNITED UTILI-TIES INC 10apr1963 02jun1972; VODAFONE GROUP PLC 16sep1991 28jul2000; VODAFONE GROUP PLC NEW 31jul2000 29dec2017
PCs	CRSP	ALTAIR CORP 29dec1972 31dec2013; APPLE COMPUTER 31dec1980 29dec2006; APPLE INC 31jan2007 31dec2013; ATARI CORP 28nov1986 28jun1996; COMMO-DORE BUSINE 31may1974 30jul1976; COMMODORE INTERN 31aug1976

		29apr1994; COMPAQ COMPUTER, 30dec1983 31may2002; DELL COMPUTER CO 30jun1988 30jun2003; DELL INC | 31jul2003 31oct2013; DIGITAL EQUIPMENT 30nov1966 30jun1998; GATEWAY 2000 INC 31dec1993 28may1999; GATEWAY INC 30jun1999 31oct2007; J T S CORP 31jul1996 29may1998; PRIME COMPUTER I 29mar1974 31jan1990; SILICON GRAPHICS 31oct1986 30nov2005; SUN MICROSYSTEMS 31mar1986 29jan2010
Office software	CRSP	ALDUS CORP 16jun1987 01sep1994; ASHTON TATE 30nov1983 14oct1991; LOTUS DEVELOPMENT CORP 06oct1983 06jul1995; MICROSOFT CORP 13mar1986 29dec2017; SOFTWARE PUBLISHING CORP 15nov1984 30dec1996
Media file compression	CRSP	24 7 MEDIA INC 14aug1998 07dec2001; 24 7 REAL MEDIA INC 10dec2001 13jul2007; ARTISTDIRECT INC 28mar2000 09may2003; AUDIBLE INC 16jul1999 19mar2008; BROADCAST COM INC 17jul1998 21jul1999; BROADVISION INC 21jun1996 30dec2016; DIGITAL RIVER INC 11aug1998 13feb2015; FLYCAST COMMUNICATIONS CORP 04may1999 14jan2000; GREAT ELM CAPITAL GROUP INC 17jun2016 30dec2016; IBEAM BROADCASTING CORP 18may2000 15nov2001; INTERACTIVE PICTURES CORP 05aug1999 20jan2000; LAUNCH MEDIA INC 23apr1999 14aug2001; LIQUID AUDIO INC 09jul1999 05jun2003; M P 3 COM INC 2 1jul1999 28aug2001; MUSICMAKER COM INC 07jul1999 27aug2001; NET2PHONE INC 29jul1999 14mar2006; NETRADIO CORP 14oct1999 19oct2001; OPENWAVE SYSTEMS INC 20nov2000 08may2012; OP-TIKA IMAGING SYSTEMS INC 26jul1996 08dec1998; OPTIKA INC 09dec1998 01jun2004; P C TEL INC 19oct1999 30dec2016; PHONE COM INC 11jun1999 17nov2000; PINNACOR INC 01nov2002 20jan2004; QUOKKA SPORTS INC 28jul1999 18may2001; REALNETWORKS INC 21nov1997 30dec2016; SCREAM-INGMEDIA INC 03aug2000 31oct2002; SPORTSLINE COM INC 22nov1999 13dec2004; SPORTSLINE USA INC 13nov1997 19nov1999; STARMEDIA NET-WORK INC 26may1999 01feb2002' STREAMLINE COM 18jun1999 01dec2000; SUNRISE TELECOM INC 13jul2000 16dec2005; UNWIRED PLANET INC 09may2012 16jun2016; WEBEX COMMUNICATIONS INC 28jul2000 29may2007

(continued)

TABLE A.3 (*continued*)

Technology	Source	Included firms for author-created indices with dates of inclusion
Social networking	CRSP	CHANGYOU COM LTD 02apr2009 29dec2017; FACEBOOK INC 18may2012 29dec2017; JIVE SOFTWARE INC 13dec2011 12jun2017; LINKEDIN CORP 19may2011 08dec2016; MATCH GROUP INC 19nov2015 29dec2017; MEETME INC 05jun2012 07apr2017; MOMO INC 11dec2014 29dec2017; PROFESSIONAL DIVERSITY NETWK INC 05mar2013 29dec2017; RENREN INC 04may2011 29dec2017; SPARK NETWORKS INC 09jul2007 03nov2017; SPARK NETWORKS PLC 14feb2006 09jul2007; THE MEET GROUP INC 10apr2017 29dec2017; TWITTER INC 07nov2013 29dec2017; Y Y INC 21nov2012 29dec2017; ZYNGA INC 16dec2011 29dec2017
Internet	CRSP	~800 firms
Online shopping	CRSP	~400 firms
MRI	CRSP	FONAR CORP 29oct1981 29dec2017
Open-source software	CRSP	GEEKNET INC 06nov2009 17jul2015; RED HAT INC 11aug1999 29dec2017; SOURCEFORGE INC 24may2007 05nov2009; V A LINUX SYSTEMS INC 09dec1999 05dec2001; V A SOFTWARE CORP 06dec2001 23may2007

Sources: Alfred Cowles 3rd, *Common-Stock Indices*, 2nd ed. (Bloomington, IN: Principia Press, 1939); *Standard & Poor's Statistical Service* (New York: Standard and Poor's Corporation, 1962). CRSP: Calculated (or derived) based on data from CRSP US Stock Database © 2016 Center for Research in Security Prices (CRSP), The University of Chicago Booth School of Business.

NOTES

Introduction

1. Robert J. Shiller, *Irrational Exuberance* (Crown Publishers, 2006). Toys "R" Us declared bankruptcy in March 2018 after failing to successfully compete in a transformed retail space. The failure of Toys "R" Us is attributed to increased competition not from specialized retailers such as eToys, but rather from general retailers such as Walmart and Amazon.

2. Erick Schonfeld, "How Much Are Your Eyeballs Worth? Placing a Value on a Website's Customers May Be the Best Way to Judge a Net Stock. It's Not Perfect, but on the Net, What Is?" *Fortune*, February 21, 2000, http://archive.fortune .com/magazines/fortune/fortune_archive/2000/02/21/273860/index.htm. See also Brett M. Trueman, M. H. Franco Wong, and Xiao-Jun Zhang, "The Eyeballs Have It: Searching for the Value in Internet Stocks," *Journal of Accounting Research* 38 (2000): 137–62.

3. Heather Green, "The Great Yuletide Shakeout," *Businessweek*, November 1, 1999, 22.

4. Michael Sokolove, "How to Lose $850 Million—and Not Really Care," *New York Times*, June 9, 2002; Erin Kelly, "The Last E-Store on the Block: Toby Lenk's Toy Shop May Be the Best-Run Specialty Store on the Web, Which Raises a Question: If eToys Can't Make Money Online, Can Anyone?" *Fortune*, September 18, 2000, http://archive.fortune.com/magazines/fortune/fortune_archive/2000/ 09/18/287719/index.htm.

5. Kelly, "Last E-Store on the Block."

6. Kelly, "Last E-Store on the Block"; "eToys to Shut Down Web Site March 8," CNN, February 26, 2001, http://cnnfn.cnn.com/2001/02/26/companies/etoys/.

7. To see how powerful narratives can be in driving capitalist activity, consider that Amazon.com has sustained a price-to-equity ratio of 200 for more than 20 years, with profit margins hovering near 1%, one-quarter that of grocery stores. Notwithstanding Amazon's modest profitability, its narrative has been wildly successful, so much so that when we hear the adjective *Amazonian*, we often cannot distinguish the river from the firm.

8. Ben Eisen, "Nasdaq Tops Inflation-Adjusted High from Dot-Com Boom," *Wall Street Journal*, January 17, 2018, https://blogs.wsj.com/moneybeat/2018/01/17/nasdaq-poised-to-top-inflation-adjusted-high-from-dot-com-boom.

9. Eli Ofek and Matthew Richardson, "Dotcom Mania: The Rise and Fall of Internet Stock Prices," *Journal of Finance* 58, no. 3 (2003): 1113–38.

10. The contemporaneous and related telecommunications bust happened at the same time. See Ofek and Richardson, "Dotcom Mania"; S. Greenstein, "The Crash in Competitive Telephony," *IEEE Micro* 22, no. 4 (July 2002): 8–9, 88.

11. For a discussion of the British Railway Mania, see Ofek and Richardson, "Dotcom Mania"; Greenstein, "Crash in Competitive Telephony"; Andrew Odlyzko, "Charles Mackay's Own Extraordinary Popular Delusions and the Railway Mania," *SSRN eLibrary*, September 14, 2011, http://papers.ssrn.com/sol3/papers.cfm?abstract_id=1927396. For a discussion of market speculation in the 1960s, see Robert Sobel, *The Last Bull Market: Wall Street in the 1960s* (Norton, 1980).

12. Sobel, *Last Bull Market*; Ofek and Richardson, "Dotcom Mania."

13. Ruth Simon, "Margin Investors Learn the Hard Way That Brokers Can Get Tough on Loans," *Wall Street Journal*, April 27, 2000, C1.

14. Robin Greenwood and Stefan Nagel, "Inexperienced Investors and Bubbles," *Journal of Financial Economics* 93, no. 2 (August 2009): 239–58.

15. Based on author calculations using VentureXpert, June 2008, from Securities Data Company.

16. Brent Goldfarb, Michael D. Pfarrer, and David A. Kirsch, "Searching for Ghosts: Business Survival, Unmeasured Entrepreneurial Activity, and Private Equity Investment in the Dot-Com Era," 2005, https://doi.org/10.2139/ssrn.825687.

17. It was not true that no one was making money. Like those selling the tools to miners during the gold rush, firms that relied on business models from the old economy did quite well. For example, purveyors such as the web development firm Scient, network infrastructure firm Cisco, Wall Street investment houses that earned a cut from IPOs, and commercial real estate agents all did quite well—at least for a time.

18. Of course, that would not be enough, either. What if owners who feed their horses more oats and grains than vegetables also live in more northern climates, and the colder weather there enhances their horses' performance? Absent the ability to run a controlled experiment, we can look for other clues. For example, can we measure greater metabolic efficiency in the horses' muscles and relate this to diet? Does variation in the diet of individual horses change their speed when training? We ask these types of secondary questions in this book as well.

19. Ours is the first to develop a rich historical and institutional narrative to study intermarket variation in the formation of bubbles. Some statistical studies

do exploit intermarket variation to identify antecedents: e.g., Gerard Hoberg and Gordon Phillips, "Real and Financial Industry Booms and Busts," *Journal of Finance* 65, no. 1 (February 1, 2010): 45–86; and Matthew Rhodes-Kropf, David Robinson, and S. Viswanathan, "Valuation Waves and Merger Activity: The Empirical Evidence," *Journal of Financial Economics* 77 (2005): 561–603.

20. Christopher Freeman, *Long Waves in the World Economy* (F. Pinter, 1984).

21. S. F. LeRoy, "Rational Exuberance," *Journal of Economic Literature* 42, no. 3 (2004): 783–804.

22. Fred R. Shapiro, *The Yale Book of Quotations* (Yale University Press, 2006).

23. Luboš Pástor and Pietro Veronesi, "Was There a Nasdaq Bubble in the Late 1990s?," *Journal of Financial Economics* 81, no. 1 (July 2006): 61–100.

24. Lubos Pastor and Pietro Veronesi, "Learning in Financial Markets," *Annual Review of Financial Economics* 1, no. 1 (2009): 361–81; Andrea Devenow and Ivo Welch, "Rational Herding in Financial Economics," *European Economic Review* 403 (1996): 603–15; B. Goldfarb, D. Kirsch, and D. A. Miller, "Was There Too Little Entry During the Dot Com Era?" *Journal of Financial Economics* 86 (2007): 100–144.

25. Adherents to the efficient markets hypothesis suggest that boom and bust episodes can be explained in ways that are consistent with rational behavior. We consider this idea in Chapter 2.

26. We follow C. Zott and R. Amit, "Business Model Design and the Performance of Entrepreneurial Firms," *Organization Science* (2007): 181, http://pubsonline.informs.org/doi/abs/10.1287/orsc.1060.0232, in which a business model is defined as "the content, structure, and governance of transactions designed so as to create value through the exploitation of business opportunities."

27. Similar phenomena are observed in technology prize competitions, where cash prizes are able to elicit aggregate investments that appear to be above the total prize amounts. Kevin J. Boudreau, Nicola Lacetera, and Karim R. Lakhani, "Incentives and Problem Uncertainty in Innovation Contests: An Empirical Analysis," *Management Science* 57, no. 5 (April 1, 2011): 843–63.

28. Gleason Leonard Archer, *History of Radio to 1926* (Arno Press, 1971).

29. See Charles Bazerman, *The Languages of Edison's Light* (MIT Press, 1999); "The Electric Light," *New York Times*, April 22, 1878.

30. "Curious Features of the Electric Lighting Business," *Scientific American* 53, no. 15 (October 10, 1885).

31. From the perspective of a financial economist, this uncertainty can be thought of as the variance surrounding the expected returns to the innovation, although in some cases, such factors affect the mean as well.

32. The option value also decreases with the elimination of competitive uncertainty (although this might be counteracted by an increase in the expected value).

33. Christopher Beauchamp, "Who Invented the Telephone? Lawyers, Patents, and the Judgments of History," *Technology and Culture* 51, no. 4 (2010): 854–78.

34. Experimental economists have demonstrated bubbles in the lab when there is no uncertainty in fundamental value but there is uncertainty in what others might be willing to pay for an asset. Vernon L. Smith, Gerry L. Suchanek, and Arlington W. Williams, "Bubbles, Crashes, and Endogenous Expectations in Experimental Spot Asset Markets," *Econometrica: Journal of the Econometric Society* 56, no. 5 (September 1988): 1119.

35. The resolution of business model uncertainty may be closely related to the emergence of a dominant design, a concept first introduced by J. Utterback and W. Abernathy, in "A Dynamic Model of Product and Process Innovation," *Omega* 3 (1975): 638–56.

36. Richard Thomas Stillson, *Spreading the Word: A History of Information in the California Gold Rush* (University of Nebraska Press, 2006).

37. Mary O'Sullivan, "The Expansion of the US Stock Market, 1885–1930: Historical Facts and Theoretical Fashions," *Enterprise and Society* 8, no. 3 (2007): 489–542; Goldfarb, Kirsch, and Miller, "Was There Too Little Entry?"

38. Charles Mackay, *Memoirs of Extraordinary Popular Delusions and the Madness of Crowds*, 2nd ed., vol. 1 (1841; Office of the National Illustrated Library, 1852).

39. See J. Bradford De Long, Andrei Shleifer, Lawrence H. Summers, and Robert J. Waldmann, "Noise Trader Risk in Financial Markets," *Journal of Political Economy* 98 (1990): 703–38. While many models rely on restrictions of short selling to limit the ability of rational traders to sell overvalued stocks, more recent work suggests that some sophisticated traders who possess "strategic IQ" may be better than others at anticipating novice irrationality, then buy overvalued stocks with the expectation of selling them. Sheen S. Levine, Evan P. Apfelbaum, Mark Bernard, Valerie L. Bartelt, Edward J. Zajac, and David Stark, "Ethnic Diversity Deflates Price Bubbles," *Proceedings of the National Academy of Sciences of the United States of America* 111, no. 52 (December 30, 2014): 18524–29, examine how the diversity of market participants can attenuate bubbles. See also Brad M. Barber and Terrance Odean, "All That Glitters: The Effect of Attention and News on the Buying Behavior of Individual and Institutional Investors," *Review of Financial Studies* 21, no. 2 (April 1, 2008): 785–818.

40. We think of novices broadly: they may be new to investing, or alternatively, they may be new to a particular investment environment or asset class and overestimate similarities between investment environments or asset classes they understand and those they do not. To wit, we do not predict that investors with experiences in a new class of assets that is substantially similar to another in which they are experienced will exhibit investor sentiment. For example, biotechnology investors investing in nanotechnology may behave rationally. Instead, we suggest

that the key insight that allows investors to avoid sentimentality is an understanding of what they do not understand about particular assets. Savvy investors understand what they know and what they do not know and make decisions accordingly. Less savvy investors fail to understand what they do not know and are in this sense over-confident. Such investors may mistakenly make analogies between particular asset classes, which may lead to more pricing errors.

41. There are, of course, exceptions to this, as in the case of electronics firms that served the growing military industrial complex. We note in our discussion of the transistor that Sputnik may have been a coordinating event.

42. Gur Huberman, "Familiarity Breeds Investment," *Review of Financial Studies* 14, no. 3 (July 1, 2001): 659–80; R. Zeckhauser, "Investing in the Unknown and Unknowable," *Capitalism and Society* 1, no. 2 (2006): 5.

43. It may also manifest in heterogeneity in beliefs across investor classes. Different information sets can be attributable to information asymmetry. For example, some investors may have access to insider information before it is available more generally. A strong argument can be made that this was of significant importance in explaining the bubble in the gold market that led to Black Friday on September 24, 1869. Charles Poor Kindleberger and Robert Z. Aliber, *Manias, Panics, and Crashes: A History of Financial Crises* (John Wiley & Sons, 2005). Others have linked the crash of dot-com stocks to the expiration of lock-up provisions of insiders (Ofek and Richardson, "Dotcom Mania"), although this has been more recently challenged (LeRoy, "Rational Exuberance"). Conceptually, the presence of novice or unsophisticated investors may be thought of as increasing the mean expected return for a given innovation because expected returns of the more naïve investors are biased.

44. Carolyn Marvin, *When Old Technologies Were New: Thinking About Electric Communication in the Late Nineteenth Century* (Oxford University Press, 1990); Wolfgang Schivelbusch, *Disenchanted Night: The Industrialization of Light in the Nineteenth Century* (University of California Press, 1995).

45. Naomi R. Lamoreaux, Margaret C. Levenstein, and Kenneth Lee Sokoloff, "Financing Invention During the Second Industrial Revolution: Cleveland, Ohio, 1870–1920," in *Financing Innovation in the United States, 1870 to the Present*, ed. Naomi R. Lamoreaux and Kenneth Lee Sokoloff (MIT Press), 50.

46. Lamoreaux, Levenstein, and Sokoloff, "Financing Invention During the Second Industrial Revolution," 50, 57.

47. Lamoreaux, Levenstein, and Sokoloff, "Financing Invention During the Second Industrial Revolution," 57. The lack of liquidity for assets in the market for early electric company assets is striking: "Completely missing from the [description of financing of new electric ventures] is any formal role for formal financial institutions in the founding of the original Brush Electric Company or the many

startups and spin-offs that came out of [the] Brush cluster. The entrepreneurs who organized and promoted these new ventures secured investment capital largely by relying on personal connections. These could be familial, as when the father of Eugene and Alfred Cowles provided much of the initial capital for the Cowles Electric Smelting and Aluminum Company; they could result from friendships, as when George Stockly agreed to support Brush's initial work in electrical lighting; or they could be based on the recommendations of men who had established their expertise in the community, as when Brush secured backing for the Linde Air Products Company simply by assuring local businessmen of the merits of the technology. Association with a hub enterprise such as Brush could in and of itself be a means of attracting both attention and funds. Thus, Bentley and Knight, as well as Short, were able to use their very visible association with Brush to raise local capital for their streetcar companies." Lamoreaux, Levenstein, and Sokoloff, "Financing Invention During the Second Industrial Revolution," 56–57.

48. Lamoreaux, Levenstein, and Sokoloff, "Financing Invention During the Second Industrial Revolution," 50.

49. See Ranald C. Michie, "The London and New York Stock Exchanges, 1850–1914," *Journal of Economic History* 46, no. 1 (March 1, 1986): 171–87. While there may have been a speculative episode on the Curb or Consolidated exchanges in New York, it was underdeveloped during this period, and we have found no evidence in the historical literature of such an event. These exchanges were outdoor, unregulated markets that traded in less established securities. The Consolidated Exchange folded, and the Curb moved indoors in 1922, becoming the American Stock Exchange in the 1950s. Robert Sobel, *The Curbstone Brokers: The Origins of the American Stock Exchange* (Beard Books, 2000).

50. Thomas Parke Hughes, "British Electrical Industry Lag: 1882–1888," *Technology and Culture* 3 (1962): 27–44.

51. Goldfarb, Kirsch, and Miller, "Was There Too Little Entry?"

52. Robert J. Shiller, "Narrative Economics," *American Economic Review* 107, no. 4 (2017): 967–1004.

Chapter 1

1. While it is not disputed that Tulip prices collapsed in this way, it is disputed whether there were many, if any, transactions completed at these asking prices. See Peter M. Garber, "Famous First Bubbles," *Journal of Economic Perspectives: A Journal of the American Economic Association* 4 (1990): 35–54; Earl A. Thompson, "The Tulipmania: Fact or Artifact?," *Public Choice* 130 (2007): 99–114. On the Beanie Baby Bubble, see Zac Bissonnette, *The Great Beanie Baby Bubble: Mass Delusion and the Dark Side of Cute* (Portfolio, 2015).

2. Alternatively, "rational" bubbles occur when investors understand that the asset is overvalued, but also believe that others will purchase the asset at an inflated

price. Thus, it is rational to buy, since a profit will be made by selling to some "greater fool." Financial economists use various strategies to determine if prices at a particular point in time actually reflected future profits (measured after the fact). This strategy has two shortcomings. First, beliefs may have been well informed but wrong. Or beliefs may have been crazy but right.

3. Bubbles unfold over time. While we have recently witnessed the rise of so-called "flash crashes," these are a new phenomenon and likely differ in fundamental ways from the larger, macro-economic events in which we are interested. Stock bubbles expand (or to keep the metaphor precise, "inflate") over time as more and more investors (a) become aware of the existence of a new investment opportunity and (b) decide to invest in it.

4. Bissonnette, *Great Beanie Baby Bubble*, chap. 3.

5. J. W. Stehman, *The Financial History of the American Telephone and Telegraph Company* (Houghton Mifflin, 1925).

6. Overall, the 2,000 shares yielded $430,000 for the National Bell treasury. The implied average price of $215 per share was well in excess of par; see Stehman, *Financial History of the American Telephone and Telegraph Company*.

7. Stehman (*Financial History of the American Telephone and Telegraph Company*, 19) observes that "the $600 per share paid for last 500 shares of the National Bell's stock was probably the highest price at which any considerable amount of the stock changed hands."

8. Stehman, *Financial History of the American Telephone and Telegraph Company*, 19.

9. Average annual earnings were $347 in 1880. Clarence D. Long, "Wages and Earnings in the United States, 1860–1890," *NBER Books*, 1960, https://ideas.repec.org/b/nbr/nberbk/long60-1.html.

10. Claude S. Fischer, *America Calling: A Social History of the Telephone to 1940* (University of California Press, 1994). 41.

11. Christopher Beauchamp, "Who Invented the Telephone? Lawyers, Patents, and the Judgments of History," *Technology and Culture* 51, no. 4 (2010): 854–78.

12. Michael Bliss, "Who Discovered Insulin?," *Physiology*, February 1, 1986, https://doi.org/10.1152/physiologyonline.1986.1.1.31.

13. Receiving the Nobel Prize within such a short time of having made a fundamental scientific discovery underscores how unique insulin was. Typically, such prizes are awarded 10 and even 20 years after the initial discovery. See Francesco Becattini et al., "The Nobel Prize Delay," *arXiv* [physics.soc-Ph], May 28, 2014, arXiv, http://arxiv.org/abs/1405.7136.

14. "TWO IMPORTANT CURES ANNOUNCED: New Insulin Treatment Reported Used with Success in Case of Diabetic Coma," *New York Times*, December 6, 1922, p. 17.

15. Michael Bliss, *The Discovery of Insulin* (University of Chicago Press, 2013), 174–75.

16. Susan J. Douglas, "Early Radio," in *Communications in History: Technology, Culture, Society*, ed. David Crowley and Paul Heyer (Routledge, 2015), 210–17.

17. E. Barnouw, *A History of Broadcasting in the United States*, vol. 1, *A Tower in Babel* (Oxford University Press, 1966), 99–105.

18. The federal government nationalized all radio patents as part of the war effort during World War I. RCA was created as part of an agreement between General Electric and the government after the war.

19. Barnouw, *History of Broadcasting in the United States*, 1:81, 117.

20. Steven Klepper and Kenneth L. Simons, "Dominance by Birthright: Entry of Prior Radio Producers and Competitive Ramifications in the U.S. Television Receiver Industry," *Strategic Management Journal* 21, nos. 10–11 (2000): 997–1016.

21. Frothiness is similar to volatility, used by financial professionals, except that it is a retrospective measure based on future and past price movements.

22. To operationalize this, when we consider the trend, we need to think about how far into the future we should look to consider the trend. We use a seven-year time frame in this analysis, although our results do not change if we use shorter frames. The time frame has to be long enough to pick up the underlying trend otherwise the boom and bust will dominate, but not too long because the future needs to be discounted. To implement our procedure, we calculate the time trend at every point in time looking backwards in time and forwards in time up to 84 months (seven years), if available. Very early in industries we may not observe a full 84 months looking backward. The data and Stata code used for these calculations are available online.

23. From Alfred Cowles III, *Common-Stock Indexes*, 2nd ed. (Principia Press, 1939), and authors' calculations. This index includes general rubber goods. However, the vast majority of rubber during the period was used in the manufacture of automobile tires.

24. This biased sampling was what Charles Kindleberger did in his classic study of the history of bubbles: *Manias, Panics, and Crashes: A History of Financial Crises*, 5th ed. (John Wiley & Sons, 2005). At the time, Kindleberger had identified an important, underappreciated economic phenomenon, and sampling strategy was a luxury he could not afford. Thirty-five years later, we can do better.

25. The theory, though intuitive, has been difficult to empirically validate. See C. Perez, *Technological Revolutions and Financial Capital* (Edward Elgar Publishing, 2003). This strategy for understanding growth proved a dead end, mostly because it ignored the high level of interdependencies between technologies, as well as the role of business in developing and diffusing new innovations. Thus, although it was possible to follow the role of an innovation or technology within the context of an industry study, because of these interdependencies it was much more difficult to tie specific industries or even groups of industries to macroeconomic events such as aggregate growth and the business cycle. These general ideas have been super-

seded by a literature that studies "general purpose technologies." See T. F. Bresna-han and M. Trajtenberg, "General Purpose Technologies: 'Engines of Growth'?" *Journal of Econometrics* (1995): http://www.sciencedirect.com/science/article/pii/030440769401598T.

26. Mea culpa. We, too, have sampled on bubbles and made claims as to their causes: B. Goldfarb, D. Kirsch, and D. A. Miller, "Was There Too Little Entry During the Dot Com Era?," *Journal of Financial Economics* 86 (2007): 100–144.

27. Christopher Freeman, *Long Waves in the World Economy* (F. Pinter, 1984).

28. J. J. Van Duijn, "Fluctuations in Innovations Overtime," *Futures* 13, no. 4 (1981): 264–75; A. Kleinknecht, "Observations on the Schumpeterian Swarm-ing of Innovations* 1," *Futures* 13, no. 4 (1981): 293–307; J. Clark, C. Freeman, and L. Soete, "Long Waves, Inventions, and Innovations," *Futures* 13, no. 4 (1981): 308–22.

29. A potential solution to the problem of isolating the role of a particular event on stock prices in large, diversified firms is an event history methodology. Isolated events hypothesized to affect stock prices are identified, and short-term prices are measured to see if they fluctuate after the time of the event. Given the nature of our theory and the long-term patterns we seek to identify, this method-ology would not allow us to measure the effect of new technologies on long-term price trends.

30. In particular, we searched a set of eight newspapers that were continually published throughout our sample period for the name of the technology together with the words *stock* or *share* (singular or plural) and the word *speculate* or any of its derivatives beginning with the character string *speculat**. Details of this exercise are available in our online Appendix.

31. David A. Hounshell, *From the American System to Mass Production, 1800–1932* (Johns Hopkins University Press, 1984).

32. Steven Klepper, *Experimental Capitalism: The Nanoeconomics of American High-Tech Industries* (Princeton University Press, 2015); Hounshell, *From the American System to Mass Production*; Brent Goldfarb, "Three Essays in Technological Change" (PhD diss., Stanford University, 2002).

33. William Rupert Maclaurin, *Invention & Innovation in the Radio Industry* (Mac-millan, 1949); Mary O'Sullivan, "Funding New Industries: A Historical Perspec-tive on the Financing Role of the U.S. Stock Market in the Twentieth Century," in *Financing Innovation in the United States, 1870 to the Present*, ed. Naomi R. Lamoreaux and Kenneth L. Sokoloff (MIT Press, 2007), 162–216.

34. The curb market data demonstrate that in May 1926 investors experi-enced a 90% decline when it was realized that few radio ventures would ever make a profit (RCA fared better). The IPO window closed for radio stocks until February 1928, after which an additional twenty-five firms raised almost $40 million primar-ily to roll up existing firms. The window again closed in September 1929.

Chapter 2

1. There were a few, high-profile demonstrations recounted in news reports, but for most people, the "original media spectacle" was their first experience with electric lights; see Carolyn Marvin, *When Old Technologies Were New: Thinking About Electric Communication in the Late Nineteenth Century* (Oxford University Press, 1990); Wolfgang Schivelbusch, *Disenchanted Night: The Industrialization of Light in the Nineteenth Century* (University of California Press, 1995).

2. Limited liability is part of modern corporate law. It means that shareholders cannot be sued by debtors for the value of their personal possessions. Before the rise of modern capitalism and the corporations, merchants were personally liable for their business debts and could be sent to "debtors" prison if they failed to pay them. Some professions today retain personal liability in organizational structures, although debtors' prisons have been superseded by personal bankruptcy proceedings in current law. Understanding the role of limited downside and unlimited upside in the pricing of options led to the joint Nobel Prize for Robert Merton and Myron Scholes. Presumptive corecipient and collaborator Fischer Black died before the prize was awarded in 1997.

3. For a wonderful, accessible description of the central role of narratives in decision making, and the biases that often appear with their use, see Daniel Kahneman, *Thinking, Fast and Slow* (Macmillan, 2011), in particular chap. 19, "The Illusion of Understanding."

4. Robert J. Shiller, "Narrative Economics," *American Economic Review* 107, no. 4 (2017): 967–1004.

5. Ellen O'Connor, "Storytelling to Be Real: Narrative, Legitimacy Building and Venturing," in *Narrative and Discursive Approaches in Entrepreneurship: A Second Movements in Entrepreneurship Book*, ed. Daniel Hjorth (Edward Elgar, 2004), 105–24. More recently, Raghu Garud and his coauthors have reintroduced this approach to strategy and entrepreneurship scholars. See Raghu Garud, Henri A. Schildt, and Theresa K. Lant, "Entrepreneurial Storytelling, Future Expectations, and the Paradox of Legitimacy," *Organization Science* 25, no. 5 (May 30, 2014): 1479–92.

6. Martin L. Martens, Jennifer E. Jennings, and P. Devereaux Jennings, "Do the Stories They Tell Get Them the Money They Need? The Role of Entrepreneurial Narratives in Resource Acquisition," *Academy of Management Journal. Academy of Management* 50, no. 5 (2007): 1109. "Technological narratives" is a term first introduced in John M. Staudenmaier, "Rationality, Agency, Contingency: Recent Trends in the History of Technology," *Reviews in American History* 30, no. 1 (2002): 168–81.

7. Harro van Lente, "Navigating Foresight in a Sea of Expectations: Lessons from the Sociology of Expectations," *Technology Analysis & Strategic Management* 24, no. 8 (2012): 772; Jens Beckert, in *Imagined Futures* (Harvard University Press, 2016),

10, describes how "fictional expectations take a narrative form and become articulated as stories that tell how the future will look and how the economy will unfold into the future."

8. Alex Preda, "The Sociological Approach to Financial Markets," *Journal of Economic Surveys* 21, no. 3 (July 2007): 506–33; Michel Callon, "Introduction: The Embeddedness of Economic Markets in Economics," *Sociological Review* 46, no. S1 (May 1, 1998): 1–57; Robert K. Merton, "The Self-Fulfilling Prophecy," *Antioch Review* 8, no. 2 (1948): 193–210.

9. Kahneman, *Thinking, Fast and Slow*, 200.

10. Frans Berkhout, "Normative Expectations in Systems Innovation," *Technology Analysis & Strategic Management* 18, nos. 3–4 (July 2006): 299–311.

11. Timothy G. Pollock, Violina P. Rindova, and Patrick Maggitti, "Market Watch: Information and Availability Cascades among the Media and Investors in the US IPO Market," *Academy of Management Journal* 51, no. 2 (2008): 335–58.

12. Kahneman, *Thinking, Fast and Slow*, 201.

13. Violina P. Rindova and Antoaneta P. Petkova, "When Is a New Thing a Good Thing? Technological Change, Product Form Design, and Perceptions of Value for Product Innovations," *Organization Science* 18, no. 2 (2007): 217–32.

14. van Lente, "Navigating Foresight in a Sea of Expectations," 775.

15. van Lente, "Navigating Foresight in a Sea of Expectations."

16. James G. March, "The Future, Disposable Organizations and the Rigidities of Imagination," *Organization* 2, nos. 3–4 (1995): 437.

17. Malcolm J. Abzug and E. Eugene Larrabee, *Airplane Stability and Control*, vol. 14 of *A History of the Technologies That Made Aviation Possible* (Cambridge University Press, 2005).

18. Mary O'Sullivan, "Funding New Industries: A Historical Perspective on the Financing Role of the U.S. Stock Market in the Twentieth Century," in *Financing Innovation in the United States, 1870 to the Present*, ed. Naomi R. Lamoreaux and Kenneth L. Sokoloff (MIT Press, 2007), 183.

19. "Aviation and Investment," *Wall Street Journal*, June 26, 1928.

20. "Highlights and Sidelights in Aviation's March of Progress Throughout World: AVIATION USED AS STOCK BAIT Leaders of Industry Join to Stop Exploitation Fake Schemes Find Field Fertile for Work Many Good Securities on Financial Market," *Los Angeles Times*, January 20, 1929.

21. "Economic and Aviation Experts Advise Caution in Buying Stocks," *Christian Science Monitor*, September 18, 1928, http://search.proquest.com/docview/512505098.

22. "YOUNG INDUSTRIES DEVELOP RAPIDLY: Airplanes, Rayon, Radio and Other Lines Make Broad Strides During Past Year," *Wall Street Journal*, December 31, 1928.

23. Earle E. Crowe, "ENGINE MAKERS TAKE LEAD: Rival Groups in Aviation Concentrating on Development of New Types; Diesel Experiments Popular," *Los Angeles Times*, May 26, 1929.

24. Brent Goldfarb and David Kirsch, "Time to Commercial Viability in Nascent Industries: A Historical Study," September 30, 2017, https://papers.ssrn .com/sol3/papers.cfm?abstract_id=3049537.

25. O'Sullivan, "Funding New Industries"; Goldfarb and Kirsch, "Time to Commercial Viability in Nascent Industries."

26. Although Wickham was later knighted for his deeds, he never again set foot in Brazil.

27. Rubber history is taken from "The International Natural Rubber Market, 1870–1930," *EH.Net*, ed. Robert Whaples, March 16, 2008, http://eh.net/ encyclopedia/the-international-natural-rubber-market-1870-1930/.

28. Zephyr Frank and Aldo Musacchio, "The International Natural Rubber Market, 1870–1930," *EH.Net*, ed. Robert Whaples, March 16, 2008, https://eh .net/encyclopedia/the-international-natural-rubber-market-1870-1930/. See also Richard T. Stillson, "The Financing of Malayan Rubber, 1905–1923," *Economic History Review* 24, no. 4 (November 1, 1971): 589–98.

29. Wall Streeter and rubber baron Bernard Baruch formed the Intercontinental Rubber Company. By 1905, 19% of American rubber was supplied by the Mexican indigenous plant the *guayule*—although the supply fell into disfavor due to its lower quality.

30. "Auto Tire Prices Will Remain High," *New York Times*, October 1, 1909, 11.

31. "Demand for Rubber: Brazilian Government Has Virtually Cornered the Market," *New York Times*, April 17, 1910, 69.

32. "NO CRUDE RUBBER FAMINE IN SIGHT; British Speculation in Shares and Increased Demand for Auto Tires Influence Price," *New York Times*, May 15, 1910, 40.

33. "RUBBER GOODS GO UP TEN PER CENT MORE; Advance, Following Rise in Raw Materials in London Only One of Many in a Year," *New York Times*, April 21, 1910, 6.

34. Stehman, *Financial History of the American Telephone and Telegraph Company*, 13.

35. Christopher Beauchamp, *Invented by Law: Alexander Graham Bell and the Patent That Changed America* (Harvard University Press, 2015).

36. The more commonly accepted view of this is that entrants are overconfident when they believe their abilities will increase the likelihood of success. There is some evidence that this effect is present only when the probability space over which outcomes realize is ill defined. See Colin Camerer and Dan Lovallo, "Overconfidence and Excess Entry: An Experimental Approach," *American Economic Review* (1999): 306–18; Daniela Grieco and Robin Hogarth, "Excess Entry, Ambiguity Seeking and Competence: An Experimental Investigation" (Econom-

ics Working Papers No. 778, Department of Economics and Business, Universitat Pompeu Fabra, 2004).

37. William Rupert Maclaurin, *Invention & Innovation in the Radio Industry* (Macmillan, 1949), quoted in O'Sullivan, "Funding New Industries."

38. Erik Barnouw, *A History of Broadcasting in the United States*, vol. 1, *A Tower of Babel* (Oxford University Press, 1966), 96–100.

39. See H. H. Cory, "Modern Methods Roll up Big: Radio Sales for Steussy," *Radio Record* 10 (1930): 4–5.

40. Gleason Leonard Archer, *Big Business and Radio* (American Historical Company, 1939), 55–56.

41. In 1929, the effectiveness of broadcast advertising was still being debated; see e.g., "Sales Method Investigation: Experience of 127 Firms with Radio Broadcasting" (Dartnell Corp., 1929).

42. "Bombarded with Energy," *Saturday Evening Post*, December 1, 1929, 81.

43. For a discussion of this episode in the context of financial markets, See Brent Goldfarb, David A. Kirsch, and April Shen, "Financing New Industries," in *Handbook of Entrepreneurial Finance*, ed. Douglas Cumming (Oxford University Press, 2012). See Kirsch (2000) for an in-depth discussion of the early history of electric vehicles.

44. U.S. Census, *Statistical Abstract of the United States, 1990*, 885, table 1439. In 1915 there were twenty-three autos per thousand U.S. population and average household size was about 4.5 individuals (873, table 1419).

45. *Automotive Industries* 37 (4): 604. See also the following for general bewilderment as to differences in stock prices reflected in the press: "Topics on Wall Street," *New York Times*, August 27, 1916, E4.

46. Alfred Cowles III, *Common-Stock Indices*, 2nd ed. (Principia Press, 1939).

47. Quentin R. Skrabec Jr., *Rubber: An American Industrial History* (McFarland, 2013), 95; Steven Klepper and Kenneth L. Simons, "The Making of an Oligopoly: Firm Survival and Technological Change in the Evolution of the U.S. Tire Industry," *Journal of Political Economy* 108, no. 4 (August 1, 2000): 728–60.

Chapter 3

1. Daniel Beunza and Raghu Garud, "Calculators, Lemmings or Frame-Makers? The Intermediary Role of Securities Analysts," *Sociological Review* 55 (October 1, 2007): 13–39.

2. See C. Heath and D. Heath, *Made to Stick: Why Some Ideas Survive and Others Die* (Random House, 2007).

3. National Public Radio's *Planet Money* podcast has an informative series on the oil business. It begins with the episode "Oil #1: We Buy Oil," https://www.npr.org/sections/money/2016/08/10/489457747/oil-1-we-buy-oil.

4. Brad M. Barber, Chip Heath, and Terrance Odean, "Good Reasons Sell: Reason-Based Choice among Group and Individual Investors in the Stock Market," *Management Science* 49, no. 12 (2003): 1636–52.

5. Brad M. Barber and Terrance Odean, in "All That Glitters: The Effect of Attention and News on the Buying Behavior of Individual and Institutional Investors," *Review of Financial Studies* 21, no. 2 (April 1, 2008): 785–818, calculate number imbalance (NI), which is the aggregate number of buy trades of stocks in the top volume decile, less the aggregate number of sell trades over the total number of trades. The ratio is more intuitive, and a rough estimate of this ratio is buys / sells = (1 + NI) / (1 − NI).

6. Attention-based bias can also be traced to Daniel Kahneman and Amos Tversky's early work on the availability heuristic: Tversky and Kahneman, "Availability: A Heuristic for Judging Frequency and Probability," *Cognitive Psychology* 5, no. 2 (1973): 207–32. Underlying these ideas, academic psychologists have identified two fallacies in which individuals fail to recognize the independence of random sequences. The gambler's fallacy suggests that some will believe that there will be a reversion to the mean—ignoring the fact that events may be independently distributed (i.e., the past is not a good predictor of the future). The fallacy's opposite-twin sibling is the hot-hand fallacy—in which immediate past performance is assumed to be predictive of the future. In 1971, Tversky and Kahneman, in "Belief in the Law of Small Numbers," *Psychological Bulletin* 76, no. 2 (1971): 105–10, identified this as the law of small numbers—or the overgeneralization from recent events. In our context, individual events may be overweighted if they are reinforced by unexpected or dramatic news reports, or recent performance. Joseph Johnson and Gerard J. Tellis, in "Blowing Bubbles: Heuristics and Biases in the Run-Up of Stock Prices," *Journal of the Academy of Marketing Science* 33, no. 4 (2005): 486–503, try to understand why mutual funds highlight recent performance in their ads. Their review of the academic literature together with their own experiments suggest that these biases affect markets.

7. Jonah Berger explores the motivations people have to spread ideas in *Contagious: Why Things Catch On* (Simon and Schuster, 2016).

8. Robert J. Shiller's *Irrational Exuberance* (Crown Publishers, 2006) is an important exception in that he describes why certain stories command our attention. Indeed, his thinking influenced this book greatly. For example, he provides a splendid example of the narrative behind the *Mona Lisa*. He does not, however, test his ideas by comparing assets that may or may not develop into stories.

9. "James K. Polk: Fourth Annual Message," December 5, 1848, http://www.presidency.ucsb.edu/ws/index.php?pid=29489.

10. His friend David Gussarsky, to the best of his recollection, held his Isramco shares and lost most of his money. Today, David is a partner at a successful venture capital firm.

11. Moreover, this effect is stronger for inexperienced investors: buying and selling are fundamentally different activities because investors choice set for selling is constrained to what they own, whereas buying is an exercise in choice from a much larger set. See Barber and Odean, "All That Glitters." For this reason, events that focus attention are important determinants of price movements because they "inform" potential buyers as to what to buy. When this focus is driven by random publicity events, we should expect prices to revert to their prepublicity levels. This attention-focus effect is more prevalent among inexperienced investors, as experienced investors are better equipped to make choices from a broad range of potential stocks. Mark S. Seasholes and Guojun Wu, "Predictable Behavior, Profits, and Attention," *Journal of Empirical Finance* 14, no. 5 (December 2007): 590–610; Barber and Odean, "All That Glitters"; Zhi Da, Joseph Engelberg, and Pengjie Gao, "In Search of Attention," *Journal of Finance* 66, no. 5 (October 1, 2011): 1461–99.

12. Gur Huberman, "Familiarity Breeds Investment," *Review of Financial Studies* 14, no. 3 (July 1, 2001): 659–80; Richard Zeckhauser, "Investing in the Unknown and Unknowable," *Capitalism and Society* 1, no. 2 (2006).

13. We think of novices broadly. They may be new to investing. Alternatively, they may be new to a particular investment environment and overestimate similarities between investment environments they understand and those they do not. To wit, we do not predict that investors experiencing a new class of assets that is substantially similar to another in which they are experienced will exhibit investor sentiment. For example, biotechnology investors investing in nanotechnology may behave rationally. Instead, we suggest that the key insight that allows investors to avoid sentimentality is an understanding of what they do not understand about particular assets. That is, savvy investors understand what they know and what they do not know, and make decisions accordingly. Less savvy investors fail to understand what they do not know, and are in this sense, overconfident. Such investors may mistakenly make analogies between particular asset classes, which may lead to more pricing errors.

14. There are, of course, exceptions to this, as in the case of electronics firms that served the growing military industrial complex. Sputnik may have been a coordinating event.

15. Daniel Kahneman, *Thinking, Fast and Slow* (Farrar, Straus & Giroux, 2011).

16. Bertrand Russell, "The Triumph of Stupidity," in *Mortals and Others*, vol. 2 of *American Essays 1931–1935*, ed. Harry Ruja (Routledge, 2009).

17. Dražen Prelec, "A Bayesian Truth Serum for Subjective Data," *Science* 306, no. 5695 (October 15, 2004): 462–66; Dražen Prelec, H. Sebastian Seung, and John McCoy, "Finding Truth Even If the Crowd Is Wrong," 2013, http://seunglab.org/wp-content/uploads/2015/07/FindingTruth16-copy.pdf; Colin Camerer, George Loewenstein, and Dražen Prelec, "Neuroeconomics: How

Neuroscience Can Inform Economics," *Journal of Economic Literature* 43, no. 1 (March 1, 2005): 9–64. For an accessible version of this research, see George Musser, "A Mathematical BS Detector Can Boost the Wisdom of Crowds," *Aeon Essays*, July 6, 2016, https://aeon.co/essays/a-mathematical-bs-detector-can-boost-the-wisdom-of-crowds.

18. J. B. De Long et al., "Noise Trader Risk in Financial Markets," *Journal of Political Economy* 98 (1990): 703–38. An implication is that experts lose money when novices have a strong enough influence on market prices.

19. Ronald R. King et al., "The Robustness of Bubbles and Crashes in Experimental Stock Markets," in *Nonlinear Dynamics and Evolutionary Economics*, ed. Richard Day and Ping (Oxford University Press, 1993), 183–200.

20. Gunduz Caginalp, David Porter, and Vernon L. Smith, "Momentum and Overreaction in Experimental Asset Markets," *International Journal of Industrial Organization* 18 (2000): 187–204; Gunduz Caginalp, David Porter, and Vernon L. Smith, "Overreactions, Momentum, Liquidity, and Price Bubbles in Laboratory and Field Asset Markets," *Journal of Psychology and Financial Markets* 1, no. 1 (2000): 24–48.

21. Edward Renshaw, "The Crash of October 19 in Retrospect," *Market Chronicle* 22, no. 1 (1988). However, this study cannot rule out the possibility that bubbles are simply rare events.

22. Gerald F. Davis, "A New Finance Capitalism? Mutual Funds and Ownership Re-Concentration in the United States," *European Management Review* 5, no. 1 (March 1, 2008): 11–21; John V. Duca, "The Democratization of America's Capital Markets," *Economic and Financial Policy Review*, no. QII (2001): 10–19.

23. In 2015, the average price of a share was just $20, and 99% of shares could be had for less than $200.

24. U.S. Census Bureau, "QuickFacts: United States," https://www.census.gov/quickfacts/table/PST045215/00.

25. This number relates to a manufacturing worker from Brandywine county in Pennsylvania. It's difficult to come by wage data from the early 1800s, and this is a decent proxy.

26. We have collected biweekly stock prices from the Curb Exchange from 1896 to 1931. Substituting Curb prices for NYSE prices leads to substantially similar conclusions. Starting in 1900, average Curb share prices average 75% and vary from 50% to 100% of NYSE prices. In 1926 CRSP data are available for NYSE data; before that we rely on the Yale NYSE database. See Rose Razaghian, "Financial Credibility in the United States: The Impact of Institutions, 1789–1860," Yale School of Management, July 29, 2013, https://som.yale.edu/faculty-research/our-centers-initiatives/international-center-finance/data/historical-newyork. The CRSP data suggest that the Yale database omits lower price shares, as the year of overlap (1925) shows that the average price in the Yale database is almost double

that in CRSP. The average CRSP NYSE prices from 1926 to 1931 are only 75% of the Curb prices in our databases.

27. Only 50% of new corporations took advantage of the limited statute of general incorporation; the remainder thought it better to get the legislature to pass an act for their companies. See W. C. Kessler, "A Statistical Study of the New York General Incorporation Act of 1811," *Journal of Political Economy* 48, no. 6 (1940): 877–82.

28. There was some room for investment for the general populace. For example, there was significant public participation in the financing of railroads throughout the period, and both stock and bond instruments were used. We also know that there were several boom and bust episodes in railroad securities. See Brent Goldfarb, David A. Kirsch, and April Shen, "Financing New Industries," in *Handbook of Entrepreneurial Finance* (Oxford University Press, 2012), chap. 1, for a discussion.

29. Numerous sources, summarized in Goldfarb, Kirsch, and Shen, "Financing New Industries."

30. See William L. Cary, "Federalism and Corporate Law: Reflections upon Delaware," *Yale Law Journal* 83, no. 4 (1974): 663–705, for a description of this process and the "race to the bottom" of the 1800s. See also D. R. Fischel, "Race to the Bottom Revisited: Reflections on Recent Developments in Delaware's Corporation Law," *Northwestern University Law Review* (1981): http://heinonline.org/hol-cgi-bin/get_pdf.cgi?handle=hein.journals/illlr76&section=38.

31. Alex Preda, "Socio-Technical Agency in Financial Markets: The Case of the Stock Ticker," *Social Studies of Science* 36, no. 5 (October 1, 2006): 753–82.

32. The initial killer app of the Victorian internet was the coordination of railroad schedules. It has been estimated that single tracking—a technology enabled by the telegraph—saved huge amounts of steel, thus making physical trade much cheaper.

33. William Orton saw ticker service as "the great future of telegraphy." See D. Hochfelder, "Where the Common People Could Speculate: The Ticker, Bucket Shops, and the Origins of Popular Participation in Financial Markets, 1880–1920," *Journal of American History* 93, no. 2 (2006): n9.

34. See Hochfelder, "Where the Common People Could Speculate," 340, although the estimates of the numbers vary. See, e.g., Preda, "Socio-Technical Agency in Financial Markets." There is no question that diffusion was quick and the technology revolutionized the market.

35. The first transatlantic cable enhanced intercontinental trading in 1878.

36. Preda, "Socio-Technical Agency in Financial Markets."

37. Hochfelder, "Where the Common People Could Speculate," 341.

38. Hochfelder, "Where the Common People Could Speculate."

39. Clarence D. Long, "Wages by Occupational and Individual Character-istics," in *Wages and Earnings in the United States, 1860–1890*, ed. Clarence D. Long (Princeton University Press, 1960), 94–108.

40. Hochfelder, "Where the Common People Could Speculate," describes a variety of tactics that unregulated bucket shops exploited. These involved either not purchasing the stock or making aggressive margin calls to close out margin-ally losing positions. The speculative nature of these activities—deemed as such because stocks were never transacted—led to a Supreme Court holding that the NYSE owned its quotations and could restrict bucket shops' access to them. Justice Oliver Wendell Holmes wrote in the majority decision that "incompetent persons bring themselves to ruin by undertaking to speculate" (352). It is unclear whether investors' cumulative behavior moved markets as often purchase and sell orders were never consummated in the actual markets. The evidence suggests that they may have commanded a substantial share of trades. For example in Buffalo it was estimated that 40% of shares were traded by bucket shops.

41. Mary O'Sullivan, "The Expansion of the US Stock Market, 1885–1930: Historical Facts and Theoretical Fashions," *Enterprise and Society* 8, no. 3 (2007): 489–542.

42. "The Financial World," *New York Times*, May 1, 1891, 5. The word *indus-trials* began to appear only in 1889 in London. Thomas R. Navin and Marian V. Sears, "The Rise of a Market for Industrial Securities, 1887–1902," *Business History Review* 29, no. 2 (June 1955): 105–38.

43. O'Sullivan, "The Expansion of the US Stock Market, 1885–1930"; Alexan-der James Field, "The Magnetic Telegraph, Price and Quantity Data, and the New Management of Capital," *Journal of Economic History* 52, no. 2 (June 1992): 401–13.

44. Goldfarb, Kirsch, and Shen, "Financing New Industries."

45. Hochfelder, "Where the Common People Could Speculate," 340.

46. Perhaps the most remarkable story of the era was the (current dollars) half-billion-dollar investment in electric vehicle companies on the New York Curb market, which suggests a strong appetite for industrial securities. Goldfarb, Kirsch, and Shen, "Financing New Industries."

47. Charles Arthur Conant, *Wall Street and the Country: A Study of Recent Financial Tendencies* (G. P. Putnam's Sons, 1904). Our estimate of individual stockholders in 1900 leverages the assumption discussed in Appendix K in Adolf A. Berle and Gardiner C. Means, *The Modern Corporation and Private Property* (Harcourt, Brace, and World, Inc., 1968), that one might estimate the total number of individual stock-holders by dividing the total number of book stockholders by 4.

48. By 1930 there were 1,582 companies traded on the Curb, up from 178 in 1911 and perhaps 50 at the turn of the century.

49. Hochfelder, "Where the Common People Could Speculate"; O'Sullivan, "The Expansion of the US Stock Market, 1885–1930"; Julia Ott, *When Wall*

Street Met Main Street: The Quest for an Investors' Democracy (Harvard University Press, 2011).

50. G. C. Means, "The Diffusion of Stock Ownership in the United States," *Quarterly Journal of Economics* 44, no. 4 (1930): 561.

51. Joe Nocera, *A Piece of the Action: How the Middle Class Joined the Money Class* (Simon and Schuster, 2013), 38.

52. Ott, *When Wall Street Met Main Street.*

53. O'Sullivan, "The Expansion of the US Stock Market, 1885–1930."

54. O'Sullivan, "The Expansion of the US Stock Market, 1885–1930"; Ott, *When Wall Street Met Main Street*; Mary A. O'Sullivan, *Dividends of Development: Securities Markets in the History of US Capitalism, 1866–1922* (Oxford University Press, 2016).

55. O'Sullivan, "The Expansion of the US Stock Market, 1885–1930."

56. Gardiner C. Means, "The Diffusion of Stock Ownership in the United States," *Quarterly Journal of Economics* 44, no. 4 (1930): 574.

57. Gene Smiley and Richard H. Keehn, "Margin Purchases, Brokers' Loans and the Bull Market of the Twenties" (paper presented at the annual meeting of the Business History Conference, 1988).

58. Robert Sobel, *The Last Bull Market: Wall Street in the 1960's* (Norton, 1980); Victor Perlo, "'People's Capitalism' and Stock-Ownership," *American Economic Review* 48, no. 3 (1958): 333–47.

59. Sobel, *Last Bull Market.*

60. U.S. Department of Commerce, *Survey of Current Business* (November 1974), 19.

61. Sobel, *Last Bull Market,* 22.

62. Although we can quibble with this particular estimate, others show a similar ballpark figure but lack the fidelity to see trends. For example, ten million households in 1962: James M. Poterba et al., "Stock Ownership Patterns, Stock Market Fluctuations, and Consumption," *Brookings Papers on Economic Activity*, no. 2 (1995): 295–372.

Chapter 4

1. Jeremy Norman, "The First Working Phototypesetting Machine and the First Book It Typeset (1946–1953)," *History of Information*, http://www.historyofinformation.com/expanded.php?id=867.

2. Management scholar Mary Tripsas has noted that 90% of Mergenthaler's existing capabilities were rendered obsolete by the new technology: "Unraveling the Process of Creative Destruction: Complementary Assets and Incumbent Survival in the Typesetter Industry," *Strategic Management Journal* 18 (1997): 119–42; and "Surviving Radical Technological Change Through Dynamic Capability: Evidence from the Typesetter Industry," *Industrial & Corporate Change* 6, no. 2 (1997).

3. "F. D. Roosevelt Jr. Is in Boston Hospital," *New York Times*, November 27, 1936.

4. "Young Roosevelt Saved by New Drug," *New York Times*, December 17, 1936.

5. "Prevailing dogma [held] that chemotherapeutic agents would only render minimal beneficial effects against generalized bacterial infections." See R. P. Rubin, "A Brief History of Great Discoveries in Pharmacology: In Celebration of the Centennial Anniversary of the Founding of the American Society of Pharmacology and Experimental Therapeutics," *Pharmacological Reviews* 59, no. 4 (2007): 316.

6. Andrea Frances Balis, "Miracle Medicine: The Impact of Sulfa Drugs on Medicine, the Pharmaceutical Industry and Government Regulation in the United States in the 1930s" (PhD diss., City University of New York, 2000), 133.

7. P. M. Wax, "Elixirs, Diluents, and the Passage of the 1938 Federal Food, Drug and Cosmetic Act," *Annals of Internal Medicine* 122, no. 6 (1995): 456–61.

8. "MENINGITIS DEATHS 'UNBELIEVABLY' CUT," *New York Times*, October 19, 1938; "PNEUMONIA CURBED BY A NEW CHEMICAL," *New York Times*, November 20, 1938; William L. Laurence, "SAY DRUG CHECKS TUBERCLE BACILLI," *New York Times*, April 6, 1939; Anne Petersen, "Agencies Hail Mortality Drop in Birth Cases," *New York Times*, April 9, 1939; "RHEUMATIC FEVER YIELDS," *New York Times*, September 7, 1939.

9. The list of firms is drawn from Balis, "Miracle Medicine." American Cyanamid patented sulfadiazine, while Merck controlled the related sulfapyridine—both of which appeared to have superior therapeutic properties than sulfanilamide. However, sales did not take off until the early 1940s, when these firms learned to produce safely, effectively, and in large quantities. By 1942, American Cyanamid sales of sulfadiazine reached $16 million ($273 million in 2017 dollars).

10. "American Cyanamid Uncovering New Products in Its Calcium Field," *Wall Street Journal*, June 5, 1941.

11. See the columns "Purely Gossip: A Daily Column of Comment in Wall Street," in the *Wall Street Journal*, from September 16, 1941; January 2, 1942; and July 24, 1942.

12. J. Ratcliff, "HERE'S MEDICAL MAGIC! Meet one of the most powerful microbe destroyers ever found: Penicillin. It's a brand-new wonder drug that will save thousands of soldiers' lives," *Atlanta Constitution*, May 16, 1943.

13. To be absolutely sure, we constructed a sulfa drug index of these companies. The index did rise and fall but not dramatically relative to the market. Its frothiness peaked at 1.05 in March 1939, but this is identical to the frothiness of the entire market in 1939. Moreover, if the movements of this index were closely related to sulfa drugs, we would almost certainly have seen an accompanying emergent narrative in the press. Speculation in sulfa drugs, if there was any, was possible only via direct entry by companies like S. K. Massengill. Thus, it is possible that

there was a brief bubble in the private equity markets for those investing in the new drug but no public bubble.

14. "First Offering of Nylon Hosiery Sold Out; Out-of-Town Buyers Swamp Wilmington," *New York Times*, October 25, 1939.

15. David A. Hounshell and John Kenly Smith, "The Nylon Drama," *American Heritage of Invention and Technology* 4, no. 2 (1988): 40–55.

16. "SALES BEGIN TODAY OF NYLON HOSIERY; Only Limited Supply of New du Pont Product, However, Will Be Available MAKERS WARN OF MIRACLE Caution Against Exaggerated Statements on Durability and Ending 'Runs,'" *New York Times*, May 15, 1940.

17. "NYLON HOSIERY PUT AT 17–20% OF TOTAL; Constantine Revises Downward Earlier Estimates on '41 Shipments to Stores," *New York Times*, May 1, 1941.

18. "NYLON HOSE SALES HEAVY AT OPENING; Price War on Unbranded Lines Marks Introduction—Many Stores Sell Out Quickly," *New York Times*, May 16, 1940.

19. Hounshell and Smith, "The Nylon Drama," 55.

20. For more detail on research and development at DuPont, see David A. Hounshell and John Kenly Smith, *Science and Corporate Strategy: DuPont Research and Development, 1902–1980* (Cambridge University Press, 1988).

21. Robert Sobel, *The Last Bull Market: Wall Street in the 1960's* (Norton, 1980). Sobel's methodology is to largely summarize the business press narrative of the 1950s and 1960s and is ideal for our purposes of identifying major narratives related to market speculation.

22. As the age of jet travel began, there were many tragic accidents—dozens in single years in the late 1950s and early 1960s. Nevertheless, the promise of speed led to a fourfold increase in passenger miles flown in the early 1960s.

23. Michael L. Tushman and Philip Anderson, "Technological Discontinuities and Organizational Environments," *Administrative Science Quarterly* 31, no. 3 (1986): 439–465.

24. John S. Reed and Glen R. Moreno, "The Role of Large Banks in Financing Innovation," in *The Positive Sum Strategy: Harnessing Technology for Economic Growth*, ed. Ralph Landau (National Academies Press, 1986), 453–66.

25. Sobel, *Last Bull Market*.

26. See Sandeep Devantha Pillai, "The Value of Contextual Richness: An Empirical Exploration of Production Scaling in the Early Automobile Industry" (working paper, University of Maryland, February 2018), for an investigation into the importance of this production know-how in the context of automobiles.

27. Howard Mingos, "FORD PREPARES TO DEVELOP FLYING 'FLIVVER': His Use of Cargo Planes a Step Toward Airplane Production on Large Scale—To Make Commercial Aviation a Success, He Says," *New York Times*, April 19, 1925.

28. "Economic and Aviation Experts Advise Caution in Buying Stocks," *Christian Science Monitor*, September 18, 1928.

29. "AVIATION EMPLOYED AS FAKE STOCK BAIT," *Washington Post*, October 7, 1928.

30. For a broader discussion, see E. P. Warner, "Commercial Aviation—Illusion or Fact," *Yale Review* 20 (1931): 707.

31. Brent Goldfarb and David Kirsch, "Time to Commercial Viability in Nascent Industries: A Historical Study" (2017), https://papers.ssrn.com/sol3/papers.cfm?abstract_id=3049537.

32. "AVIATION EMPLOYED AS FAKE STOCK BAIT."

33. Goldfarb and Kirsch, "Time to Commercial Viability in Nascent Industries."

34. Authors' calculations.

35. Agis Salpukas, "Wankel Fever Is Now Widespread," *New York Times*, November 5, 1972.

36. Jan P. Norbye, "A Wankel in Your Future," *New York Times*, April 2, 1972.

37. Richard E. Mooney, "GERMAN CAR USES NEW-TYPE ENGINE; N.S.U. Installing Wankel—Others Prepare Models," *New York Times*, October 26, 1964; Richard E. Mooney, "Citroen to Develop A Pistonless Auto; CITROEN PLANNING PISTONLESS AUTO," *New York Times*, April 1, 1965.

38. John B. Hege, *The Wankel Rotary Engine: A History* (McFarland, 2006).

39. "U.S. Business: German Engine is in U.S. via Japan," *New York Times*, July 19, 1970.

40. Jan P. Norbye, "What G.M. Sees in the Wankel," *New York Times*, November 15, 1970.

41. "U.S. Business."

42. The United States had tighter emissions regulations than did Europe in early 1970. One might wonder why we score this technology as having low technology and business uncertainty when its technical failure was central to the story. Technical and business uncertainty aggregates other items as well, including whether it was believed that the new technology would disrupt incumbents or require novel business models. The Wankel was decidedly not believed to have been likely to cause such upheaval in the automobile market, and hence on aggregate, this score comes out low.

43. John J. Abele, "WALL STREET: Hutton Suggests a Hedge on Wankel," *New York Times*, March 5, 1972.

44. Elizabeth M. Fowler, "PRICES ON AMEX SHOW SLIM DROP," *New York Times*, June 10, 1972.

45. Charles G. Burck, "A Car That May Reshape the Industry's Future," *Fortune* 86 (July 1972): 75.

46. Gene Smith, "G.M. PLAYS DOWN WANKEL REPORT," *New York Times*, July 13, 1972.

47. Agis Salpukas, "G.M. Will Produce the Wankel Engine in Limited Quantity," *New York Times*, August 29, 1972.

48. Richard Wadell, "The Wankel Comes of Age," *New York Times*, April 8, 1973, https://www.nytimes.com/1973/04/08/archives/the-wankel-comes-of-age-challenge-conceded-license-agreement-there.html.

49. It appears to have found a niche when size may matter. See Hege, *Wankel Rotary Engine*; Wikipedia contributors, "Wankel Engine," *Wikipedia*, February 3, 2018, https://en.wikipedia.org/w/index.php?title=Wankel_engine&oldid=823720951.

50. Nathan Rosenberg, "Uncertainty and Technological Change," in *The Mosaic of Economic Growth*, ed. T. Taylor Ralph Landau and Gavin Wright (Stanford University Press, 1996), 334–56.

51. Burton Gordon Malkiel, *Random Walk Down Wall Street: Including a Life-Cycle Guide to Personal Investing* (W. W. Norton, 1991).

52. "Stock Spree: Many Investors Shun 'Blue Chips,' Bid Up Cheaper Issues," *Wall Street Journal*, April 24, 1961.

53. Sobel, *Last Bull Market*.

54. Our index includes AT&T, General Electric, IBM, Raytheon, Texas Instruments, Fairchild & Philco.

55. SBICs (small-business investment corporations) invested directly in small start-ups but then sold shares of the upside on the public markets. SBICs eventually failed. See Brent Goldfarb, Magnus Henrekson, and Nathan Rosenberg, "Demand vs. Supply Driven Innovations: US and Swedish Experiences in Academic Entrepreneurship" (SSE/EFI Working Paper Series in Economics and Finance, 2001), http://hdl.handle.net/10419/56272. However, the additional uncertainty given the investment instrument contributed to the mania. See Sobel, *Last Bull Market*.

56. For a broader discussion of this process and industry, see Steven Klepper, *Experimental Capitalism: The Nanoeconomics of American High-Tech Industries* (Princeton University Press, 2015).

57. We should not confuse the 1960s with the events of 1929. Even at the height of excitement in the early 1960s, descriptions of the hot electronics stocks were mostly confined to the business pages. See Steve Fraser, *Every Man a Speculator: A History of Wall Street in American Life* (HarperCollins, 2005), 492; Sobel, *Last Bull Market*.

58. As described in Chapter 3, we also might believe that lack of stock market regulation increases the probability of a bubble. Our ability to measure times of lower and higher regulation is quite blunt. We evaluated a modified scheme where we added 2 points to the total factor score if the window of bubble opportunity ended before 1913, when the Federal Reserve was established following the Panic of 1907. We added an additional point if the window of bubble opportunity ended

before 1933, the year of the Glass-Steagall Act, which led to the formation of the Securities and Exchange Commission. In doing this, the correlation between factors and frothiness fell slightly, to 0.36. That is, taking into account financial regulation does not change our understanding of the patterns in the data.

59. Robert C. Kennedy, "On This Day: February 11, 1865," *New York Times on the Web Learning Network*, http://www.nytimes.com/learning/general/onthisday/harp/0211.html.

Chapter 5

1. Knowledge@Wharton, "Top 30 Innovations of the Last 30 Years," *Forbes Magazine*, February 19, 2009, https://www.forbes.com/2009/02/19/innovation-internet-health-entrepreneurs-technology_wharton.html.

2. Brent Goldfarb and Andrew A. King, "Scientific Apophenia in Strategic Management Research: Significance Tests & Mistaken Inference," *Strategic Management Journal* 37, no. 1 (January 1, 2016): 168.

3. Another example of this problem was exposed by Thomas Piketty and Emmanuel Saez, who found that the belief that economic inequality decreased with economic growth in the United States was an artifact of initial studies that focused on the years 1945–1973. Once a more general sample of countries and periods was examined, it could be seen that this period in economic history was quite special. See Thomas Piketty and Emmanuel Saez, "Income Inequality in the United States, 1913–1998," *Quarterly Journal of Economics* 118, no. 1 (February 1, 2003): 1–41.

4. Samuel Kortum and Josh Lerner, "Does Venture Capital Spur Innovation?" in *Entrepreneurial Inputs and Outcomes: New Studies of Entrepreneurship in the United States*, ed. Gary D. Libecap, Advances in the Study of Entrepreneurship, Innovation & Economic Growth 13 (JAI, 2001), 1–44.

5. Brent Goldfarb, Andrew A. King, and Timothy S. Simcoe, "Replication Is Good, but Will Not Save Us" (working paper, University of Maryland, February 23, 2018).

6. In 1998, almost half of US households held stocks, and more than half of those held stocks outside of retirement accounts. From 1989 until 1998, the number of investors increased by one-third—with most of that increase occurring between 1995 and 1998. This represented a 100% increase from 1975. The period from 1998 and 2001 tells a dramatic tale of shifting investor portfolios. Although the total number of households holding stocks went up just under 10%, the number holding stocks in their retirement portfolios went up by 60%. Investors were shifting holdings in their retirement accounts from fixed assets or bonds to stocks dramatically during this period. See Ana M. Aizcorbe, Arthur B. Kennickell, and Kevin B. Moore, *Recent Changes in U.S. Family Finances: Evidence from the 1998 and 2001 Survey of Consumer Finances* (Federal Reserve Bulletin, 2003).

7. V. Bogan, "Stock Market Participation and the Internet," *Journal of Financial and Quantitative Analysis* 43, no. 1 (2006): 191–212.

8. B. M. Barber and T. Odean, "Online Investors: Do the Slow Die First?" *Review of Financial Studies* 15 (2002): 455–88. Margin investment figures are from Ruth Simon, "Margin Investors Learn the Hard Way That Brokers Can Get Tough on Loans," *Wall Street Journal*, April 27, 2000, based on data from Smith Barney and the New York Stock Exchange. Barber and Odean also point out that internet trading is different from older trading technologies in two important ways. First, internet trading eliminates human intermediaries and makes the entire trading process quicker. Second, the internet allows access to a much greater amount of information than was previously available to investors. They argue that this will lead to overconfidence, as investors will sift through the overwhelming amounts of information and seek only that information which confirms their beliefs. Importantly, they note that ease of trading is indeed associated with lower returns and that investors trade more when they do so using internet technologies.

9. Bogan, "Stock Market Participation and the Internet," 194.

10. James J. Choi, David Laibson, and Andrew Metrick, "How Does the Internet Affect Trading? Evidence from Investor Behavior in 401(k) Plans," *Journal of Financial Economics* 64, no. 3 (June 1, 2002): 397–421; Bogan, "Stock Market Participation and the Internet."

11. The trend continued to increase even after the market crash.

12. M. L. Goldstein and I. Krutov, *The Future of Money Management in America* (Bernstein Research, 2000).

13. Authors' calculations based on *VentureXpert*, August 2006, available from Securities Data Company.

14. Robert H. Reid, *Architects of the Web: 1,000 Days That Built the Future of Business* (New York: Wiley, 1997), 37.

15. We discuss the rise of the "get big fast" beliefs in greater detail in David Kirsch and Brent Goldfarb, "Small Ideas, Big Ideas, Bad Ideas, Good Ideas: 'Get Big Fast' and Dot Com Venture Creation," in *The Internet and American Business*, ed. William Aspray and Paul E. Ceruzzi (MIT Press, 2008).

16. Even eBay's market potential was overestimated—turns out that the format works best for one-of-a-kind items, not commodities.

17. Heather Green, "The Great Yuletide Shakeout," *BusinessWeek*, November 1, 1999, 18–28.

18. Michael Sokolove, "How to Lose $850 Million—and Not Really Care," *New York Times*, June 9, 2002, http://www.nytimes.com/2002/06/09/magazine/09LENK.html.

19. Sokolove, "How to Lose $850 Million."

20. "A Netscape Moment?" *The Economist*, February 4, 2010, https://www .economist.com/node/15464481.

21. Daniel Roth, "My, What Big Internet Numbers You Have!" *Fortune* 139, no. 5 (1999): 114–18.

22. Kirsch and Goldfarb, "Small Ideas, Big Ideas."

23. Brent D. Goldfarb, Michael D. Pfarrer, and David Kirsch, "Searching for Ghosts: Business Survival, Unmeasured Entrepreneurial Activity and Private Equity Investment in the Dot-Com Era" (Robert H. Smith School Research Paper No. RHS 06-027, October 12, 2005), https://ssrn.com/abstract=825687 or http://dx.doi.org/10.2139/ssrn.825687.

24. Goldfarb, Kirsch, and Miller, "Was There Too Little Entry."

25. Goldfarb, Kirsch, and Miller, "Was There Too Little Entry."

26. For a less sophisticated example, see Marian Betancourt, *The Best Internet Businesses You Can Start* (Adams Media Corporation, 1999).

27. Jeff Hecht, *City of Light: The Story of Fiber Optics* (Oxford University Press, 2004); Shane Greenstein, *How the Internet Became Commercial: Innovation, Privatization, and the Birth of a New Network* (Princeton University Press, 2015).

28. *Personal computers* and *laptops* refer to two of at least three separate waves in the evolution of the technology. Technically, minicomputers were PCs. Companies such as Wang and DEC produced these products in the 1970s and 1980s before losing market share to the client-server model we are familiar with today. Minicomputers were expensive business machines used for computationally intensive applications such as oil exploration models. We explore the history of the microcomputer, which is the technology commonly thought of as a PC today.

29. "Apple II Series," *Wikipedia*, January 27, 2018, https://en.wikipedia.org/ w/index.php?title=Apple_II_series&oldid=822619419.

30. Matt Nicholson, *When Computing Got Personal* (Matt Publishing, 2014), loc. 1301.

31. New York Times Labs (shut down in 2017), http://chronicle.nytlabs.com/ ?keyword=PErsonal%20computer.Internet.

32. Andrew S. Grove, *Only the Paranoid Survive: How to Exploit the Crisis Points That Challenge Every Company and Career* (Currency Doubleday, 1996); Timothy F. Bresnahan, Shane Greenstein, and Rebecca M. Henderson, "Schumpeterian Competition and Diseconomies of Scope: Illustrations from the Histories of Microsoft and IBM," in *The Rate and Direction of Inventive Activity Revisited* (University of Chicago Press, 2011), 203–71.

33. For example, Steve Jobs believed strongly that the Macintosh would be the future of Apple. Then Apple CEO John Scully disagreed—and this, together with Jobs's somewhat imperfect interpersonal skills, led to Jobs being fired. The Macintosh was both expensive and underpowered compared to its competitors. However,

it did have a killer app: a laser printer. This allowed the Macintosh to attract a new cohort of desktop publishers and sustained the company as it lost its dominance in the more general PC market.

34. Peter J. Schuyten, "Commodore Prepares Challenge to U.S. Home-Computer Giants," *New York Times*, October 1, 1980, D26.

35. Karen W. Arenson, "A 'Hot' Offering Retrospective: Genentech and Apple Varied Greatly," *New York Times*, December 30, 1980, D1.

36. Andrew Pollack, "Computer Makers in a Severe Slump: Problems Such as Oversupply Resist Speedy Resolution Computer Industry in a Severe Slump," *New York Times*, June 10, 1985, A1.

37. Samuel Reynard, "Financial Market Participation and the Apparent Instability of Money Demand," *Journal of Monetary Economics* 51, no. 6 (September 2004): 1297–1317.

38. Thomas Murtha, Stefanie Lenway, and Jeffrey Hart, *Managing New Industry Creation: Global Knowledge Formation and Entrepreneurship in High Technology* (Stanford University Press, 2001), 46.

39. Murtha, Lenway, and Hart, *Managing New Industry Creation*.

40. Murtha, Lenway, and Hart, *Managing New Industry Creation*, 172.

41. Murtha, Lenway, and Hart, *Managing New Industry Creation*, 3.

42. Dennis Normile, "Flat TV Arrives," *Popular Science* 250, no. 5 (May 1997): 69–73.

43. As reported by John Markoff, "Advances in Asia Propel Wider Use of Flat-Panel Displays," *New York Times*, May 20, 1996, D7: "For decades engineers have been promising television sets that would hang on the wall like a picture. That fabled day may finally be coming, based on evidence from a technical conference last week in San Diego, where engineers demonstrated so-called flat-panel displays with screens big enough to begin rivaling television monitors—and with costs low enough that flat screens may soon become a viable alternative to the bulky cathode-ray tube, or CRT, monitors now standard on desktop computers."

44. Laparoscopy is, as defined by *Merriam-Webster's Dictionary*, "a visual examination of the abdomen by means of a laparoscope, or an operation (as tubal ligation or gall bladder removal) involving laparoscopy" (see https://www.merriam-webster.com).

45. K. Nakajima, J. W. Milsom, and B. Böhm, "History of Laparoscopic Surgery," in *Laparoscopic Colorectal Surgery* (Springer, 2006).

46. These articles are the results of searching for the words *laparoscopic surgery* in all articles in 1993 in the *New York Times* archives (conducted on March 3, 2018).

47. These articles are the results of the same search as noted previously, in year 1995 (conducted on March 3, 2018).

48. Aaron K. Chatterji, "Spawned with a Silver Spoon? Entrepreneurial Performance and Innovation in the Medical Device Industry," *Strategic Management Journal* 30, no. 2 (February 1, 2009): 185–206.

49. In the language of empirical social scientists, we used up our data in the development of the theory in Chapter 4, and to some extent—due to problems of external validity—we have done so here with the Wharton 30 as well. See also Goldfarb, King, and Simcoe, "Replication Is Good."

50. Sometimes the bundling was done by additional intermediaries, but that is not critical for our story here. At the time of the writing, Fannie Mae and Freddie Mac purchase and hold the bulk of mortgages in US residential markets.

51. For a short history of this emergence of mortgage-backed securities, see Elena Loutskina and Philip E. Strahan, "Informed and Uninformed Investment in Housing: The Downside of Diversification," *Review of Financial Studies* 24, no. 5 (May 1, 2011): 1447–80.

52. Fannie Mae and Freddie Mac contributed to the crises. They held a disproportionate share of private-label subprime and Alt-A mortgage backed securities. In 2004 they bought 10% of the total, and 4.5% in 2007. Martin Neil Baily, Robert E. Litan, and Matthew S. Johnson, *The Origins of the Financial Crisis* (Initiative on Business and Public Policy at Brookings, 2008), 34.

53. Baily, Litan, and Johnson, *Origins of the Financial Crisis*.

54. Douglas W. Diamond and Raghuram Rajan, "The Credit Crisis: Conjectures About Causes and Remedies" (National Bureau of Economic Research, 2009), http://www.nber.org/papers/w14739.pdf. Diamond and Rajan also point out that assessing the risk associated with new types of securities is difficult—as one cannot determine whether financial excess returns are attributable to shrewd investment or whether enough time has passed to assess the true risk.

55. Manuel Adelino, "Do Investors Rely Only on Ratings? The Case of Mortgage-Backed Securities" (Working paper, MIT Sloan School of Management and Federal Reserve Bank of Boston, 2009); Manuel Adelino, W. Scott Frame, and Kristopher S. Gerardi, "The Effect of Large Investors on Asset Quality: Evidence from Subprime Mortgage Securities," *Journal of Monetary Economics* 87 (2017): 34–51.

56. "Profile of Home Buyers and Sellers" (National Association of Realtors, 2007).

57. There were many cities with high levels of inexperienced buyers but no bubble. Ron Martin, "The Local Geographies of the Financial Crisis: From the Housing Bubble to Economic Recession and Beyond," *Journal of Economic Geography* 11, no. 4 (2011): 587–618. That is, it appears that inexperienced buyers did not take out mortgages they could not afford in absence of signals of increasing prices.

58. Phil Angelides, Brooksley Born, Byron Georgiou, Bob Graham, Heather H. Murren, and John W. Thompson, *Financial Crisis Inquiry Report: Final Report of the*

National Commission on the Causes of the Financial and Economic Crisis in the United States (Financial Crisis Inquiry Commission, Washington, DC, 2011).

59. Michael Brian Schiffer, *Taking Charge: The Electric Automobile in America* (Smithsonian, 2003).

60. Brent Goldfarb, "Why Tesla Is Overhyped—and Overvalued," *Vox*, June 26, 2017, https://www.vox.com/the-big-idea/2017/6/26/15872468/tesla-gm -ford-valuation-justifying-disruption.

61. Lithium Americas Corp., Western Lithium US Corp., and American Lithium Minerals are three good examples of lithium pure plays.

Chapter 6

1. "Fisher Sees Stocks Permanently High," *New York Times*, October 16, 1929.

2. "Says Stock Slump Is Only Temporary," *New York Times*, October 24, 1929.

3. It is also true that there was speculation in department stores. Though this innovation is not on our list, it is particularly interesting in that Merrill Lynch developed his brokerage business by underwriting department store shares and then selling these shares to his clients—who shopped at the underwritten department stores. See Steve Fraser, *Every Man a Speculator: A History of Wall Street in American Life* (HarperCollins, 2005).

4. "City and Suburban News," *New York Times*, April 22, 1878.

5. Authors' calculations based on *VentureXpert*, August 2006, available from Securities Data Company. All VC firms operating for five years or less were counted as new.

6. Ruth Simon, "Margin Investors Learn the Hard Way That Brokers Can Get Tough on Loans," *Wall Street Journal*, April 27, 2000.

7. "James K. Polk: Fourth Annual Message," December 5, 1848, http://www .presidency.ucsb.edu/ws/index.php?pid=29489.

8. Robert D. Hof, "Commentary: 'Please God, Just One More Bubble,'" *Bloomberg News*, August 16, 2004, https://www.bloomberg.com/news/articles/ 2004-08-15/commentary-please-god-just-one-more-bubble.

9. See *Financial Crisis Inquiry Report: Final Report of the National Commission on the Causes of the Financial and Economic Crisis in the United States*, U.S. Government Edition (Financial Crisis Inquiry Commission, 2011).

10. Robert H. Fetridge, "Highways and Byways of Finance," *New York Times*, February 27, 1949.

11. Fetridge, "Highways and Byways."

12. All of Kranzberg's laws discuss the very human nature of technology: we create it and it changes us. Melvin Kranzberg, "Technology and History: 'Kranzberg's Laws,'" *Technology and Culture* 27, no. 3 (1986): 544–60.

13. Ramana Nanda and Matthew Rhodes-Kropf, "Investment Cycles and Startup Innovation," *Journal of Financial Economics* 110, no. 2 (November 1, 2013): 403–18.

14. Jorge Guzman and Scott Stern, "The State of American Entrepreneurship: New Estimates of the Quantity and Quality of Entrepreneurship for 15 US States, 1988–2014" (working paper, National Bureau of Economic Research, March 2016), https://doi.org/10.3386/w22095.

15. Erik Gerding, *Law, Bubbles, and Financial Regulation* (Routledge, 2013).

16. You can read more about this in Brent Goldfarb, David Kirsch, and Dave Kressler, "Business Exercise Starts with $5 in Seed Money," *Entrepreneur & Innovation Exchange*, February 13, 2018, https://doi.org/10.17919/X9566C.

17. Colin Camerer and Dan Lovallo, "Overconfidence and Excess Entry: An Experimental Approach," *American Economic Review* (1999): 306–18.

18. Steven Klepper and Kenneth L. Simons, "The Making of an Oligopoly: Firm Survival and Technological Change in the Evolution of the U.S. Tire Industry," *Journal of Political Economy* 108, no. 4 (August 1, 2000): 728–60; Steven Klepper, *Experimental Capitalism: The Nanoeconomics of American High-Tech Industries* (Princeton University Press, 2015).

19. Robert J. Shiller, *Irrational Exuberance* (Crown Publishers, 2006).

20. Gerding, *Law, Bubbles, and Financial Regulation*.

REFERENCES

Abele, John J. 1972. "Wall Street: Hutton Suggests a Hedge on Wankel." *New York Times*, March 5.

Abzug, Malcolm J., and E. Eugene Larrabee. 2005. *Airplane Stability and Control: A History of the Technologies That Made Aviation Possible*. Vol. 14. Cambridge: Cambridge University Press.

Adelino, Manuel. 2009. "Do Investors Rely Only on Ratings? The Case of Mortgage-Backed Securities." Job market paper, MIT Sloan School of Management and Federal Reserve Bank of Boston.

Adelino, Manuel, W. Scott Frame, and Kristopher S. Gerardi. 2017. "The Effect of Large Investors on Asset Quality: Evidence from Subprime Mortgage Securities." *Journal of Monetary Economics* 87: 34–51.

Aizcorbe, Ana M., Arthur B. Kennickell, and Kevin B. Moore. 2003. "Recent Changes in U.S. Family Finances: Evidence from the 1998 and 2001 Survey of Consumer Finances." *Federal Reserve Bulletin* 89: 1–32.

"American Cyanamid Uncovering New Products in Its Calcium Field." 1941. *Wall Street Journal*, June 5.

Angelides, Phil, Brooksley Born, Byron Georgiou, Bob Graham, Heather H. Murren, and John W. Thompson. 2011. *Financial Crisis Inquiry Report: Final Report of the National Commission on the Causes of the Financial and Economic Crisis in the United States*. Washington, DC: Financial Crisis Inquiry Commission.

Archer, Gleason Leonard. 1939. *Big Business and Radio*. New York: American Historical Co.

———. 1971. *History of Radio to 1926*. New York: Arno Press.

Arenson, Karen W. 1980. "A 'Hot' Offering Retrospective: Genentech and Apple Varied Greatly." *New York Times*, December 30.

"Auto Tire Prices Will Remain High." 1909. *New York Times*, October 1.

"Aviation and Investment." 1928. *Wall Street Journal*, June 26.

"Aviation Employed as Fake Stock Bait." 1928. *Washington Post*, October 7.

Baily, Martin Neil, Robert E. Litan, and Matthew S. Johnson. 2008. *The Origins of the Financial Crisis*. Initiative on Business and Public Policy at Brookings.

Balis, Andrea Frances. 2000. "Miracle Medicine: The Impact of Sulfa Drugs on Medicine, the Pharmaceutical Industry and Government Regulation in the United States in the 1930s." PhD diss., City University of New York, 2000.

Barber, Brad M., Chip Heath, and Terrance Odean. 2003. "Good Reasons Sell: Reason-Based Choice Among Group and Individual Investors in the Stock Market." *Management Science* 49 (12): 1636–52.

Barber, B. M., and T. Odean. 2002. "Online Investors: Do the Slow Die First?" *Review of Financial Studies* 15: 455–88.

Barber, Brad M., and Terrance Odean. 2008. "All That Glitters: The Effect of Attention and News on the Buying Behavior of Individual and Institutional Investors." *Review of Financial Studies* 21 (2): 785–818.

Barnouw, Erik. 1966. *A Tower of Babel*. Vol. 1 of *A History of Broadcasting in the United States*. New York: Oxford University Press.

Bazerman, Charles. 1999. *The Languages of Edison's Light*. Cambridge, MA: MIT Press.

Beauchamp, Christopher. 2010. "Who Invented the Telephone? Lawyers, Patents, and the Judgments of History." *Technology and Culture* 51 (4): 854–78.

———. 2015. *Invented by Law: Alexander Graham Bell and the Patent That Changed America*. Cambridge, MA: Harvard University Press.

Becattini, Francesco, Arnab Chatterjee, Santo Fortunato, Marija Mitrović, Raj Kumar Pan, and Pietro Della Briotta Parolo. 2014. "The Nobel Prize Delay." *arXiv* [physics.soc-Ph]. http://arxiv.org/abs/1405.7136.

Beckert, Jens. 2016. *Imagined Futures*. Cambridge, MA: Harvard University Press.

Berger, Jonah. 2016. *Contagious: Why Things Catch On*. New York: Simon and Schuster.

Berkhout, Frans. 2006. "Normative Expectations in Systems Innovation." *Technology Analysis & Strategic Management* 18 (3–4): 299–311.

Berle, Adolf A., and Gardiner C. Means. 1968. *The Modern Corporation and Private Property*. New York: Harcourt, Brace, and World, Inc.

Betancourt, Marian. 1999. *The Best Internet Businesses You Can Start*. Holbrook, MA: Adams Media Corp.

Beunza, Daniel, and Raghu Garud. 2007. "Calculators, Lemmings or Frame-Makers? The Intermediary Role of Securities Analysts." *Sociological Review* 55 (October): 13–39.

Bissonnette, Zac. 2015. *The Great Beanie Baby Bubble: Mass Delusion and the Dark Side of Cute*. New York: Portfolio.

Bliss, Michael. 1986. "Who Discovered Insulin?" *Physiology*, February. https://doi.org/10.1152/physiologyonline.1986.1.1.31.

———. 2013. *The Discovery of Insulin*. Chicago: University of Chicago Press.

Bogan, Vicki. 2008. "Stock Market Participation and the Internet." *Journal of Financial and Quantitative Analysis* 43 (1): 191–212.

"Bombarded with Energy." 1929. *Saturday Evening Post*, December 1.

Bresnahan, Timothy F., Shane Greenstein, and Rebecca M. Henderson. 2011. "Schumpeterian Competition and Diseconomies of Scope: Illustrations from the Histories of Microsoft and IBM." In *The Rate and Direction of Inventive Activity Revisited*, edited by Josh Lerner and Scott Stern, 203–71. Chicago: University of Chicago Press.

Bresnahan, T. F., and M. Trajtenberg. 1995. "General Purpose Technologies 'Engines of Growth'?" *Journal of Econometrics* 65 (1): 83–108. http://www.sciencedirect.com/science/article/pii/030440769401598T.

Burck, Charles G. 1972. "A Car That May Reshape the Industry's Future." *Fortune* 86 (July): 75.

Caginalp, Gunduz, David Porter, and Vernon L. Smith. 2000a. "Momentum and Overreaction in Experimental Asset Markets." *International Journal of Industrial Organization* 18: 187–204.

———. 2000b. "Overreactions, Momentum, Liquidity, and Price Bubbles in Laboratory and Field Asset Markets." *Journal of Psychology and Financial Markets* 1 (1): 24–48.

Callon, Michel. 1998. "Introduction: The Embeddedness of Economic Markets in Economics." *Sociological Review* 46 (S1): 1–57.

Camerer, Colin, George Loewenstein, and Dražen Prelec. 2005. "Neuroeconomics: How Neuroscience Can Inform Economics." *Journal of Economic Literature* 43 (1): 9–64.

Camerer, Colin, and Dan Lovallo. 1999. "Overconfidence and Excess Entry: An Experimental Approach." *American Economic Review* 89 (1): 306–18.

Cary, William L. 1974. "Federalism and Corporate Law: Reflections upon Delaware." *Yale Law Journal* 83 (4): 663–705.

Casson, Herbert N. 1910. *The History of the Telephone*. Chicago: A. C. McClurg & Co.

Chatterji, Aaron K. 2009. "Spawned with a Silver Spoon? Entrepreneurial Performance and Innovation in the Medical Device Industry." *Strategic Management Journal* 30 (2): 185–206.

Choi, James J., David Laibson, and Andrew Metrick. 2002. "How Does the Internet Affect Trading? Evidence from Investor Behavior in 401(k) Plans." *Journal of Financial Economics* 64 (3): 397–421.

"City and Suburban News." 1878. *New York Times*, April 22.

Clark, J., C. Freeman, and L. Soete. 1981. "Long Waves, Inventions, and Innovations." *Futures* 13 (4): 308–22.

Conant, Charles Arthur. 1904. *Wall Street and the Country: A Study of Recent Financial Tendencies*. New York: G. P. Putnam's Sons.

Cory, H. H. 1930. "Modern Methods Roll Up Big: Radio Sales for Steussy." *Radio Record* 10: 4–5.

Cowles, Alfred, III. 1939. *Common-Stock Indices*. 2nd ed. Bloomington, IN: Principia Press.

Crowe, Earle E. 1929. "Engine Makers Take Lead: Rival Groups in Aviation Concentrating on Development of New Types; Diesel Experiments Popular." *Los Angeles Times*, May 26.

"Curious Features of the Electric Lighting Business." 1885. *Scientific American*, October 10.

Da, Zhi, Joseph Engelberg, and Pengjie Gao. 2011. "In Search of Attention." *Journal of Finance* 66 (5): 1461–99.

Dartnell Corporation. 1929. "Sales Method Investigation: Experience of 127 Firms with Radio Broadcasting." Research Report No. 306. Chicago: Dartnell Corporation.

Davis, Gerald F. 2008. "A New Finance Capitalism? Mutual Funds and Ownership Re-Concentration in the United States." *European Management Review* 5 (1): 11–21.

De Long, J. Bradford, Andrei Shleifer, Lawrence H. Summers, and Robert J. Waldmann. 1990. "Noise Trader Risk in Financial Markets." *Journal of Political Economy* 98: 703–38.

"Demand for Rubber: Brazilian Government Has Virtually Cornered the Market." 1910. *New York Times*, April 17.

Devenow, Andrea, and Ivo Welch. 1996. "Rational Herding in Financial Economics." *European Economic Review* 403: 603–15.

Diamond, Douglas W., and Raghuram G. Rajan. 2009. "The Credit Crisis: Conjectures About Causes and Remedies." *American Economic Review* 99 (2): 606–10.

Douglas, Susan J. 2015. "Early Radio." In *Communications in History: Technology, Culture, Society*, edited by David Crowley and Paul Heyer, 210–17. New York: Routledge.

Duca, John V. 2001. "The Democratization of America's Capital Markets." *Economic and Financial Policy Review* (Federal Reserve Bank of Dallas), no. QII: 10–19.

"Economic and Aviation Experts Advise Caution in Buying Stocks." 1928. *Christian Science Monitor*, September 18.

Eisen, Ben. 2018. "Nasdaq Tops Inflation-Adjusted High from Dot-Com Boom." *Wall Street Journal*. January 17. https://blogs.wsj.com/moneybeat/2018/01/17/nasdaq-poised-to-top-inflation-adjusted-high-from-dot-com-boom/.

"The Electric Light." 1878. *New York Times*, April 22.

"eToys to Shut down Web Site March 8." 2001. *CNN Money*, February 26. http://cnnfn.cnn.com/2001/02/26/companies/etoys/.

"F. D. Roosevelt Jr. Is in Boston Hospital." 1936. *New York Times*, November 27.

Fetridge, Robert H. 1949. "Highways and Byways of Finance." *New York Times*, February 27.

Field, Alexander James. 1992. "The Magnetic Telegraph, Price and Quantity Data, and the New Management of Capital." *Journal of Economic History* 52 (2): 401–13.

"The Financial World." 1891. *New York Times*, May 1.

"First Offering of Nylon Hosiery Sold Out; Out-of-Town Buyers Swamp Wilmington." 1939. *New York Times*, October 25.

Fischel, D. R. 1981. "Race to the Bottom Revisited: Reflections on Recent Developments in Delaware's Corporation Law." *Northwestern University Law Review*. HeinOnline. http://heinonline.org/hol-cgi-bin/get_pdf.cgi?handle=hein .journals/illlr76&section=38.

Fischer, Claude S. 1994. *America Calling: A Social History of the Telephone to 1940*. Berkeley: University of California Press.

"Fisher Sees Stocks Permanently High." 1916. *New York Times*, October 16.

Fowler, Elizabeth M. 1972. "Prices on AMEX Show Slim Drop." *New York Times*, June 10.

Frank, Zephyr, and Aldo Musacchio. 2008. "The International Natural Rubber Market, 1870–1930." *EH.Net Encyclopedia, Edited by Robert Whaples*. https://eh .net/encyclopedia/the-international-natural-rubber-market-1870–1930/.

Fraser, Steve. 2005. *Every Man a Speculator: A History of Wall Street in American Life*. New York: HarperCollins.

Freeman, Christopher. 1984. *Long Waves in the World Economy*. London: F. Pinter.

Garber, Peter M. 1990. "Famous First Bubbles." *Journal of Economic Perspectives: A Journal of the American Economic Association* 4: 35–54.

Garud, Raghu, Henri A. Schildt, and Theresa K. Lant. 2014. "Entrepreneurial Storytelling, Future Expectations, and the Paradox of Legitimacy." *Organization Science* 25 (5): 1479–92.

Gerding, Erik. 2013. *Law, Bubbles, and Financial Regulation*. New York: Routledge.

Goldfarb, Brent Daniel. 2002. "Three Essays in the Economics of Technological Change." PhD diss., Stanford University.

———. 2017. "Why Tesla Is Overhyped—and Overvalued." *Vox*, June 26. https:// www.vox.com/the-big-idea/2017/6/26/15872468/tesla-gm-ford-valuation -justifying-disruption.

Goldfarb, Brent, Magnus Henrekson, and Nathan Rosenberg. 2001. "Demand vs. Supply Driven Innovations: US and Swedish Experiences in Academic Entrepreneurship." Working Paper No. 436, SSE/EFI Working Paper Series in Economics and Finance. http://hdl.handle.net/10419/56272.

Goldfarb, Brent, and Andrew A. King. 2016. "Scientific Apophenia in Strategic Management Research: Significance Tests & Mistaken Inference." *Strategic Management Journal* 37 (1): 167–76.

Goldfarb, Brent, Andrew A. King, and Timothy S. Simcoe. 2018. "Replication Is Good, but Will Not Save Us." Working paper, University of Maryland.

Goldfarb, Brent, and David Kirsch. 2017. "Time to Commercial Viability in Nascent Industries: A Historical Study." Working paper, University of Maryland.

Goldfarb, B., D. Kirsch, and D. A. Miller. 2007. "Was There Too Little Entry During the Dot Com Era?" *Journal of Financial Economics* 86: 100–144.

Goldfarb, Brent, David Kirsch, and Dave Kressler. 2018. "Business Exercise Starts with $5 in Seed Money." *Entrepreneur & Innovation Exchange*, February. https://doi.org/10.17919/X9566C.

Goldfarb, Brent, David A. Kirsch, and April Shen. 2012. "Financing New Industries." In *Handbook of Entrepreneurial Finance*, edited by Douglas Cumming, 9–46. New York: Oxford University Press.

Goldfarb, Brent D., Michael D. Pfarrer, and David Kirsch. 2005. "Searching for Ghosts: Business Survival, Unmeasured Entrepreneurial Activity and Private Equity Investment in the Dot-Com Era." Robert H. Smith School Research Paper No. RHS 06-027. http://dx.doi.org/10.2139/ssrn.825687.

Goldstein, M. L., and I. Krutov. 2000. *The Future of Money Management in America.* New York: Bernstein Research Report.

Green, Heather. 1999. "The Great Yuletide Shakeout." *Business Week*, November 1.

Greenstein, S. 2002. "The Crash in Competitive Telephony." *IEEE Micro* 22 (4): 8–9, 88.

Greenstein, Shane. 2015. *How the Internet Became Commercial: Innovation, Privatization, and the Birth of a New Network.* Princeton, NJ: Princeton University Press.

Greenwood, Robin, and Stefan Nagel. 2009. "Inexperienced Investors and Bubbles." *Journal of Financial Economics* 93 (2): 239–58.

Grieco, Daniela, and Robin Hogarth. 2004. "Excess Entry, Ambiguity Seeking and Competence: An Experimental Investigation." Economics Working Papers No. 778, Department of Economics and Business, Universitat Pompeu Fabra.

Grosvener, Dannelet A., ed. 1974. *Survey of Current Business, Volume 54.* Washington, DC: US Department of Commerce.

Grove, Andrew S. 1996. *Only the Paranoid Survive: How to Exploit the Crisis Points That Challenge Every Company and Career.* New York: Currency Doubleday.

Guzman, Jorge, and Scott Stern. 2016. "The State of American Entrepreneurship: New Estimates of the Quantity and Quality of Entrepreneurship for 15 US States, 1988–2014." Working Paper No. 22095, National Bureau of Economic Research. https://doi.org/10.3386/w22095.

Heath, C., and D. Heath. 2007. *Made to Stick: Why Some Ideas Survive and Others Die.* New York: Random House.

Hecht, Jeff. 2004. *City of Light: The Story of Fiber Optics.* New York: Oxford University Press.

Hege, John B. 2006. *The Wankel Rotary Engine: A History.* Jefferson, NC: McFarland.

"Highlights and Sidelights in Aviation's March of Progress Throughout World: Aviation Used as Stock Bait; Leaders of Industry Join to Stop Exploitation Fake Schemes Find Field Fertile for Work Many Good Securities on Financial Market." 1929. *Los Angeles Times*, January 20.

Hoberg, Gerard, and Gordon Phillips. 2010. "Real and Financial Industry Booms and Busts." *Journal of Finance* 65 (1): 45–86.

Hochfelder, D. 2006. "Where the Common People Could Speculate: The Ticker, Bucket Shops, and the Origins of Popular Participation in Financial Markets, 1880–1920." *Journal of American History* 93 (2): 335.

Hof, Robert D. 2004. "Commentary: 'Please God, Just One More Bubble.'" *Bloomberg News*, August 16. https://www.bloomberg.com/news/articles/2004–08-15/commentary-please-god-just-one-more-bubble.

Hounshell, David A. 1984. *From the American System to Mass Production, 1800–1932.* Baltimore, MD: Johns Hopkins University Press.

Hounshell, David A., and John Kenly Smith. 1988a. "The Nylon Drama." *American Heritage of Invention and Technology* 4 (2): 40–55.

———. 1988b. "Science and Corporate Strategy, DuPont Research and Development 1902–1980." New York: Cambridge University Press.

Huberman, Gur. 2001. "Familiarity Breeds Investment." *Review of Financial Studies* 14 (3): 659–80.

Hughes, Thomas Parke. 1962. "British Electrical Industry Lag: 1882–1888." *Technology and Culture* 3: 27–44.

"The International Natural Rubber Market, 1870–1930." 2008. *EH.Net Encyclopedia, Edited by Robert Whaples.* March 16. http://eh.net/encyclopedia/the-international-natural-rubber-market-1870–1930/.

Johnson, Joseph, and Gerard J. Tellis. 2005. "Blowing Bubbles: Heuristics and Biases in the Run-Up of Stock Prices." *Journal of the Academy of Marketing Science* 33 (4): 486–503.

Kahneman, Daniel. 2011. *Thinking, Fast and Slow.* New York: Farrar, Straus & Giroux.

Kelly, Erin. 2000. "The Last E-Store on the Block: Toby Lenk's Toy Shop May Be the Best-Run Specialty Store on the Web, Which Raises a Question: If eToys Can't Make Money Online, Can Anyone?" *Fortune*, September 18. http://archive.fortune.com/magazines/fortune/fortune_archive/2000/09/18/287719/index.htm.

Kennedy, Robert C. 2001. "On This Day: February 11, 1865." *New York Times.* http://www.nytimes.com/learning/general/onthisday/harp/0211.html.

Kessler, W. C. 1940. "A Statistical Study of the New York General Incorporation Act of 1811." *Journal of Political Economy* 48 (6): 877–82.

Kindleberger, Charles Poor, and Robert Z. Aliber. 2005. *Manias, Panics, and Crashes: A History of Financial Crises.* 5th ed. Hoboken, NJ: John Wiley & Sons.

King, Ronald R., Vernon L. Smith, Arlington W. Williams, and Mark Van Boening. 1993. "The Robustness of Bubbles and Crashes in Experimental Stock Markets." In *Nonlinear Dynamics and Evolutionary Economics*, edited by Richard Day and Ping, 183–200. Oxford: Oxford University Press.

Kirsch, David A. 2000. *The Electric Vehicle and the Burden of History*. New Brunswick, NJ: Rutgers University Press.

Kirsch, David, and Brent Goldfarb. 2008. "Small Ideas, Big Ideas, Bad Ideas, Good Ideas: 'Get Big Fast' and Dot Com Venture Creation." In *The Internet and American Business*, edited by William Aspray and Paul E. Ceruzzi. Cambridge, MA: MIT Press.

Kleinknecht, A. 1981. "Observations on the Schumpeterian Swarming of Innovations." *Futures* 13 (4): 293–307.

Klepper, Steven. 2015. *Experimental Capitalism: The Nanoeconomics of American High-Tech Industries*. Princeton, NJ: Princeton University Press.

Klepper, Steven, and Kenneth L. Simons. 2000a. "Dominance by Birthright: Entry of Prior Radio Producers and Competitive Ramifications in the U.S. Television Receiver Industry." *Strategic Management Journal* 21 (10–11): 997–1016.

———. 2000b. "The Making of an Oligopoly: Firm Survival and Technological Change in the Evolution of the U.S. Tire Industry." *Journal of Political Economy* 108 (4): 728–60.

Knowledge@Wharton. 2009. "Top 30 Innovations of The Last 30 Years." *Forbes Magazine*, February 19. https://www.forbes.com/2009/02/19/innovation -internet-health-entrepreneurs-technology_wharton.html.

Kortum, Samuel, and Josh Lerner. 2001. "Does Venture Capital Spur Innovation?" In *Entrepreneurial Inputs and Outcomes: New Studies of Entrepreneurship in the United States*, edited by Gary D. Libecap, 1–44. Amsterdam: JAI.

Kranzberg, Melvin. 1986. "Technology and History: 'Kranzberg's Laws.'" *Technology and Culture* 27 (3): 544–60.

Lamoreaux, Naomi R., Margaret C. Levenstein, and Kenneth Lee Sokoloff. 2007. "Financing Invention During the Second Industrial Revolution: Cleveland, Ohio, 1870–1920." In *Financing Innovation in the United States, 1870 to the Present*, edited by Naomi R. Lamoreaux and Kenneth Lee Sokoloff (Cambridge, MA: MIT Press).

Laurence, William L. 1939. "Say Drug Checks Tubercle Bacilli." *New York Times*, April 6.

LeRoy, S. F. 2004. "Rational Exuberance." *Journal of Economic Literature* 42 (3): 783–804.

Levine, Sheen S., Evan P. Apfelbaum, Mark Bernard, Valerie L. Bartelt, Edward J. Zajac, and David Stark. 2014. "Ethnic Diversity Deflates Price Bubbles." *Proceedings of the National Academy of Sciences of the United States of America* 111 (52): 18524–29.

Long, Clarence D. 1960a. Introduction to *Wages and Earnings in the United States, 1860–1890*, edited by Clarence D. Long, 94–108. Princeton, NJ: Princeton University Press.

———. 1960b. "Wages by Occupational and Individual Characteristics." In *Wages and Earnings in the United States, 1860–1890*, edited by Clarence D. Long, 94–108. Princeton, NJ: Princeton University Press.

Loutskina, Elena, and Philip E. Strahan. 2011. "Informed and Uninformed Investment in Housing: The Downside of Diversification." *Review of Financial Studies* 24 (5): 1447–80.

Mackay, Charles. 1852. *Memoirs of Extraordinary Popular Delusions and the Madness of Crowds.* 2nd ed. Vol. 1. London: Office of the National Illustrated Library.

Maclaurin, William Rupert. 1949. *Invention & Innovation in the Radio Industry.* New York: Macmillan.

Malkiel, Burton Gordon. 1991. *Random Walk Down Wall Street: Including a Life-Cycle Guide to Personal Investing.* New York: W. W. Norton & Co.

March, James G. 1995. "The Future, Disposable Organizations and the Rigidities of Imagination." *Organization* 2 (3–4): 427–40.

Margo, Robert A. 2006. "Hourly and Weekly Earnings of Production Workers in Manufacturing: 1909–1995, Table Ba4361-4366." In *Historical Statistics of the United States, Earliest Times to the Present: Millennial Edition*, edited by Susan B. Carter, Scott Sigmund Gartner, Michael R. Haines, Alan L. Olmstead, Richard Sutch, and Gavin Wright. New York: Cambridge University Press.

Markoff, John. 1996. "Advances in Asia Propel Wider Use of Flat-Panel Displays." *New York Times*, May 20.

Martens, Martin L., Jennifer E. Jennings, and P. Devereaux Jennings. 2007. "Do the Stories They Tell Get Them the Money They Need? The Role of Entrepreneurial Narratives in Resource Acquisition." *Academy of Management Journal* 50 (5): 1107–32.

Martin, Ron. 2011. "The Local Geographies of the Financial Crisis: From the Housing Bubble to Economic Recession and beyond." *Journal of Economic Geography* 11 (4): 587–618.

Marvin, Carolyn. 1990. *When Old Technologies Were New: Thinking About Electric Communication in the Late Nineteenth Century.* New York: Oxford University Press.

Means, G. C. 1930. "The Diffusion of Stock Ownership in the United States." *Quarterly Journal of Economics* 44 (4): 561–600.

"Meningitis Deaths 'Unbelievably' Cut." 1938. *New York Times*, October 19.

Merton, Robert K. 1948. "The Self-Fulfilling Prophecy." *Antioch Review* 8 (2): 193–210.

Michie, Ranald C. 1986. "The London and New York Stock Exchanges, 1850–1914." *Journal of Economic History* 46 (1): 171–87.

Mingos, Howard. 1925. "Ford Prepares to Develop Flying 'Flivver': His Use of Cargo Planes a Step Toward Airplane Production on Large Scale—To Make Commercial Aviation a Success, He Says." *New York Times*, April 19.

Mooney, Richard E. 1964. "German Car Uses New-Type Engine; N.S.U. Installing Wankel—Others Prepare Models." *New York Times*, October 26.

———. 1965. "Citroen to Develop a Pistonless Auto; Citroen Planning Pistonless Auto." *New York Times*, April 1.

Murtha, Thomas, Stefanie Lenway, and Jeffrey Hart. 2001. *Managing New Industry Creation: Global Knowledge Formation and Entrepreneurship in High Technology.* Stanford, CA: Stanford University Press.

Musser, George. 2016. "A Mathematical BS Detector Can Boost the Wisdom of Crowds." *Aeon Essays*, July 6. https://aeon.co/essays/a-mathematical-bs-detector-can-boost-the-wisdom-of-crowds.

Nakajima, Kiyokazu, Jeffrey W. Milsom, and Bartholomäus Böhm. 2006. "History of Laparoscopic Surgery." In *Laparoscopic Colorectal Surgery*, 2nd ed., edited by Jeffrey W. Milsom, Bartholomäus Böhm, and Kiyokazu Nakajima, 1–9. New York: Springer.

Nanda, Ramana, and Matthew Rhodes-Kropf. 2013. "Investment Cycles and Startup Innovation." *Journal of Financial Economics* 110 (2): 403–18.

National Association of Realtors. "Profile of Home Buyers and Sellers." 2007. Chicago: National Association of Realtors.

Navin, Thomas R., and Marian V. Sears. 1955. "The Rise of a Market for Industrial Securities, 1887–1902." *Business History Review* 29 (2): 105–38.

"A Netscape Moment?" 2010. *The Economist,* February 4. https://www.economist.com/node/15464481.

Nicholson, Matt. 2014. *When Computing Got Personal.* Bristol, UK: Matt Publishing.

Nocera, Joe. 2013. *A Piece of the Action: How the Middle Class Joined the Money Class.* New York: Simon and Schuster.

"No Crude Rubber Famine in Sight; British Speculation in Shares and Increased Demand for Auto Tires Influence Price." 1910. *New York Times,* May 15.

Norbye, Jan P. 1970. "What G.M. Sees in the Wankel." *New York Times,* November 15.

———. 1972. "A Wankel in Your Future." *New York Times,* April 2.

Norman, Jeremy. N.d. "The First Working Phototypesetting Machine and the First Book It Typeset (1946–1953)." HistoryofInformation.com. http://www.historyofinformation.com/expanded.php?id=867.

Normile, Dennis. 1997. "Flat TV Arrives." *Popular Science* 250 (5): 69–73.

"Nylon Hose Sales Heavy at Opening; Price War on Unbranded Lines Marks Introduction—Many Stores Sell Out Quickly." 1940. *New York Times,* May 16.

"Nylon Hosiery Put at 17–20% of Total; Constantine Revises Downward Earlier Estimates on '41 Shipments to Stores." 1941. *New York Times,* May 1.

O'Connor, Ellen. 2004. "Storytelling to Be Real: Narrative, Legitimacy Building and Venturing." In *Narrative and Discursive Approaches in Entrepreneurship: A Second Movements in Entrepreneurship Book,* edited by Daniel Hjorth and Chris Steyaert, 105–24. Northampton, MA: Edward Elgar.

Odlyzko, Andrew. 2011. "Charles Mackay's Own Extraordinary Popular Delusions and the Railway Mania." *SSRN eLibrary,* September. http://papers.ssrn.com/sol3/papers.cfm?abstract_id=1927396.

Ofek, Eli, and Matthew Richardson. 2003. "Dotcom Mania: The Rise and Fall of Internet Stock Prices." *Journal of Finance* 58 (3): 1113–38.

O'Sullivan, Mary. 2007a. "Funding New Industries: A Historical Perspective on the Financing Role of the U.S. Stock Market in the Twentieth Century." In *Financing Innovation in the United States, 1870 to the Present*, edited by Naomi R. Lamoreaux and Kenneth L. Sokoloff, 162–216. Cambridge, MA: MIT Press.

———. 2007b. "The Expansion of the US Stock Market, 1885–1930: Historical Facts and Theoretical Fashions." *Enterprise and Society* 8 (3): 489–542.

———. 2016. *Dividends of Development: Securities Markets in the History of US Capitalism, 1866–1922*. Oxford: Oxford University Press.

Ott, Julia. 2011. *When Wall Street Met Main Street: The Quest for an Investors' Democracy*. Cambridge, MA: Harvard University Press.

Pástor, Luboš, and Pietro Veronesi. 2006. "Was There a Nasdaq Bubble in the Late 1990s?" *Journal of Financial Economics* 81 (1): 61–100.

———. 2009. "Learning in Financial Markets." *Annual Review of Financial Economics* 1 (1): 361–81.

Perez, C. 2003. *Technological Revolutions and Financial Capital*. Cheltenham, UK: Edward Elgar.

Perlo, Victor. 1958. "'People's Capitalism' and Stock-Ownership." *American Economic Review* 48 (3): 333–47.

Petersen, Anne. 1939. "Agencies Hail Mortality Drop In Birth Cases." *New York Times*, April 9.

Piketty, Thomas, and Emmanuel Saez. 2003. "Income Inequality in the United States, 1913–1998." *Quarterly Journal of Economics* 118 (1): 1–41.

Pillai, Sandeep Devanatha. 2018. "The Value of Contextual Richness: An Empirical Exploration of Production Scaling in the Early Automobile Industry." Working paper, University of Maryland.

"Pneumonia Curbed by a New Chemical." 1938. *New York Times*, November 20.

Polk, James K. 1848. "James K. Polk: Fourth Annual Message." December 5. http://www.presidency.ucsb.edu/ws/index.php?pid=29489.

Pollack, Andrew. 1985. "Computer Makers in a Severe Slump: Problems Such as Oversupply Resist Speedy Resolution Computer Industry in a Severe Slump." *New York Times*, June 10.

Pollock, Timothy G., Violina P. Rindova, and Patrick Maggitti. 2008. "Market Watch: Information and Availability Cascades Among the Media and Investors in the US IPO Market." *Academy of Management Journal* 51 (2): 335–58.

Poterba, James M., Andrew A. Samwick, Andrei Shleifer, and Robert J. Shiller. 1995. "Stock Ownership Patterns, Stock Market Fluctuations, and Consumption." *Brookings Papers on Economic Activity* 1995 (2): 295–372.

Preda, Alex. 2006. "Socio-Technical Agency in Financial Markets: The Case of the Stock Ticker." *Social Studies of Science* 36 (5): 753–82.

————. 2007. "The Sociological Approach to Financial Markets." *Journal of Economic Surveys* 21 (3): 506–33.

Prelec, Dražen. 2004. "A Bayesian Truth Serum for Subjective Data." *Science* 306 (5695): 462–66.

Prelec, Dražen, H. Sebastian Seung, and John McCoy. 2013. "Finding Truth Even If the Crowd Is Wrong." Working paper, MIT. http://seunglab.org/wp -content/uploads/2015/07/FindingTruth16-copy.pdf.

Ratcliff, J. 1943. "Here's Medical Magic!: Meet One of the Most Powerful Microbe Destroyers Ever Found: Penicillin. It's a Brand-New Wonder Drug That Will Save Thousands of Soldiers' Lives." *Atlanta Constitution*, May 16.

Razaghian, Rose. 2013. "Financial Credibility in the United States: The Impact of Institutions, 1789–1860." Yale ICF Working Paper No. 00-13. https:// som.yale.edu/faculty-research/our-centers-initiatives/international-center -finance/data/historical-newyork.

Reed, John S., and Glen R. Moreno. 1986. "The Role of Large Banks in Financing Innovation." In *The Positive Sum Strategy: Harnessing Technology for Economic Growth*, edited by Ralph Landau and Nathan Rosenberg, 453–66. Washington, DC: National Academies Press.

Reid, Robert H. 1997. *Architects of the Web: 1,000 Days That Built the Future of Business*. New York: Wiley.

Renshaw, Edward. 1988. "The Crash of October 19 in Retrospect." *Market Chronicle* 22 (1): 1.

Reynard, Samuel. 2004. "Financial Market Participation and the Apparent Instability of Money Demand." *Journal of Monetary Economics* 51 (6): 1297–1317.

"Rheumatic Fever Yields." 1939. *New York Times*, September 7.

Rhodes-Kropf, Matthew, David Robinson, and S. Viswanathan. 2005. "Valuation Waves and Merger Activity: The Empirical Evidence." *Journal of Financial Economics* 77: 561–603.

Rindova, Violina P., and Antoaneta P. Petkova. 2007. "When Is a New Thing a Good Thing? Technological Change, Product Form Design, and Perceptions of Value for Product Innovations." *Organization Science* 18 (2): 217–32.

Rosenberg, Nathan. 1996. "Uncertainty and Technological Change." In *The Mosaic of Economic Growth*, edited by T. Taylor Ralph Landau and Gavin Wright, 334–56. Stanford, CA: Stanford University Press.

Roth, Daniel. 1999. "My, What Big Internet Numbers You Have!" *Fortune* 139 (5): 114–18.

"Rubber Goods Go Up Ten Per Cent More; Advance, Following Rise in Raw Materials in London Only One of Many in a Year." 1910. *New York Times*, April 21.

Rubin, Ronald P. 2007. "A Brief History of Great Discoveries in Pharmacology: In Celebration of the Centennial Anniversary of the Founding of the American

Society of Pharmacology and Experimental Therapeutics." *Pharmacological Reviews* 59 (4): 289–359.

Russell, B. 2009. "The Triumph of Stupidity." In *Mortals and Others*, vol. 2, *American Essays 1931–1935*, edited by Harry Ruja. New York: Routledge.

"Sales Begin Today of Nylon Hosiery; Only Limited Supply of New Du Pont Product, However, Will Be Available. Makers Warn Of Miracle, Caution Against Exaggerated Statements on Durability and Ending 'Runs.'" 1940. *New York Times*, May 15.

Salpukas, Agis. 1972a. "G.M. Will Produce the Wankel Engine in Limited Quantity." *New York Times*, August 29.

———. 1972b. "Wankel Fever Is Now Widespread." *New York Times*, November 5.

"Says Stock Slump Is Only Temporary." 1929. *New York Times*, October 24.

Schiffer, Michael Brian. 2003. *Taking Charge: The Electric Automobile in America*. Washington, DC: Smithsonian.

Schivelbusch, Wolfgang. 1995. *Disenchanted Night: The Industrialization of Light in the Nineteenth Century*. Berkeley: University of California Press.

Schonfeld, Erick. 2000. "How Much Are Your Eyeballs Worth? Placing a Value on a Website's Customers May Be the Best Way to Judge a Net Stock. It's Not Perfect, but on the Net, What Is?" *Fortune*, February 21.

Schuyten, Peter J. 1980. "Commodore Prepares Challenge To U.S. Home-Computer Giants." *New York Times*, October 1, D26.

Seasholes, Mark S., and Guojun Wu. 2007. "Predictable Behavior, Profits, and Attention." *Journal of Empirical Finance* 14 (5): 590–610.

Shapiro, Fred R. 2006. *The Yale Book of Quotations*. New Haven, CT: Yale University Press.

Shiller, Robert J. 2006. *Irrational Exuberance*. New York: Crown Publishers.

———. 2017. "Narrative Economics." *American Economic Review* 107 (4): 967–1004.

Simon, Ruth. 2000. "Margin Investors Learn the Hard Way That Brokers Can Get Tough on Loans." *Wall Street Journal*, April 27.

Skrabec, Quentin R., Jr. 2013. *Rubber: An American Industrial History*. Jefferson, NC: McFarland.

Smiley, Gene, and Richard H. Keehn. 1988. "Margin Purchases, Brokers' Loans and the Bull Market of the Twenties." *Business and Economic History: Papers Presented at the Annual Meeting of the Business History Conference* 17: 129–42.

Smith, Gene. 1972. "G.M. Plays Down Wankel Report." *New York Times*, July 13.

Smith, Vernon L., Gerry L. Suchanek, and Arlington W. Williams. 1988. "Bubbles, Crashes, and Endogenous Expectations in Experimental Spot Asset Markets." *Econometrica: Journal of the Econometric Society* 56 (5): 1119.

Sobel, Robert. 1980. *The Last Bull Market: Wall Street in the 1960's*. New York: Norton.

———. 2000. *The Curbstone Brokers: The Origins of the American Stock Exchange*. Washington, DC: Beard Books.

Sokolove, Michael. 2002. "How to Lose $850 Million—and Not Really Care." *New York Times*, June 9.

Staudenmaier, John M. 2002. "Rationality, Agency, Contingency: Recent Trends in the History of Technology." *Reviews in American History* 30 (1): 168–81.

Stehman, Jonas Warren. 1925. *The Financial History of the American Telephone and Telegraph Company*. Boston: Houghton Mifflin.

Stillson, Richard T. 1971. "The Financing of Malayan Rubber, 1905–1923." *Economic History Review* 24 (4): 589–98.

———. 2006. *Spreading the Word: A History of Information in the California Gold Rush*. Lincoln: University of Nebraska Press.

"Stock Spree: Many Investors By-Pass 'Blue Chips,' Bid Up Lesser Known Shares." 1961. *Wall Street Journal*, April 24.

Thompson, Earl A. 2007. "The Tulipmania: Fact or Artifact?" *Public Choice* 130: 99–114.

"Topics on Wall Street." 1916. *New York Times*, August 27. http://search.proquest.com/docview/97866489.

Tripsas, Mary. 1997a. "Surviving Radical Technological Change Through Dynamic Capability: Evidence from the Typesetter Industry." *Industrial & Corporate Change* 6 (2): 341–77.

———. 1997b. "Unraveling the Process of Creative Destruction: Complementary Assets and Incumbent Survival in the Typesetter Industry." *Strategic Management Journal* 18: 119–42.

Trueman, Brett M., M. H. Franco Wong, and Xiao-Jun Zhang. 2000. "The Eyeballs Have It: Searching for the Value in Internet Stocks." *Journal of Accounting Research* 38: 137–62.

Tushman, Michael L., and Philip Anderson. 1986. "Technological Discontinuities and Organizational Environments." *Administrative Science Quarterly* 31 (3): 439–65.

Tversky, Amos, and Daniel Kahneman. 1971. "Belief in the Law of Small Numbers." *Psychological Bulletin* 76 (2): 105–10.

———. 1973. "Availability: A Heuristic for Judging Frequency and Probability." *Cognitive Psychology* 5 (2): 207–32.

"Two Important Cures Announced: New Insulin Treatment Reported Used with Success in Case of Diabetic Coma." 1922. *New York Times*. December 6, 17.

"U.S. Business: German Engine Is in U.S. via Japan." 1970. *New York Times*, July 19.

US Census Bureau. 1990. *Statistical Abstract of the United States, 1990*. https://www.census.gov/prod/99pubs/99statab/sec31.pdf.

US Census Bureau. N.d. "U.S. Census Bureau QuickFacts: United States." https://www.census.gov/quickfacts/table/PST045215/00.

Utterback, J., and W. Abernathy. 1975. "A Dynamic Model of Product and Process Innovation." *Omega* 3: 638–56.

Van Duijn, J. J. 1981. "Fluctuations in Innovations Overtime." *Futures* 13 (4): 264–75.

Vanek Smith, Stacy, and Robert Smith. 2016. "Oil #1: We Buy Oil." *NPR Planet Money.* https://www.npr.org/sections/money/2016/08/10/489457747/oil-1 -we-buy-oil.

van Lente, Harro. 2012. "Navigating Foresight in a Sea of Expectations: Lessons from the Sociology of Expectations." *Technology Analysis & Strategic Management* 24 (8): 769–82.

Vartan, Vartanig G. 1972. "Market Dawdles at a Snail's Pace." *New York Times,* July 4.

Wadell, Richard. 1973. "The Wankel Comes of Age." *New York Times,* April 8. https://www.nytimes.com/1973/04/08/archives/the-wankel-comes-of-age -challenge-conceded-license-agreement-there.html.

Warner, E. P. 1931. "Commercial Aviation—Illusion or Fact." *Yale Review* 20 (June): 707.

Wax, P. M. 1995. "Elixirs, Diluents, and the Passage of the 1938 Federal Food, Drug and Cosmetic Act." *Annals of Internal Medicine* 122 (6): 456–61.

"Young Industries Develop Rapidly: Airplanes, Rayon, Radio and Other Lines Make Broad Strides During Past Year." 1928. *Wall Street Journal,* December 31.

"Young Roosevelt Saved by New Drug." 1936. *New York Times,* December 17.

Zeckhauser, R. 2006. "Investing in the Unknown and Unknowable." *Capitalism and Society* 1 (2): 5.

Zott, C., and R. Amit. 2007. "Business Model Design and the Performance of Entrepreneurial Firms." *Organization Science* 18 (2): 181–99. http://pubsonline .informs.org/doi/abs/10.1287/orsc.1060.0232.

INDEX